13

A
PEMBROKESHIRE
ANTHOLOGY

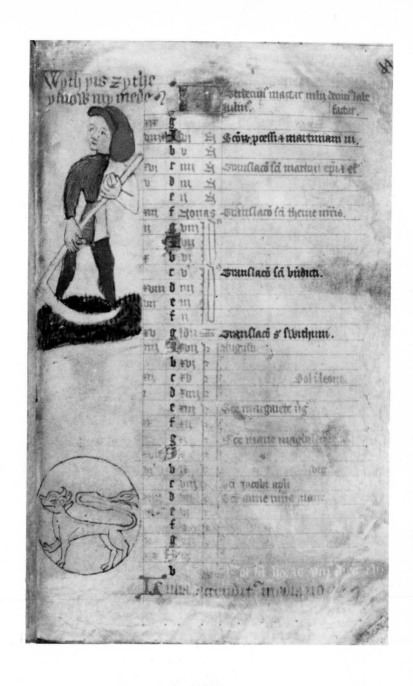

A page from the Haroldston Calendar: the month of July 'With this zythe I mow my mede' (XV century). British Library.

A PEMBROKESHIRE ANTHOLOGY

Dillwyn Miles

Published by
Hughes & Son (Publishers) Ltd
Rawlings Road
Llandybïe, Dyfed SA18 3YD

ISBN 0 85284 018 7

*Printed in Wales by
Salesbury Press Ltd
Llandybïe, Dyfed*

*Especially for
my grandchildren –
Andrew and Tamsin
Emily and Max.*

Foreword

Pembrokeshire is that magical south-western peninsula of Wales which has now become one of the most sought-after holiday counties in Britain. Modern administrators have done their best to hide it under the blanket title of 'Dyfed', but Pembrokeshire has an obstinate life of its own. It remains a separate, unique and astonishingly beautiful county in its own right, — with its wide sandy beaches, rugged sea cliffs and lonely moorlands. Here are magnificent castles, curious cromlechs standing amongst the heather on lost hillsides, strange church towers as strong as fortresses. The visitor, the expatriot and those of us who have neglected our heritage are eager to know their story, but where are we to find it? There are learnéd works on the shelves of the copyright libraries but none that can so easily be handled or come by conveniently. Now Dillwyn Miles has given us the perfect *passe partout* to the literature of Pembrokeshire.

This was an excellent idea — to make an anthology of all the best and most fascinating passages in previous writing about the county. Pembrokeshire has produced its own best interpreters of life in the past. Giraldus Cambrensis — one of the most vivid and important writers of the Middle Ages — was a Pembrokeshire man. In George Owen the county possessed one of the finest chroniclers of Elizabethan life. The reader of this book will be surprised, I am sure, with George Owen's description of the wild game of knappan, which was surely the origin of modern rugby, especially the Welsh variety. But this is only one of the many pleasures that lie between the covers of *A Pembrokeshire Anthology*.

No one is better qualified to make this anthology than Dillwyn Miles. He is a Pembrokeshire man, Welsh speaking and a previous Director of the Dyfed Rural Council. He is also a scholar and a local historian of distinction. He knows his county as few people can, for he has been in the forefront of the battle to protect its natural beauty and safeguard its heritage. He has obviously enjoyed every minute of the long task of selecting these intriguing extracts from the men of the past who travelled the Pembrokeshire highways and byeways; and he communicates his enthusiasm to his readers. Here is the history of Pembrokeshire in the words of those who saw it being made.

Fishguard 1982   *Wynford Vaughan Thomas*

Introduction

Pembrokeshire is beautiful. Its face, moulded from features that range from the most ancient rocks to soft sand dunes, reveals a natural diversity of spectacular landscapes and remarkable scenery.

The oldest rocks are the product of intense igneous activity that took place a thousand million years ago and more. The chiselled, leonine group of Maiden Castle at Treffgarne and the thrust of molten magma upon which Roch Castle stands are visible survivals of this remote period. But in the main, the older rocks lie deep under later deposits, folded, buckled, contorted by movements and forces over the millenia. The sea rose and fell hundreds of feet above its present level, so that Carn Llidi and Penbiri stood upon the waters as the off-shore islands do today. It sank as much at other times, and it is sinking still, an inch every hundred years.

More than once, great ice sheets smoothed its features and cut deep meltwater channels to form low-slung valleys. When the last ice receded some ten thousand years ago, man came and sought shelter in the limestone caves of the south coast from the cold, dry winds of the tundra that then was. He left his simple tools and the remains of his diet — reindeer, hyaena, horse and mammoth — on the cave floors at Hoyle's Mouth and Longbury Bank near Tenby, Nanna's Cave on Caldey, and Catshole Quarry at Pembroke.

Milder weather enabled his successors to live in flimsy dwellings on river banks and coastal sites. The small flint implements they used for fishing and hunting have been found on Nab Head, Ord Point, Little Furzenip, Swan Lake, and on the banks of the Nevern at Newport, the first evidence of human settlement in the northern part of the county. Many of their hunting grounds are now the submerged forests of Newgale and Amroth: the skeleton of a piglet found at Lydstep with a flint arrowhead between its ribs was the unretrieved quarry of one of these Mesolithic hunters.

For the past five thousand years man has had a direct hand in shaping the face of Pembrokeshire, for the Neolithic people brought with them a knowledge of the arts of agriculture. The time between sowing and reaping enabled man to think on life, and on life hereafter. These people buried their dead with ceremony in great chambered tombs, of which Pentre Ifan is the most splendid specimen. The Presely Hills were of such significance to them that they went to the trouble of transporting over eighty 'bluestone' pillars over land and water all the way to Stonehenge.

Bronze Age man travelled the ancient trackways towards Ireland in pursuit of copper to mix with Cornish tin and, later, of gold from the Wicklow Hills. Their round barrows mark the burials of those who died along the ridgeways, and their wide distribution elsewhere indicates a settlement by these people over the greater part of Pembrokeshire.

The defensive settlements of those who brought iron to this land, in about 500 B.C., were also widespread: promontory forts such as Warriors' Dyke on St David's Head, and hill forts like Moel Drygarn, Garn Fawr and Carn Ingli. Fields and folds stone-walled by these early Celtic farmers can still be traced on Skomer Island. Their language became the language of the people of Wales.

When the Romans occupied the rest of Britain, this south-western peninsula of Wales was the home of Welsh tribes whom Ptolemy called the Demetae, and their land Demetia, which the Welsh called Dyfed. They may have entered into a compact with the Romans, or may have proved themselves too troublesome: whatever the reason, there are no more than traces of Roman trade and of fortified farm-steads occupied, perhaps, by Romanized natives.

From prehistoric time, the sea was the highway, and the grey waters of the Irish Sea were 'bright with Neolithic argonauts'. The intense maritime activity that existed from remote antiquity brought Wales and Ireland under a common culture from megalithic times. Evidence of this continuing connection is provided by the settlement of the Deisi from County Waterford in the fourth century, who estab-lished an Irish dynasty in Dyfed that lasted several centuries. They are commemorated in placenames like Pencnwc and Maenclochog, and their literacy is revealed by their invention of the ogham alphabet for more easily inscribing, often bilingually in Latin and Goidelic, on stone the names of those whom they considered should be remembered. These inscriptions date from the fifth century onward, and they are our first written words.

Early Christian missionaries, the Celtic 'saints', sailed their skin boats along the western seaways, and avoided the dangerous promontories of Brittanny, Cornwall and Dyfed by following trans-peninsular routes. They built small coastal chapels where they could place themselves in God's mercy during their perilous journeys, and thank Him for safe landings. Their monastic cells became churches dedicated to them: dedications to Brynach, David, Padarn, Teilo and other 'saints' are legion. The shrine of St David acquired such fame that throughout the Middle Ages, two pilgrimages to it equalled one to Rome. For the Irish, upon whose main route to the Holy See it lay, it was a bonus.

St David's suffered more than anywhere from the pillaging of the Norsemen. They sacked the cathedral time and again and, in 999, murdered its bishop. Nothing is known of their settlement, nor did they leave any tangible evidence save for a small metal object bearing a Norse dragon, but they are remembered out of proportion to their impact by the names they bestowed on islands and islets — Skomer, Skokholm, Ramsey, Caldey, Tusker, Goscar, — and coastal settlements, like Angle, Dale, Gelliswick, Musselwick, Fishguard and Milford.

The Normans crossed Wales diagonally under Roger, Earl of Shrewsbury, and his son Arnulph, and established their headquarters in Pembroke in 1094 and built 'a slender fortress of stakes and turf' there. The old Welsh hundred of Penfro became the county palatine of Pembroke in 1138, hence the 'premier county of Wales', with Gilbert de Clare as its first Earl. The earldom was conferred on Jasper Tudor in 1452, and on the Prince of Wales in 1479; it was erected into a marquessate for Anne Boleyn, and reverted to an earldom in 1551 when it was granted to William Herbert, ancestor of the present Earl. In the north of the county, Robert FitzMartin sailed across from Combe Martin and occupied the ancient 'cantref' of Cemais.

The Normans built more than fifty castles in Pembrokeshire, some two-thirds of which were earthworks. The stone castles were mostly sited on or near navigable waters, except for the sweep of frontier castles from Roch to Tenby erected to protect 'Little England beyond Wales'. They established towns and boroughs, hitherto unknown in Pembrokeshire, and granted charters to their inhabitants

The Tudor period came about with the birth of Henry Tudor at Pembroke Castle, and his landing at Dale in 1485 to march on Bosworth. His son, Henry VIII, fortified Milford Haven and established the boundaries of the county as they were to remain until the reorganisation of 1974.

The Civil Wars saw Pembrokeshire divided. The Welshry was

mostly for the King; the English south for Parliament. But then John Poyer, mayor, refused to surrender Pembroke Castle and declared for the Royalists, and was shot at Covent Garden, but not before Cromwell himself had come 'to suppress the Welsh insolence'.

Religious dissent and disaffection persisted throughout the seventeenth and the following two centuries. Lewis David and his fellow Quakers fled to Pennsylvania in 1686 and called their townships Haverford and Narberth. The Moravian Brethren built themselves a chapel at Haverfordwest. John Wesley was encouraged to visit Pembrokeshire on no less than fourteen different occasions.

The eighteenth century ended in excitement with the 'great fiasco of the French invasion' of 1797 which caused a stir among the local gentry and peasantry alike, and made a legend of the women of Fishguard. Forty years later, men dressed as women destroyed the toll-gate at Efailwen as a first strike against oppression in what came to be known as the Rebecca Riots, an agrarian revolt that freed the roads from excessive tolls and expressed a class division.

The nineteenth century dawned with the promise of prosperity for Milford Haven. The manors of Hubberston and Pill had descended to Catherine Barlow of Slebech who became the wife of Sir William Hamilton. After her death Hamilton placed his nephew, Charles Greville, in charge of a plan to develop a harbour and a new town at Milford. Greville invited some whaling Quakers from Nantucket, whose influence has been much exaggerated, to settle there. Greville's mistress, Emma, became his aunt, Lady Hamilton. In 1802 Sir William and Lady Hamilton and Lord Nelson visited Milford at Greville's invitation. Nelson said that he considered Milford Haven and Trincomalee the finest harbours he had ever seen.

Pembrokeshire, with coasts on three sides, has long been engaged in sea trading. The ruined remains of quays and warehouses in almost every coastal village are the silent witnesses to a bustling trade that existed up to the earlier part of the present century. Woollen cloth, corn, malt, hides, coal, slates, herrings, oysters were exported, while imports included salt, fruit, tobacco, timber, millstones and wine. The schooners and ketches that brought these cargoes have, by today, given way to gaily coloured sailing dinghies and the leviathans that bring oil in to Milford Haven, now the largest oil port in the kingdom.

Throughout the centuries agriculture has been the main industry of Pembrokeshire. The north grew oats: the south grew oats for its horses and wheat for its people. Barley was grown everywhere. As dairy farming represents about a half of the total agricultural output,

Friesian cows polka-dot the landscape, but Pembrokeshire is proud of its own breed of Castlemartin Black Cattle — as it is of the Pembrokeshire Corgi and the Sealyham Terrier. It produces the earliest potatoes and rivals Norfolk for turkeys. There are more sheep than people and as many pigs as there are families, even though it is no longer the case of every man having a pig in his cot. The ancient tales will tell you that pigs first appeared here, sent to the Prince of Dyfed by the King of the Other World.

Pembrokeshire emerges from the twilight world as *gwlad hud a lledrith* — the land of magic and enchantment. In so many ways it remains so.

DILLWYN MILES

Haverfordwest, 1982

By the same author:
The Castles of Pembrokeshire
The Sheriffs of the County of Pembroke
The Royal National Eisteddfod of Wales

As Editor
Nature in Wales
The Pembrokeshire Historian
Pembrokeshire Coast National Park (H.M.S.O. Guide)

CONTENTS

IV.   CASTLES AND PLACES

V.   HOLY PLACES

VI.   SAINTS

VII.   MEN OF PEMBROKE

VIII.   THE QUALITY

XII SHIPS AND THE SEA

XIII FOOD

XIV SPORT AND LEISURE

XV WAR AND STRIFE

XVI   DIVERS WONDERS

List of Illustrations

I

The Land

1. The Look of Pembrokeshire

Stones, the sea and the weather have moulded the look of Pembrokeshire. Man has merely scratched its surface.

The oldest rocks are those in the north; volcanic and slaty, and the surface soil has boulder clays and gravel, most of which is poor in quality, wet, heavy and deficient in lime. In the south are fertile loams of underlying Old Red Sandstone and Carboniferous Limestone; in the centre again the soil is thin and less fertile, a gradation from one to the other.

The climate is mild and humid: rarely baking hot and rarely freezing. Along the coast rainfall averages thirty-two inches a year; in the Prescellies nearly double. Winter gales condition the landscape, and shape the trees like porcupines' backs and horses' manes. But spring comes early, and luxuriant growth quickly; along the banks of deep-set lanes, and on cliffs and among the lichen-mottled boulders, gorse, sedum, seathrift and thyme change the colour of all. Foxgloves in Pembrokeshire often grow as tall as men. Ferns are prolific. Things that strike a visitor because they are likely to be a change to his eyes are the stone walls, fine bleached grass, bushes and small trees — gorse, hazel and oak often blown into odd shapes. And in winter the pale, tall trunks of big trees near white-walled or pink-walled farms, and the sheets of snowdrops — often miles from the nearest dwelling. Then the thin, clear light; and the stretches of undeveloped seaboard, the fierce, romantic cliffs with their caves and contortions and the many dark beaches difficult or impossible to get to, and the few with wide sand and blue-grey pebble banks.

Vyvyan Rees, *South-West Wales,* 1963.

2. *The Ice Age*

There are few signs in the landscape of any intensity of glacial erosion in Pembrokeshire; and only one or two steep-sided hollows on the north face of the Presely Hills mildly hint at the cirques and rock basins of North Wales. There is, however, impressive evidence of ice-movement across the area, partly in the exposure of ice-scratched rock surfaces (well developed on Carn Llidi at 500 feet, and in Whitesand Bay) but especially in the occurrence of a widespread veneer of boulder clay and fluvioglacial gravels that reveal oscillations of climatic change during Pleistocene times. Along the north coast, notably in some of the bays between Strumble Head and Cardigan, there appear to be two layers of boulder clay, separated by intervening water-borne sand and gravel, that are clear indication of advance of the ice, and of a local melting during a mild interlude. Elsewhere such a tripartite division of the deposits is not so readily recognised, but drift to thicknesses of tens of feet, as stiff stony till or as well-washed melt-water sands and shingle, together with 'head' and solifluvial loams, is commonly met in shallow diggings inland and is well seen in Whitesand Bay and in Milford Haven.

The pebbles in the boulder clay are often ice-scratched and polished and reveal their mode of transport. Many of them were derived from local sources, but a number are of rock types not found in place in Pembrokeshire: these include pebbles of granite matched by rock-in-place in Arran, Ailsa Craig, and Galloway in Scotland, and in the Isle of Man, and it is to be inferred that a regional ice-sheet that traversed Pembrokeshire from the north-west had its origins far to the north in the Clyde estuary and the Irish Sea. Very large boulders of such 'foreign' erratics are scattered over the low ground of southern Pembrokeshire — one from Scotland lies in Bosherston village, another from North Wales overhangs the extremity of St Govan's Head. Some of the drift deposits contain marine shells (mussels, cockles, tellens, whelks, periwinkles) dredged from the sea floor as the ice moved on to the land from the north-west.

The Irish Sea ice, fed from an extensive hinterland, underwent slow melting as the Ice Age came to an end. In one interpretation, it continued to impinge on the Pembrokeshire coast long after the small local glaciers of Welsh ice had disappeared. It formed a barrier to the free outflow of the rivers into Cardigan Bay and St George's Channel, and dammed up temporary lakes in the river valleys along the north and west coasts. The pattern of these lakes may still be recognised, although they were drained when the Irish Sea ice finally melted, by the marshy flats of their lake floor sediments, notably the sediments of 'Lake Maenorowen' south-west of Fishguard. They are also defined by the abandoned gaps through which overspill from the temporary lakes found its way to the sea: the Gwaun valley, now dry at its north-eastern limit, drained 'Lake Nevern' into Fishguard Bay; the Jordanston channel drained 'Lake Maenorowen' into the Cleddau; Cwmyreglwys briefly took over from the Gwaun valley as a late spillway from 'Lake Nevern' and separated Dinas 'Island' from the mainland; Barry 'Island' between Porthgain and Abereiddi matches Dinas 'Island' in being similarly cut off by an abandoned spillway; Dale Roads formed the exit of a spillway at one stage from St Bride's Haven 3 miles to the north, and at another stage from Westdale Bay a mile to the west; and the Wooltack peninsula and the Neck of Skomer are isolated by similar overflow channels.

In an alternative interpretation, ice-dammed lakes at best had a brief life; and the anomalous drainage channels, now dry, are not to be regarded as lake outlets but as subglacial melt-water courses temporarily occupied under a waning ice cover and abandoned when the ice finally melted.

Temporary amelioration of climate during the Ice Age is indicated by cave deposits, notably in Hoyle's Mouth near Tenby and on Caldey, that have yielded an abundance of bones of 'cold' animals including mammoth, reindeer, Irish elk, woolly rhino, cave bear, hyena, and cave lion.

T. Neville George, 'Geology and Scenery' in *Pembrokeshire Coast National Park Guide,* No. 10 ed. Dillwyn Miles, 1973.

3.   *As Cornwall is to England* . . .

As Cornwall is to England so Pembrokeshire is to Wales. It lies in the far south-west with the sea on three sides and this remoteness, coupled with its strong links with Ireland, made it an enchanted country in the minds of the legend makers. Most of the stories in the *Mabinogion* took place here in Dyfed, or have some strong connection with it.

It is impossible to stand more than eight miles from salt water anywhere in Pembrokeshire, for the tide runs up Milford Haven and on far up the Cleddau estuaries. That unprovincial consciousness of the outside world which is often found among seafaring people may manifest itself in the name of a bungalow or small-holder's cottage: St Helena or Constantinople.

   The gales in the west are tremendous, but the climate is such that optimists leave geraniums out all the year and pessimists say they will have to mow their lawns on Boxing Day . . .

Peter Howell & Elisabeth Beazley,
The Companion Guide to South Wales, 1977.

4.   PENINSULA RUN

A shock orange sunball
hit the windscreen
when we crunched off the red beach
at Manorbier, under the ruin.
High-altitude jets
made trails like snail-creep
as we perched on the coast,
two ants mobile in speeding tin.

Flutter of pheasant into hedges,
bits of picnic mess and plastic cup
scattered on the sponge tussock
above the limestone loft of Stack Rocks —
two crags lifting from the sea
breaking on the wine-streaked bulk
of St Govan cliff.

             Then
to Freshwater West, the huge
crater dunes bunkered in gorse
rolling back layer on layer;
skidding through tunnelled driftsand
banked up to the roof,
closing in for a wing-touch
as we curved round to Angle —

that long blockhouse out in the bay
at the end of a western shore
in ramshackle splendour,
at the end of history's province.

John Tripp from *Pembrokeshire Poems*, 1976.

5. *The Primeval Forest of Newgale*

We then passed over Niwegal sands, at which place (during the winter that King Henry II spent in Ireland), as well as in almost all the other western ports, a very remarkable circumstance occurred. The sandy shores of South Wales, being laid bare by the extraordinary violence of a storm, the surface of the earth, which had been covered for many ages, re-appeared, and discovered the trunks of trees cut off, standing in the very sea itself, the strokes of the hatchet appearing as if made only yesterday. The soil was very black, and the wood like ebony. By a wonderful revolution, the road for ships became impassable, and looked, not like a shore, but like a grove cut down, perhaps, at the time of the deluge, or not long after, but certainly in very remote ages, being by degrees consumed and swallowed up by the violence and encroachments of the sea. During the same tempest many sea fish were driven, by the violence of the wind and waves, upon dry land. We were well lodged at St David's by Peter, bishop of the see, a liberal man, who had hitherto accompanied us during the whole of our journey.

Giraldus Cambrensis, *The Itinerary through Wales*, 1188.

6. *Life on the Seashore*

The cold-water common starfish (*Asterias rubens*) and, despite its name, the warm-water spiny starfish (*Marthasterias glacialis*) are both found in Pembrokeshire. The butterfish (*Centronotus gunnellus*) is at its extreme southern limit here, the male guarding the yellow eggs which the female had attached to the underside of a stone very low on the shore; while its relation Montagu's blenny (*Blennius montagui*) only just reaches us from the south. The Mediterranean spiny spider crab (*Maia squinado*) is unusual in the Isle of Man but in

Pembrokeshire, particularly in summer, is a pest of lobster fishermen since it fills their pots, sometimes to overflowing.

The common octopus (*Octopus vulgaris*) and the electric ray (*Torpedo nobiliana*) both find it only just warm enough to reach us in summer. The common oyster (*Ostrea edulis*) breeds as long as the temperature is 15-16°C or more. There used to be a large commercial fishery inside Milford Haven, but inevitable tainting by oil has made its re-establishment now impossible. The Portuguese oyster (*Gryphaea angulata*) lives here but cannot breed because of the cold . . .

Some of the sand-flats have dense populations of razor-shells (*Ensis*) that at the vibration of a footfall burrow down faster than their catcher can go down after them. The little *Tellinas* live there too, up to a thousand in a square yard; and the heart urchin (*Echinocardium caudatum*); the strange burrowing anemone *Peachia hastata;* the masked crab *Corystes cassivelaunus* (a splendid polysyllable to use when swearing at the cat!).

J. H. Barrett, 'Life on the Seashore' in *Pembrokeshire Coast National Park Guide,* No. 10 ed. Dillwyn Miles, 1973.

7.   *The Gulf Stream*

Pembrokeshire is the furthest west piece of Wales, of which, as a country, westernness (with its Atlantic weather and its eroded, escarpmented terrain) is a characteristic. It is surrounded on three sides by sea, so that little of it is more than a few miles inland. The Gulf Stream, in its wanderings, apparently strikes this corner of the Irish Sea's coastline, and, in theory at any rate, makes the sea which lies off those plentiful sandy beaches warmer than most. Sometimes one would hardly think so; but the climate, possibly under the Gulf Stream's influence, is certainly fine and dry, and there are copious statistics to prove it. The lowest winter average is 40°F, and the coastal rainfall, one of Britain's lowest, is 32 inches per year. Both sunshine and wind replace our national murky rainclouds. Hence the sheltering banks which form the field-boundaries, and the angle at which the very few trees which can survive in the salt gales lean their strained branches. The sunshine, however, provides an early season; and one of the most profitable ventures of Pembrokeshire farmers is the new-potato crop.

Michael Senior, *Portrait of South Wales,* 1974.

8.   *Cliff Walk*

From Little Haven a cliff-edge path takes you on into the west. Soon you come to Goultrop on whose cliffs deciduous woodland lives in rare intimacy with the sea. Further west along the headlands you will see breeding colonies of gulls, fulmars and cormorants; stonechats call from the gorse; and choughs often pass in lovely bouncing flight. On these cliffs are several raths (the Pembrokeshire word for earthworks) which are mostly Iron Age promontory forts. Far more ancient are the traces of man found in the earth of Nab Head where Mesolithic chipped flints and pierced beads have been found. From Nab Head to Musselwick sands the cliffs get more and more colourful. Steeply tilted strata of near-black rocks alternate with beds some of palest grey, some of rich purple-red. Then the bedding place changes and for a few hundred yards the rocks are tidily horizontal until suddenly they buckle in chaos. But everywhere it is the beautiful purple rocks that predominate, coming to brilliant life when the sunlight is on them and a blue sea is washing below. Along these cliff tops you may think some disease has struck down the broom bushes. They lie with their branches on the ground, spread out like the spokes of a wheel. But fear not: this is the local botanical curiosity — the prostrate broom. Not a separate species, just an odd variety.

William Condry, *Exploring Wales*, 1970.

9.   *Perilous Abyss*

Here is the wild and perilous abyss yclept the Huntsman's Leap, from the story of some fabulous rider who, putting his horse to full gallop, plunged across the unexpected chasm, only to perish from sheer fright upon regaining his home! The nodding cliffs approach so closely upon either hand, as to have been not inaptly likened to a pair of leviathan vessels locked fast in collision.

A bowshot westward lies Bosheston Meer, a similar cavern sunk fathoms deep in the solid rock. Near it is a funnel-shaped aperture that acts in stormy weather as a blowhole; whence it is said the waves are driven high above the land, plunging back again with a roar that can be heard far inland.

Strange tales were told in bygone times of the freaks of this tempest-torn abyss. George Owen, an Elizabethan chronicler, observes: 'If Sheepe or other like Cattell be grazing neere the Pitt, offtimes they are forcibly and violently Drawne and carryed into the pitt; and if a Cloke, or other garment, bee cast on the grownd neere the Pitt, at certaine seasones, you shall stande afarre off, and see it sodainely snatch'd, drawne and swallowed up into the Pitt, and never seene againe.'

H. Thornhill Timmins, *Nooks and Corners of Pembrokeshire,* 1895.

10. *Sanctus Winnoccus*

The name of the parishe is Sanctus Winnoccus as we finde by old records, but commonly & generally call'd by the name of St Twinnells. It is a village and hath in it but 3 houses besides ye Rect: & Viccarage . . .

There is a small park wall'd round abt 6 or 7 acres of Land w'ch had deer in itt abt seven yeares past but now a Warren, it belonges to ye Whites of Henllan call'd by ye name of Lovestone Cunniger, my Lady Buckley being now proprietor if itt.

We have a lake yt goes by ye name of Treforse lake. Itt passes from ye West to ye East parte of Stackpool house & south to ye sea, it runns in ye middle of parishe & hath severall Springs & Rivulets yt falls to itt from a Hill yt lies to the North parte of the bottom.

The ground of the parishe is good for Corne and Pasture: the color of ye soile to the South (viz) the limestone land they call itt Hazeley; to the North it is Redish; very fertil & planie Champion Grounds, noe great deepness of earth, it is gravelly & rocky being all limestone; the pasture is extraordinary feeding for good Mutton & Lamb.

The generall graines they sow here is Wheat, Barley, white & grey pease, beanes, oates & rie towards ye sea being barren ground neer ye Rocks; they breed but few Cattle & Horses only what is usefull for their Husbandrie. Their greatest advantages arises from sheep & piggs.

All the south parte of ye parishe is an intire veine of Limestone, & every ffarmor hath a quarrie & Lime-kill uppon his own Land and within his own bounds.

Edward Lhuyd, *Parochialia* in *Archaeologia Cambrensis,* 1911.

11. *This Blesséd Milford*

Imogen (reading letter from her husband Posthumus Leonatus):
Justice, and your father's wrath, should he take me in his dominion,
could not be so cruel to me, as you, O the dearest of creatures, would
even renew me with your eyes. Take notice that I am in Cambria, at
Milford-Haven: what your own love will, out of this, advise you,
follow. So he wishes you all happiness that remains loyal to his vow,
and your, increasing in love, LEONATUS POSTHUMUS.

O for a horse with wings! — Hearst thou, Pisanio?
He is at Milford-Haven: read and tell me
How far 'tis thither . . . how far it is
To this same blesséd Milford: and, by the way,
Tell me how Wales was made so happy as
To inherit such a haven.

William Shakespeare, *Cymbeline* III, 2.

12. IN TWO FIELDS*

Where did it roll in from, that sea of light
Whose floor was on Weun Parc y Blawd and Parc y Blawd?
After I had quested long in the dark land
Where did it come from, that which had always existed?
Or who, who was the archer, the sudden revealer?
The sea's unroller was the field's life-giving hunter.
From on high, above bright-billed curlews, the wary swerving of
lapwings,
He brought me the great stillness.

---

*   Weun Parc y Blawd and Parc y Blawd, two flowery moorland fields with
rush-grown areas near the poet's childhood home in Pembrokeshire. 'It was
in a gap between these two fields, about forty years ago, I suddenly and
vividly realized in a very definite personal experience, that people are above
all else brothers to one another'.

He stirred my soul where nothing stirred
Save the sun's thought spinning the haze into verse,
The ripe gorse clicking in the hedgerows,
The host of rushes dreaming the blue sky.
Who is it calls when the imagination wakens,
'Rise, walk, dance, look on creation!'?
Who is it hides in the midst of the words?
— These things on Weun Parc y Blawd and Parc y Blawd.

And when the huge and fugitive pilgrim clouds
Were red with the sunset of November's tempest,
Down in the ash and the sycamore parting the fields
The song of the wind was deep as deep silence.
Who is there, amidst that extravagant splendour?
Who stands there, containing it all?
Each witness's witness, each memory's memory, life of each life.
The tranquil calmer of the turmoil of self.

Till the whole world came sometimes into the stillness,
And on the two fields his people walking;
And through them, among them, there spread all around them
The spirit rising out of concealment and making all one;
As it was for us few, when wielding our pitchforks
Or culling reluctant thatch from the heavy rushland.
How close we grew one to the other!
The silent hunter was drawing his net about us.

O through the ages of blood on the straw and through the light the
lamenting,
What whistling was that which only the heart might hear? O who was
he,
Foiler of every presumption, runner on every man's trail,
And, ho there! escaper from armies,
Whistling in recognition, recognition that asks recognition?
Glorious the soaring and fusion of hearts after their cruel freezing:
Fountains were there, breaking out heavenwards,
And falling back, their tears like the leaves of a tree.

Upon these things the day broods under sun, under cloud,
And night through the cells of her many-branched brain:
How still they are, and she with her untroubled breathing

Over Weun Parc y Blawd and Parc y Blawd,
And their hold on the object, the fields full of people.
Surely the moment will come! And what hour shall it be
When the outlaw comes, and the hunter; the claimant comes to the gap in the hedge;
The Exiled King comes, and the rushes are parted before him.

Waldo Williams, trans. Gwyn Jones, *The Oxford Book of Welsh Verse in English,* 1977.

II

Early Peoples

1. *The First Settlers*

The first settlement of man in Pembrokeshire is associated with the caves in the Carboniferous Limestone outcrops of the south. The chief sites are in the Tenby region: Hoyle's Mouth (SN 113001) and Longbury Bank in the Ritec valley, Nanna's Cave (SS 146969) on Caldey; but there is an important outlier to the west, Priory Farm or Catshole Quarry Cave, on the Pembroke river (SM 978019). Nanna's Cave differs from the others in being a relatively shallow recess or shelter; Hoyle's Mouth and the rest are deep sinuous water-formed penetrations of the solid rock whose human inhabitants lived usually near or at the opening, where their stone implements and food-bones are found in the soil which accumulated on the cave floor.

Amongst the species of animals represented in the deposits, many of them now extinct in Britain, reindeer and horse are the most numerous. They reflect the cold dry conditions which prevailed in the last phase of the Pleistocene Ice Age, and produced tundra and steppe vegetation which suited the herds of hoofed grazing animals that were the Palaeolithic hunters' chief source of food. The beginning of this period is placed at about 25,000 B.C. in round figures; but on present evidence Pembrokeshire man does not appear, at earliest, before about 10,000 B.C.

The implements left by the cave-people are characteristic of the cultures that equate with the final Ice Age. They include the scrapers and bone-working gravers and other forms common to the time: examples can be seen in Tenby Museum. The distinctive implement, however, is best described as a kind of pen-knife, which is well represented at Nanna's Cave and at Priory Farm Cave. It links these Pembrokeshire hunters directly with their contemporaries elsewhere in Britain as possessors of the Creswellian culture, so named from the caves at Creswell Crags in Derbyshire, where more clearly than anywhere else it could be seen that the cave-dwellers of Britain had developed differently from their contemporaries in south-western France and elsewhere on the Continent.

The accepted date for the end of the Ice Age in Britain generally is about 8000 B.C., but the change was in fact gradual. It would certainly not have been perceptible to those who lived through it. The evidence from Nanna's Cave shows quite clearly that 'Creswellian' people were still about as the climatic conditions improved to a warmer and wetter version of the climate of today . . .

The somewhat indeterminate remains of the Mesolithic hunter / fisher groups are succeeded in the next period by antiquities which stand in marked contrast of them in every way. These are the great stone tombs, the *cromlechau,* which were the burial monuments of the Neolithic people. The spread of knowledge of farming and its related arts from its ultimate centres of origin in the Near East was a complicated and prolonged process which affected the British Isles generally during the fourth millennium B.C. Many of the movements were seaborne. For over a thousand years Pembrokeshire shared the activity which affected all the lands round the Irish Sea, with groups of settlers moving in the area and establishing themselves on sites that were suited to their needs as primitive cultivators and stockbreeders.

The tombs are more numerous in the northern part of the county than in the south. Their chief areas of distribution are the coastal strip and its hinterland from Fishguard to St David's, the Nevern Valley, and the southern foothills of Presely. In the south there are scattered examples mainly on or near the coast in Milford Haven and between Angle and Manorbier. The tombs vary in form and it must be remembered that what survives above ground today is normally all that remains of a much more elaborate structure. The chamber itself may have had other features, entrance-passages and the like, and all were covered by mounds or cairns of stone which have been removed in more recent times but still many years ago.

By the time of the Roman occupation the people dwelling in Pembrokeshire had become the *Demetae,* so named in the later second century A.D. by the geographer Ptolemy, who also identifies the other ancient name, *Octapitae,* St David's Head. The eastern boundary of the tribe is not known, but Ptolemy records *Maridunum,* Carmarthen, as lying within it.

Carmarthen is also the most westerly known Roman fort. On

present evidence the Roman military occupation took no account of Pembrokeshire, thus depriving the modern student of a fixed point of great value for chronological purposes. It is assumed that perhaps from the beginning, unlike other Welsh tribes, the Demetae accepted the Romans peaceably, rendering military posts within their midst unnecessary.

W. F. Grimes, 'Archaeology' in *Pembrokeshire Coast, National Park Guide No. 10*, ed. Dillwyn Miles, 1973.

2.   *Pwyll Prince of Dyved*

Pwyll Prince of Dyved was lord of the seven Cantrevs of Dyved; and once upon a time he was at Narberth his chief palace, and he was minded to go and hunt, and the part of his dominions in which it pleased him to hunt was Glyn Cuch. So he set forth from Narberth that night, and went as far as Llwyn Diarwyd. And that night he tarried there, and early on the morrow he rose and came to Glyn Cuch, when he let loose the dogs in the wood, and sounded the horn, and began the chase. And as he followed the dogs, he lost his companions; and whilst he listened to the hounds, he heard the cry of other hounds, a cry different from his own, and coming in the opposite direction.

And he beheld a glade in the wood forming a level plain, and as his dogs came to the edge of the glade, he saw a stag before the other dogs. And lo, as it reached the middle of the glade, the dogs that followed the stag overtook it and brought it down. Then looked he at the colour of the dogs, staying not to look at the stag, and of all the hounds that he had seen in the world, he had never seen any that were like unto these. For their hair was of a brilliant shining white, and their ears were red; and as the whiteness of their bodies shone, so did the redness of their ears glisten. And he came towards the dogs, and drove away those that had brought down the stag, and set his own dogs upon it.

The Mabinogion, translated by Lady Charlotte Guest.

3. *Rhiannon*

And once upon a time he was at Arberth, a chief court of his, with a feast prepared for him, and great hosts of men along with him. And after the first sitting Pwyll arose to take a walk, and made for the top of a mound which was above the court and was called Gorsedd Arberth . . . And as they were sitting down, they could see a lady, on a big fine pale white horse, with a garment of shining gold brocaded silk upon her, coming along the highway that led past the mound . . . Pwyll mounted his horse, and no sooner had he mounted his horse than she passed him by. He turned after her and let his horse, mettled and prancing, take its own speed. And he thought that at the second bound or the third he would come up with her. But he was no nearer to her than before. He drove her horse to its utmost speed, but he saw that it was idle for him to follow her.

Then Pwyll spoke. 'Maiden', said he, 'for his sake whom thou lovest best, stay for me'. 'I will, gladly', said she, 'and it had been better for the horse hads't thou asked this long since' . . . 'Lady', said he, 'wilt thou tell me anything of thine errands?' 'I will, between me and God', said she. 'My main errand was to try to see thee'. 'That', said Pwyll, 'is to me the most pleasing errand thou couldst come on. And wilt thou tell me who thou art?' 'I will, Lord', said she. 'I am Rhiannon daughter of Hefeydd the Old, and I am being given to a husband against my will. But no husband have I wished for, and that out of love of thee, nor will I have him even now unless thou reject me. And it is to hear thy answer to that that I am come'. 'Between me and God', replied Pwyll, 'this is my answer to thee — that if I had choice of all the ladies and maidens in the world, 'tis thou I would choose'.

And in the third year the men of the land began to feel heaviness of heart at seeing a man whom they loved as much as their lord . . . without offspring; and they summoned him to them. The place they met was Preseleu in Dyfed. 'Lord', said they, 'we know that thou art not of an age with some of the men of this country, but our fear is lest thou have no offspring of the wife thou hast; and so, take another wife of whom thou mayest have offspring. Thou wilt not last for ever', said they . . . 'Why', said Pwyll, 'it is not long as yet since we have been together, and many a chance may yet befall. Grant me a respite herein till the end of the year; and a year from now we will appoint a time to come together, and I will submit to you counsel'.

They appointed a time. Before the end of that time came, a son was born to him, and in Arberth was he born.

The Mabinogion, translated by Gwyn Jones and Thomas Jones, 1949.

4.   *Anglia Transwallina*

Pembrokeshire is usually called *Little England beyonde Wales* and that not unworthilye, and therefore I think good to shewe my opinion whie the same was soe called: Mr Camden calleth it *Anglia Transwallina,* the reasons whie it tooke that name may well be conjectured, for that the most parte of the countrey speacketh Englishe, and in yt noe use of the Welshe. The names of the people are meere Englishe eche familye followinge the Englishe fashion in surnames. Their buildinges are Englishe like, in townreddes and villages, and not in severall and lone houses. Their dyett is as the Englishe people use, as the comon foode is beefe, mutton, pigge, goose, lambe, veale, and kydd which usually the poorest husbandman doth daylye feed on. The names of the countrey places are Englishe . . .

Soe that a stranger travellinge from Englande and haveing rydden foure score miles and more in Wales, haveinge herde no Englishe, nor Englishe names of people, or of places and comeinge hither to Penbrokshere where he shall here nothing but Englishe, and seeinge the rest agreable to Englande, would thinke that Wales were envyroned with England, and would imagine he had travelled throughe Wales and came into England againe.

These reasons and alsoe for that most of the anciente gentlemen came thither out of England . . . might verye fittlye procure it the name of *Litle England beyonde Wales.*

George Owen, *A Description of Penbrokshire,* 1603.

5.   *The Norman Invasion*

A rapid Norman thrust in the latter half of the eleventh century altered the whole political structure of West Wales, and the land known to us as Pembrokeshire became severed from Deheubarth, so that by the twelfth century it consisted of a conglomeration of feudal lordships forming part of those occupied lands known as the marches of Wales. This arrangement lasted until 1536, so that throughout the Middle Ages Pembrokeshire never achieved any unity, and its history is that of fragments, each under its own feudal lord who held the land of the King, often retaining many of the older Welsh customs, local officials such as the *maer* and *ragler,* and elements of Welsh administration that the Norman Lords incorporated into the feudal structure. And so the 'way of life' of the people — particularly in the rural areas — was not unduly disturbed. It was a change of masters rather than a change of population. Even in southern Pembrokeshire where Anglo-Norman occupation was more pronounced, the native population was not so much displaced as absorbed, as shown by the names of Welshmen in early deeds and documents, and by Welsh place-names like Tenby, Pembroke, Pwllcrochan, Llangwm, which would not have survived had the occupation been as ruthless and as thorough as it is sometimes alleged to have been. The most significant of the changes wrought by the conquerors was the establishment of towns and boroughs, almost exclusively Anglo-Norman, and as these were more numerous in southern Pembrokeshire, their influence there was more marked than in the agricultural north. Furthermore, intermarriage between the invaders and the native population, such as Martin, Mortimer, Cantington, de Windsor, Stackpole, and Perrott, to name but a few, led to an early intermingling of the races, and so to a lessening of tension and a general stabilisation. The difference between 'Little England beyond Wales' and the rest of the county is not racial but linguistic.

The Norman arrival was heralded by the advance of Roger de Montgomery (created Earl of Shrewsbury in 1071), who from Cardiganshire thrust boldly into Pembrokeshire with forces that proved sufficiently powerful to retain those areas that the rapidity of their onset had gained. These lands were conferred upon Earl Roger's younger son, Arnulph de Montgomery, who established his *caput* at Pembroke, where a fortalice, hurriedly built, was later erected into a formidable stone castle and entrusted to the care of his chief follower, Gerald de Windsor. Encouraged by this success, other Norman thrusts followed, and the land was parcelled out among the adventurous invaders.

Francis Jones, 'From Norman Times Onward' in *Pembrokeshire Coast, National Park Guide No. 10,* ed. Dillwyn Miles 1973.

6. *I Hate It*

I am sprung from the princes of Wales and from the barons of the Marches, and when I see injustice in either race, I hate it.

Giraldus Cambrensis. *The Itinerary through Wales,* 1188

7. *The Flemings*

The inhabitants of this province derived their origin from Flanders, and were sent by King Henry I to inhabit these districts; a people brave and robust, ever most hostile to the Welsh; a peope, I say, well versed in commerce and woollen manufactories; a people anxious to seek gain by sea or land, in defiance of fatigue and danger; a hardy race, equally fitted for the plough or the sword; a people brave and happy, if Wales (as it ought to have been) had been dear to its sovereign, and had not so frequently experienced the vindictive resentment and ill-treatment of its governors.

It is worthy of remark, that these people, from the inspection of the right shoulders of rams, which have been stripped of their flesh, and not roasted, but boiled, can discover future events, or those which have passed and remained long unknown. They know, also, what is transpiring at a distant place, by a wonderful art, and a prophetic kind of spirit. They declare, also, by means of signs, the undoubted symptoms of approaching peace and war, murders and fires, domestic adulteries, the state of the king, his life and death. It happened in our time, that a man of those parts, whose name was William Mangunel, a person of high rank, and excelling all others in the aforesaid art, had a wife big with child by her own husband's grandson. Well aware of the fact, he ordered a ram from his own flock to be sent to his wife, as a present from her neighbour, which was carried to the cook, and dressed. At dinner, the husband purposely gave the shoulder-bone of the ram, properly cleaned, to his wife, who was also well skilled in this art, for her examination; when, having for a short time examined the secret marks, she smiled, and threw the oracle down on the table. Her husband, dissembling, earnestly demanded the cause of her smiling, and the explanation of the matter. Overcome by his entreaties, she answered: 'The man to whose fold this ram belongs, has an adulterous wife, at this time pregnant by the commission of incest with his own grandson'. The husband, with a sorrowful and dejected countenance, replied: 'You deliver, indeed, an oracle supported by too much truth, which I have so much more reason to lament, as the ignominy you have published redounds to my own injury'. The woman, thus detected, and unable to dissemble her confusion, betrayed the inward feeling of her mind by external signs: shame and sorrow urging her by turns, and manifesting themselves, now by blushes, now by paleness, and lastly (according to the custom of women), by tears.

Giraldus Cambrensis, *The Itinerary through Wales,* 1188.

8. *The Flemish Weavers*

It is often said that the growth of the Pembrokeshire woollen industry, and particularly the introduction of fulling mills resulted from the immigration of Flemish weavers into Pembrokeshire in the twelfth and again in the fourteenth centuries. Their importance and the widespread changes attributed to them have probably been exaggerated for the first wave of immigrants came too early and the second too late to explain the establishment of fulling mills in Pembrokeshire. Between 1300 and 1330 at least seventy-one *pandai* were built in Wales, but only six were constructed during the following seventy years; yet the majority of Flemish weavers did not come to Wales before 1331. Furthermore, it is difficult to imagine that the work of a small isolated group in Pembrokeshire should have penetrated the valleys of Glamorgan and Monmouthshire, though fulling mills were as common there as they were in Pembrokeshire. The coming of the Flemings in fact, may have been evidence of the increasing importance of the woollen industry, rather than a cause of its growth.

J. Geraint Jenkins, 'Pembrokeshire and the Woollen Industry' in *The Pembrokeshire Historian,* No. 2, 1966.

9. *Little Englanders*

Good humour and cheeriness are eminently characteristic of our Little Englanders. In charm of manner, too, they yield to none, and a peculiarly pleasant voice tends to strengthen the good impression thus created. This agreeable address is indicative of their best quality. The inhabitants of South Pembrokeshire are essentially a kindly folk; they are gentle to women and children, and merciful to animals; indeed cases of wife beating or beast torture are practically unknown. On the other hand a love of making things pleasant militates against truth. It is absolutely hopeless to expect an exact statement. Disagreeable angles are rounded off, and to screen a comrade the lie downright is deemed commendable. Clannishness is very strong. These virtues and vices are perhaps ascribable to Gaelic blood. The much vaunted Irish chastity, however, is, I regret to say, not a marked characteristic of the race. 'Love children' abound, and a girl who has tripped is not considered to have erred very grievously. This tolerance seems to be of Kymric origin. Unlike the Welshmen our Little Englanders are good horsemen and bold sailors, qualities inherited from their Norse ancestors; heavy drinkers too, a failing we may perhaps attribute to the same source. They are, however, not quarrelsome when in their cups. Extremely hospitable, they are very thrifty, but lack enterprise, and save rather than make money. Slovenly in their houses, persons, and work, they are curiously unaesthetic, and at the same time passionately fond of music.

Edward Laws, *The History of Little England Beyond Wales,* 1888.

10. *The English Element*

It has been said that to understand Pembrokeshire Welsh you need only a working knowledge of English. In its context this statement was intended to emphasize the present day tendency of speakers of the dialect of north Pembrokeshire to use newly borrowed English words — a tendency, common to other parts of Wales, which has been brought about by the pervading anglicizing influence of newspapers, books, radio, television, travel, settlement, communications, inventions, and even education. But over a long period, before it began to degenerate into an adulterated patois under twentieth-century conditions, the dialect had been exposed to English influences. The Anglo-Norman conquest of south Pembrokeshire in medieval times and the settlement there of a large colony of English immigrants from the west country ousted the Welsh language from the area and replaced it with English which since then has remained the language of 'Little England beyond Wales'. Welsh survived in the northern part of the county but during the course of the centuries, in spite of a well-defined linguistic boundary across the county, the vocabulary of the Welsh dialect absorbed a considerable number of words from the English dialect of the south. This was inevitable over a long period of inter-communication between the two nations but it should be noted that there was a much greater reluctance on the part of the English to borrow Welsh words from their neighbours. Along the linguistic divide there must have been a bilingual belt: the presence of place-names with both English and Welsh forms in the border parishes go far to prove this. Another channel through which borrowing was apt to take place was that of trade, the centres of which were Haverfordwest and, to a lesser extent, Pembroke and Tenby. The Welsh made regular visits to the market and fairs of these English towns to sell their produce and stock and buy household goods and agricultural implements and utensils. English-speaking merchants from Haverfordwest were the main stall-holders in the fairs and markets of north Pembrokeshire. The traffic in goods naturally resulted in a traffic in words and must be regarded as one of the main sources of English loan-words in the dialect and, furthermore, is an important aspect of the influence of one culture upon another within this racially and linguistically divided county. Another factor was the immigration of population across the linguistic boundary, mainly perhaps through inter-marriage. Some loan-words no doubt came in through other channels such as schools, churches, the professions, travellers, and the literary language. The cumulative effect of these contacts down the centuries is reflected in the strong English element which became a feature of the Welsh dialect of north Pembrokeshire long before the influx of English words during the last thirty or forty years.

B. G. Charles, 'The English Element in Pembrokeshire Welsh' in *Studia Celtica,* Vol. VI, 1971.

III

Ancient Monuments

1. *The Most Stone Monuments*

As we enter Pembrokeshire itself, the county which for its size certainly has the most stone monuments of any in Britain, we first encounter a few sites in the relatively low-lying country round Milford Haven. Of these the dolmen of King's Quoit has a fine position near the sea at Old Castle Head, Manorbier, while the names of both King's Quoit and its opposite number, the Devil's Quoit, Broomhill Burrows, at the west end of this southern peninsula of Pembrokeshire, strike the right note for the 'Little England beyond Wales'. There is a group of standing stones near the southern end of the great sweeping curve of St Bride's Bay, but little else until, passing the romantic landmark of Castle Roch, we reach the northern part of the county where monuments crowd thickly on and between St David's and Strumble Heads.

This is attractive and interesting country which, like Cornwall, is chiefly renowned for its coasts. Many bays — from long bows of gleaming pale sand, to little pockets with no more than a few yards of sand held among the stones — are recessed between fanged headlands where the sea is always at work, whether it is with a gentle pushing and falling back, or a savage attack with spray streaming out along the cliffs. The inland scenery is more varied than in Cornwall for the plateau of the old sedimentary rocks is broken by abrupt outcrops of the much harder rocks spewed up by volcanoes. These outcrops, looking a little like South African kopjes, have attracted human settlers by offering both building material and good shelter. Each one will be seen to have a little farm with its pretty, dilapidated, out-buildings edged up against it, built of the same rock but most sharply distinguished by a coat of whitewash. It has been noticed that a very considerable number of dolmens have similarly been built against the volcanic outcrops; their architects certainly made use of the stone, but they would hardly have been interested in the advantages of shelter and one wonders whether these very striking rock masses had been endowed with spirits, local deities, and had, therefore, a sanctity which made them desirable burial-places.

Jacquetta Hawkes, *A Guide to the Prehistoric and Roman Monuments in England and Wales,* 1973.

2.   *Flamboyant Tomb*

There is something about Pentre Ifan which is almost flamboyant, a virtuoso display of skill and inspiration. Though it is built on the same form as many other cromlechs, several of which survive not far away, it is simply larger and grander, and has remained more spectacularly intact. Beautiful and clever, its elegant capstone still confidently in place, it stands out on its breeze slope as a permanent memorial of the values and aspirations of the New Stone Age. Because nobody could have built such a thing without first possessing something more than a mere animal instinct for immediate survival.

Michael Senior, *Portrait of South Wales,* 1974.

3.   ENCOUNTER AT PENTRE IFAN

It looks weird from the road,
Like a monstrous spider-crab.

Approaching through a narrow
Earth-banked path, we emerge
To a broader sky.

Stone-walled fields shelve
Mistily towards the sea,
Under the ghost of a clouded sun.

Here it is congruous:
Stone in a field of stones;

But still exotic,
With the unnatural grace
Of man.

The capstone balances
On uprights like a boat
Inverted for the winter.

It is spacious under the roof,
In the house of the dead.

Others approach; you greet them
Familiarly, with surprise.
We stand shadowed.

Inevitable that we should say,
'Wales is a small country.'

Jeremy Hooker in *Pembrokeshire Poems,* 1976.

4.   *The Bluestones of Stonehenge*

Let us start with the bluestones (the so-called bluestones, we should
say — because the word as used at Stonehenge applies to five separate
kinds of rock which have in common only a bluish tint, best seen
when wet, and an igneous origin).

Most of the bluestones are dolerite, a coarse-grained greenish blue
stone, but twelve of these stones are now buried stumps of interesting
composition: five are volcanic lava, darkish grey-blue in colour,
called rhyolite; four are a type of darkish olive-green volcanic ash;
two are a grey-blue Cosheston sandstone, and one is a bluish
calcareous ash. Geologists find much to speculate on in the varying
natures and placements and weatherings of these different types of
stones, but for the nonspecialist the most interesting fact about the
various bluestones is this: all three main types — dolerite, rhyolite
and volcanic ash — occur naturally close together in a small area

about a mile square in the Prescelly Mountains of Wales — and *only* there. 'There can thus be no doubt now,' notes Atkinson, 'that it was from this very restricted region that the bluestones were chosen and brought to Stonehenge.' That distance, as the crow flies, is 130 miles — as the rollers roll, the raft floats, and the rollers roll again, the distance is 240 miles. Bearing in mind that those eighty or more blue-stones weighed up to five tons each, that is quite a long way. Nothing like this astonishing feat of transportation was ever attempted by any other people anywhere else in prehistoric Europe. The only comparable performance, indeed, was the moving of the other big stones, the sarsens, to Stonehenge.

The probable route began at the blue-stone source in the Prescelly Mountains, went southwest to the sea at Milford Haven, followed the coast all the way to Avonmouth, then went up the Bristol Avon and Frome rivers, overland to the river Wylye, down that stream to the Salisbury Avon, and up that river to Amesbury and the Stonehenge Avenue. Total overland distance: about 25 miles. Total water distance: about 215 miles. This route seems most probable because it makes maximum use of safe waterways. Furthermore, there is circumstantial evidence: near Milford Haven occur the only two kinds of bluestones not found in the Prescellys — Cosheston sandstone and calcareous ash. Presumably the Stonehengers picked up these stones on the way.

Gerald S. Hawkins, *Stonehenge Decoded,* 1966.

5.   *Stonehenge – The Motive?*

Of all the aspects of Stonehenge — by far the most remarkable is the fact of the transport of its stones from Pembrokeshire. What can have been the motives which prompted this extraordinary undertaking, for which there is no parallel in European prehistory, apart from the transport of the Stonehenge sarsens themselves?

I am myself convinced that to the Beaker people who opened up the trade-route to Ireland along the south coast of Wales the mountain of Prescelly had a very special significance — that it was, in fact, a sacred mountain. A glance at the map shows that Prescelly Top, 1760 ft above sea-level, is the highest point anywhere in the south-western peninsula of Wales, and dominates the landscape for miles around.

On a clear day it can even be seen on the far horizon from the hills above Aberystwyth, fifty miles away to the north. To the traveller humping his pack along the ridgeways of south Pembrokeshire on the last stages of the land-route to the West, its cloud-wrapped summit must have seemed no less the home of gods than did Mount Ida to a voyager in the Cretan plain; and to the trader returning across the sea from Ireland, shielding his eyes from the spray as he peered across the bows of his laden boat, the same summit would be the first welcome sign of land ahead.

I believe, therefore, that the awe-inspiring character of Prescelly Mountain is alone sufficient to account for the special significance of the rocks which crop out along its crest. But there is another way in which a special demand for these rocks may have been created in Wessex. Among the stone battle-axes used by Necked-Beaker warriors there are a few made of preselite, that is, the spotted dolerite of Prescelly. Admittedly they are very few; but one must remember that for every object now in a museum many more must originally have been in circulation. It must be realized, too, that weapons, and axes in particular, had a significance in prehistoric times beyond that of mere efficacy or utility. Like Excalibur, they possessed symbolic and magical qualities, qualities that might well be transmitted to the material of which they were made. May it not be, then, that the particular virtues of this Prescelly rock became celebrated in Wessex through the medium of these weapons of prestige, and that when the time came to build at Stonehenge a monument of especial significance and sanctity, it was this rock, from the cloud-capped crest of the sacred mountain far to the west, that was chosen in preference to all others?

R. J. C. Atkinson, *Stonehenge,* 1956.

New evidence from radiocarbon dates and from further excavations at Stonehenge has shown that in the first instance the bluestones were probably transported from Pembrokeshire not directly to Stonehenge itself but to a site as yet undiscovered, perhaps on Salisbury Plain to the west of Stonehenge, and a date much earlier than the establishment by a Beaker people of a trade route from the west. This change of date in no way affects the remarkable character of this great feat of prehistoric transport. — See R. J. C. Atkinson, *Stonhenge,* Penguin Books, 1979, p. 214.

6. *A Glimpse of Tir-nan-Og*

Curiously enough you can see Ireland from Pembrokeshire. On an exceptionally clear day last June, when the whole western sky had been swept clean of cloud after rain and the horizon was a sharp line drawn against the pale blue, I climbed Carn Ingli, the 1,000-ft outlier of the Preseli Hills. These rolling moorlands hold secrets among the scattered rock outcrops that rival the tors of Dartmoor in their impressive shapes. From one of them came the blue stones that form the heart of Stonehenge. Great cromlechs like that of Pentre Ifan lie on the lower slopes. Everywhere you feel the presence of the megalithic tomb-builders, of the Iron Age warriors who piled their stones for the great hill-forts and of the kindly and absent-minded old Celtic saints. Deep below Carn Ingli runs the wooded valley of the Gwaun, where they have resolutely refused to accept the reform of the calendar in the 18th century and joyously celebrate the New Year 11 days later than the rest of Britain. In all this, I see a faint anticipation of Ireland.

I climbed over the tumbled walls of the Carn Ingli fort with a tingle of excitement. The conditions were just right for the long views and Carn Ingli and the Preselis are perfectly placed for those great visual leaps which stir the imagination and which you can only get on the isolated high hills of western Britain. . . .

But was the link-up with Ireland possible from Carn Ingli on that exceptionally clear June day with the green farms of North Pembrokeshire stretched below me like a map encircled by the sea? I turned my binoculars to the north-west and there, rising up over the very edge of the world, were the outlines of another land, a mysterious country like the fabled Celtic Tir-nan-Og, the land of eternal youth where no snow falls and life passes in an everlasting June.

Wynford Vaughan Thomas, *Countryside Companion,* 1979.

7.   *The Dancing Stones*

The Sagranus Stone at St Dogmell's, Pembrokeshire, was formerly used as a bridge over a brook not far from where it at present stands — luckily with its inscribed face downwards, so that the sculpture remained unharmed while generations were tramping over it. During its use as a bridge it bore the reputation of being haunted by a white lady, who was constantly seen gliding over it at the witching hour of midnight. No man or woman could be induced to touch the strange stone after dark, and its supernatural reputation no doubt helped materially in its preservation unharmed till the present time. It is considered on paleographic grounds to be of the fourth century.

In Pembrokeshire also are found the famous Dancing Stones of Stackpool. These are three upright stones standing about a mile from each other, the first at Stackpool Warren, the second further to the west, on a stone tumulus in a field known as Horestone Park, and the third still further westward. One of many traditions concerning them is to the effect that on a certain day they meet and come down to Sais's Ford to dance, and after their revel is over return home and resume their places.

Wirt Sikes, *British Goblins,* 1879.

8.   *Early Christian Monuments*

The archaeological evidence for early Christianity in Dyfed is made up almost entirely of the inscribed and carved stones which were set up to commemorate important individuals, secular and religious, of the time. No buildings of the earlier period are known; they would have been small churches and cells which in many places have been succeeded and overlaid by mediaeval parish churches. The Church was organised on a monastic basis, with religious communities (*clas*) whose task in the fifth and sixth centuries was a missionary one: the results of their efforts in gaining acceptance for Christianity through-out the country are seen in the dedications of individual churches to the saints who were the patrons of the *clas*. The chief missionary church in Pembrokeshire (as a part of Dyfed) was St David's (Mynwy); there were others at St Dogmael's, Nevern, Penally, and Caldey (Ynys Pŷr), each with its own saint.

W. F. Grimes, 'Archaeology' in *Pembrokeshire Coast, National Park Guide No. 10,* ed. Dillwyn Miles, 1973.

9. *Ogam Writing*

Ogam is an alphabetic script which consists of lines, representing consonants, and dots, representing vowels. It is, at any rate in its extant form, incised on stones, though there is a theory that an older form of it might have been cut on sticks and used for carrying short messages. The markings are organised around the corner of a pillar, the vowels being indented into the edge itself, and the lines hatched either side or obliquely across it — their position, to right, left, or across, and the number in which they are grouped (from one to five) determining the letter they represent. The inscription commonly runs from the bottom upwards.

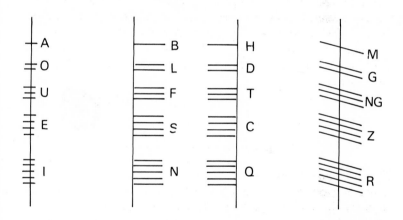

Clearly ogam inscriptions are all very early, some of them, on linguistic grounds, being thought to be of the fourth century; but the form in which they occur makes them difficult to date precisely, and their relation, at any rate as they exist today, to the Latin alphabet, means at least that the form continued well into Christian times. It was the Sagranus stone at St Dogmael's which made it possible, in 1848, for the script (which had somehow become forgotten) to be deciphered.

Michael Senior, *Portrait of South Wales,* 1974.

IV

Castles and Places

1. PRAISE OF TENBY

There is a fine fortress stands on the sea,
The bright headland is gay at the Calends,
And when the ocean puts forth its might
Commonly poets are loud over mead-cups.
The hurrying wave surges against it,
They abandon the green flood to the Picts.
And through my prayer, O God, may I find
As I keep faith, atonement with you . . .

There is a fine fortress of revel and tumult
A multitude makes, a crying of birds.
Gay was that company met at the Calends
Round a generous lord, splendid and brave.
Before he had gone to the oaken church
From a bowl of glass gave me mead and wine.

There is a fine fortress on the foreshore,
Finely to each is given his share.
I know at Tenby — pure white the seagull —
Companions of Bleiddudd, lord of the court.
The night of the Calends it was my custom
To lie by my king, brilliant in war,
With a cloak coloured purple, having such cheer
I were the tongue to the poets of Britain!

There is a fine fortress on the height,
Its feasting lavish, its revelry loud.
Lovely about it, that camp of heroes,
Is the wandering spray, long are its wings.
Hoarse sea-birds haunt the crest of the crag.
Let all anger be banished over the hills!
I wish for Bleiddudd the best bliss that may be —
Let these words of remembrance be weighed at his wake!

Anonymous, c.875, trans. Anthony Conran *The Penguin Book of Welsh Verse,* 1967,

2. *Pembroke Castle*

One night, when fifteen soldiers had deserted, and endeavoured to escape from the castle in a small boat, on the following morning Giraldus [de Windsor] invested their armour bearers with the arms and estates of their masters, and decorated them with the military order. The garrison being, from the length of the siege, reduced to the utmost want of provisions, the constable, with great prudence and flattering hopes of success, caused four hogs, which yet remained, to be cut into small pieces and thrown down to the enemy from the fortifications. The next day, having again recourse to a more refined stratagem, he contrived that a letter, sealed with his own signet, should be found before the house of Wilfred, bishop of St David's, who was then by chance in that neighbourhood, as if accidentally dropped, stating that there would be no necessity of soliciting the assistance of Earl Arnulph for the next four months to come. The contents of these letters being made known to the army, the troops abandoned the siege of the castle, and retired to their own homes. Giraldus, in order to make himself and his dependents more secure, married Nest, the sister of Gruffydd, prince of South Wales, by whom he had an illustrious progeny of both sexes.

Giraldus Cambrensis, *The Itinerary through Wales,* 1188.

3. *In Pembroke City*

In Pembroke City when I was young
I lived by the Castle Keep
Sixpence a week was my wages
For working for the chimbley sweep.
Six cold pennies he gave me
Not a farthing more or less
And all the fare I could afford
Was parsnip gin and watercress.
I did not need a knife and fork
Or a bib up to my chin
To dine on a dish of watercress
And a jug of parsnip gin.
Did you ever hear a growing boy
To live so cruel cheap
On grub that has no flesh and bones
And liquor that makes you weep?
Sweep sweep chimbley sweep,
I wept through Pembroke City
Poor and barefoot in the snow
Till a kind young woman took pity.
Poor little chimbley sweep she said
Black as the ace of spades
O nobody's swept my chimbley
Since my husband went his ways.
Come and sweep my chimbley
Come and sweep my chimbley
She sighed to me with a blush
Come and sweep my chimbley
Come and sweep my chimbley
Bring along your chimbley brush!

Dylan Thomas, *Under Milk Wood,* 1954.

4.   *Maenor Pyrr*

The castle called Maenor Pyrr, that is, the mansion of Pyrrus, who also possessed the island of Caldey, which the Welsh call Ynys Pyrr, or the island of Pyrrus, is distant about three miles from Pembroke. It is excellently well defended by turrets and bulwarks, and is situated on the summit of a hill extending on the western side towards the seaport, having on the northern and southern sides a fine fish-pond under its walls, as conspicuous for its grand appearance, as for the depth of its waters, and a beautiful orchard on the same side, inclosed on one part by a vineyard, and on the other by a wood, remarkable for the projection of its rocks, and the height of its hazel trees. This country is well supplied with corn, sea-fish, and imported wines; and what is preferable to every other advantage, from its vicinity to Ireland, it is tempered by a salubrious air. Demetia, therefore, with its seven cantreds, is the most beautiful, as well as the most powerful district of Wales; Pembroke, the finest part of the province of Demetia; and the place I have just described, the most delightful part of Pembroke. It is evident, therefore, that Maenor Pirr is the pleasantest spot in Wales; and the author may be pardoned for having thus extolled his native soil, his genial territory, with a profusion of praise and admiration.

Giraldus Cambrensis, *The Itinerary through Wales,* 1188.

5.   POEM FROM MANORBIER

I in this sun-worn house of books and flowers
open my eyes at dawn of morning light
upon a carillon of castle towers

and turrets caught in showers of larks and leaves.
An arc of sand eternally is tilled
by tides below, where wind-frilled water heaves.

I wake to the break of waves and the rake
of surf in the caves, in the architraves
of silence where dark waters lie opaque —

the cloisters of the sea where oysters share
the prayer of prawns in moist profundity,
in undine cells under the water-glare.

Gerallt grandson of Nest, Helen of Wales,
a boy in this Troy, do you walk here still
on the hill in a night of nightingales?

O Dylan son of Aranrhod, young sea-god
for whom all the waves of the ocean wept,
are these the pools you leapt, the sands you trod?

Raymond Garlick in *Pembrokeshire Poems,* 1976.

6.   *A Little Pretty Pile*

Narbarthe a litle preati pile of old Syr Rheses given onto hym by King
Henri the VIII. Ther is a poore village . . . Grifith Nicolas
graundfather to Syr Rise boute it of the Duke of York, but after loste.

John Leland, *The Itinerary in Wales,* 1536-39.

7.   *Roch*

Roch Castle stands most singularly, on the top of a high rock, rising
perpendicularly from an extensive flat, on which there is no similar
appearance elsewhere. The castle, from this circumstance, is seen at a
great distance, and so completely occupies the summit, that the
artificial fabric is scarcely to be distinguished from its natural base,
but on a near approach. According to the legendary tale, the owner
had a foreboding that he should die by the sting of an adder: he
therefore built his mansion in such a manner as to place himself as
much as possible out of his enemy's reach. The conclusion of the story
will naturally be anticipated: if he had not died by the sting of an
adder, the motive of his choice would scarcely have been worth
recording.

Benjamin Heath Malkin, *The Scenery, Antiquities and Biography of
South Wales,* 1804.

8.   *A Circumstance at Haverfordwest Castle*

A circumstance happened in the castle of Haverford during our time, which ought not to be omitted. A famous robber was fettered and confined in one of its towers, and was often visited by three boys, the son of the earl of Clare, and two others, one of whom was son of the lord of the castle, and the other his grandson, sent thither for their education, and who applied to him for arrows, with which he used to supply them. One day, at the request of the children, the robber, being brought from his dungeon, took advantage of the absence of the gaoler, closed the door, and shut himself up with the boys. A great clamour instantly arose, as well from the boys within, as from the people without, nor did he cease, with an uplifted axe, to threaten the lives of the children, until indemnity and security were assured to him in the most ample manner.

Giraldus Cambrensis, *The Itinerary through Wales,* 1188.

9.   *A Tilt and Tournament*

The most memorable circumstance in the history of this castle [Carew] is the celebration of a tilt and tournament held here by Sir Rice ap Thomas after he had indulged his taste in decorating this favourite spot, and had received the order of the garter. These exercises were proclaimed in honour of St George's day. The company assembled from all parts of Wales. Not only his own family and neighbours were present, but the Vaughans of Tretower out of Brecknockshire, the Mansels and Herberts from Glamorgan and Monmouthshire, and many other distinguished gentlemen from greater distances. These guests of the first rank were all lodged within the castle. Besides them, five or six hundred more, of decent quality, were drawn together to be spectators of these unusual solemnities. Tents and pavilions were pitched all about the domain for the reception of the inferior visitors, with provisions, beds, and every other species of accommodation. The festival lasted five days, commencing with the eve of St George's eve, when Sir Rice reviewed his military guests, amounting to five hundred, and divided them into five troops. On St George's eve they were exercised in various evolutions. On St George's day they visited the Bishop of St Davids, then residing at Lamphey Park, at the distance of little more than a mile. Sir Rice was questioned at the gate, Why he came thither in military array? He justified himself as one of St George's knights, whose duty it was to appear in soldierly equipage on that day. His object, however, was peaceable; to pray for the soul of St George, and the prosperity of King Henry, the sovereign of the honourable order; in which service he entreated the assistance of the Bishop. His petition of course was not refused; but he and his associates were required to robe themselves in their civil and scholastic livery. The Abbot of Talley and the Prior of Carmarthen assisted the bishop in doing the honours; the parties complimented each other; sang and prayed; walked thrice round the court, and then proceeded to the chapel. There the same ceremonies were performed as in St George's Chapel at Windsor; after which the clergy returned with the company to dinner at Carew. Each of the five captains had his particular tent in the park, where he entertained his soldiers and other friends, whilst Sir Rice presided in the castle. Over the great gate was a picture of St George and St David embracing. In the great hall there were two long tables, and a cross table left vacant for the king. The bishop said grace; the king's chair was turned, in token of his absence; the guests put on their hats, and dined; the bards attended in their places, and the insipidity of general conversation was relieved by music in the intervals. A solemn challenge for the honour of the ladies, service in the chapel, and a formal supper, ended the ceremonial of the day. The next day the tournament took place, between Sir William Herbert, challenger, and Sir Gruffyth Rice, son of Sir Rice ap Thomas, defendant; each with their assistants, their escutcheons and mottos. The parties tilted well, and innocently Sir Rice, the judge of the combat, laboured under a polite incapacity of deciding; and face-tiously advised the combatants to look anxiously to the honour of those ladies whom they had so manfully supported. Divine service and dinner occupied the rest of the evening. On the fifth day, the day of parting, a wager of a supper at Carmarthen was to be decided between Sir William Herbert and Sir Gruffyth Rice, by skill in gymnastic exercises. Sir Rice ap Thomas, inflexibly well bred, gave his verdict by previous agreement against his son. After dinner they rode to Carmarthen; — a long ride after dinner; — there they supped, saw a play performed by the domestics of Carew, and parted.

Benjamin Heath Malkin, *The Scenery, Antiquities and Biography of South Wales*, 1804.

10.   *A Veritable Showpiece*

But it was Sir John Perrot's magnificent home at Carew Castle that really reflected the catholicity of culture of the genuine Elizabethan aristocrat. His library contained a number of books in French and Spanish, as well as in English and the classical languages, while his music room abounded with all the known instruments of the age. There were sackbuts, cornets, a flute, two recorders, a violin, an Irish harp, hautboys and a pair of virginals, together with books of music — rare acquisition which he may have procured through his contacts at Court, and a set of psalm books for singing . . .

The gentry furnished their country mansions with a lavishness that would have astounded their grandfathers. There was little in the way of fashionable domestic ware that did not eventually find a place in their homes. Much of it was purchased in London and other English cities, but there were also Welsh craftsmen at hand to make pieces of furniture from home grown timber, and to show their skill in emulating foreign styles, as well as incorporating their own.

Most of the rooms, including bedrooms, were wainscotted either in full or in half panels, and, as a result, tapestry was gradually being superseded although pieces of it, especially of Arras manufacture continued to be used for wall hangings. Tables and chairs were made of various kinds of wood, particularly ash and walnut, but an innovation was cupboards of maple tree wood. Beds were generally built of wainscot or walnut, sometimes fastened to the walls, and having canopies and hanging draperies of silk, fustian, velvet or taffeta fringed with lace or gold and embroidered with coloured designs. Furniture of foreign make was much in vogue, and Flanders chairs and chests, Danzig chests and Lisbon stools were placed in halls and bedrooms to invest them with an air of refined gentility. Floors were being gradually covered with a variety of carpets and rugs. Sir John Perrot had a positive passion for them, and was extravagant in the purchase of carpets of Turkish, Dornex and Scottish make and of Irish rugs. In fact, Carew Castle was a veritable showpiece of contemporary taste in home furnishings. Damask cushions, taffeta curtains, sarcenet quilts and holland cloth were only a few of the foreign fabrics that competed in colour, quality and profusion with furnishings of silk, satin, velvet and the more homely fustian and flannel.

G. Dyfnallt Owen, *Elizabethan Wales,* 1964.

11. *Newport*

The lofty situation of the castle and its steep approach, give it an air of some importance, nor are its fragments without their grandeur. Little of its history is known. In the year 1215, Lhewelin ap Jorwerth, after having taken Newcastle in Emlyn, turned his arms toward this district, and in the progress of his victorious career, levelled Newport Castle with the ground. I have not been able to ascertain the date of the present structure; and it probably has not been so much a scene of action as to enable a more diligent inquirer than myself to make out any connected account of it. There is a kind of freestone found near Newport, of a dark grey colour for the most part, with some veins of white, and some of yellow, intermixed. It is well adapted for building, and has been much used in all the castles of this neighbourhood. It is dug out of the cliff. The stone in the mountain above Newport is of a different sort, rising in large masses, but not difficult to be hewn, yet sufficiently durable for common purposes of architecture. This mountain is high and sharp, and stony. The pasture of it was formerly given by the lord of the hundred to the burgesses of this town, with many other liberties and privileges. Its circumference is five or six miles, and affords excellent sheep-walks. There are slate-quarries at Newport, though their quality is not esteemed so good as that of the hills about Velindre. The working of these and the salmon and herring fishery constitute nearly the whole trade of the place. There are two or three weirs on the river Nevern. The market is very small and bad; it was anciently held on the Sunday morning at sun-rise: and there is a very great fair on the 16th of June. The town seems to have been of consequence in the time of Edward the First, when there was a large market every Thursday, and the tenants were prohibited from selling anything without first offering it at the market, and paying a toll.

Benjamin Heath Malkin, *The Scenery, Antiquities and Biography of South Wales,* 1804.

12. *Slebech*

The Knights Hospitallers of St John at Slebech were firmly established by 1198 through grants made by the son and grandson of Wizo the Fleming of Wiston. Although there were many pilgrims to the shrine at Slebech all through the Middle Ages, almost the only glimpse we get of the life of the Knights there is from Lewis Glyn Cothi in the second half of the fourteenth century, when he tells us Slebech was ever thronged with pilgrims 'seeking the pardons to purify men'.

The Knights had the coveted right of sanctuary, and although there appears to be no record of anyone who used it, there can be little doubt that many a hunted man fled there in those parlous times. At Slebech the fugitive could be sure of safety, for there was a long underground passage from the house to the banks of the tidal river, from whence he could make his way to the sea. This passage was re-discovered during the 1939-45 war by a party of VADs from the Military Hospital then at Picton Castle. They crawled through it — and came out inside Slebech House, then occupied by American troops who promptly arrested them, and kept them under guard until an officer from their Unit came over to identify them!

Two of the brothers of Bishop Barlow bought Slebech after its suppression. It remained in the family until 1773, except for a period of sequestration during the Commonwealth, for the Barlows, to their credit, remained loyal to the King when so many other Pembroke-shire gentlemen were trimming their sails to the prevailing wind.

Another tradition of Slebech — that Nelson's Lady Hamilton was a visitor and is buried there — is founded on a misapprehension. Sir William Hamilton's first wife was a Barlow, and it was she who brought him the property in Pembrokeshire which afterwards passed to Charles Greville. This first Lady Hamilton died in 1782, and was buried in the family vault of the old church at Slebech, and Sir William was buried with her in 1803, whilst his second wife, Nelson's Emma, is buried in Calais.

Maxwell Fraser, *Introducing West Wales,* 1956.

13. *Stackpole Treasures*

Stackpole is now the residence of the noble 'Thane of Cawdor', whose ancestor acquired the estate by marriage with Miss Lort, the sole heiress to all these broad acres.

The mansion contains some interesting works of art and relics of antiquity, including a portrait by Romney of the famous Lady

Hamilton; a fine painting of Admiral Sir George Campbell, GCB, who captured the French invaders at Fishguard in 1797; and a curious old map of the county, adorned with shields and armorial devices.

That famous drinking-cup the 'Hirlas horn' was formerly to be seen at Stackpole, but has since been removed to Golden Grove, in Carmarthenshire. This curious treasure is mounted in silver, and is supported upon an oval plinth by two silver quadrupeds. The latter are probably the only remaining portions of the original horn, presented by Henry of Richmond to his faithful entertainer, Dafydd ap Ievan, while resting at the castle of Llwyn Dafydd, in Cardiganshire, on his way to Bosworth Field.

H. Thornhill Timmins, *Nooks and Corners of Pembrokeshire,* 1895.

14.   *Home Life at Picton Castle*

Two delightful glimpses of life at Picton Castle have survived from different periods of the Philipps regime. The first we owe to the indefatigable Lewis Glyn Cothi, who has left us a vivid description of the hospitality of Thomas ap Phillip and his lady in the latter half of the fifteenth century. He calls her 'the golden daughter of Harri Dwnn', the 'Silken One of Pembroke, and a Rose', comparing her beauty with the Northern Lights, but his muse rises to its highest pitch of enthusiasm in describing the festive board, graced 'with more than twenty kinds of wine', including those of Mount, Normandy, Bordeaux, and Rochelle, Speyer-on-the-Rhine, sparkling Muscatel, the grape of Spain, and the home-brewed beverage of his native land — which he makes clear he appreciated at their true worth!

The second picture is given in a poem by Mary Philipps of an evening at Picton during the time of the Good Sir John's second son and namesake, usually known as the Jacobite for his enthusiastic support of the South Wales Jacobite Society, the Society of Sea Sergeants. Miss Mary describes an evening in 1754 with the five members of the family whiling away the time beside the fire. Sir John reading, and 'carefully turning o'er many a page', his lady enjoying a nap; Miss Betty 'all meekness, and mildness and merit', 'dextrously making a ruff'; Miss Kitty 'busily altering a ruffle', and Miss Mary herself, presumably, writing, for the poem ends:

Now Sir John shuts his book, and my Lady's awake,
The chambermaid's called for the candles to take,
My pen I must quit, to wish you goodnight,
May I give you more pleasure the next time I write.

Maxwell Fraser, *Introducing West Wales,* 1956.

15.   *Pembrokeshire Houses*

It remains to ask how the south-west, particularly Pembrokeshire, acquired its distinctive character — the lateral outshuts of the peasant houses, the vaulted first-floor halls of the aristocracy, not forgetting the unusually early fireplaces and the peculiarly shaped chimneys common to both.

Of the outshut development no completely satisfactory explanation has been advanced. The most likely cause is the independent development of simple stone building in a remote area, far from the conventions of timber construction, and free from the discipline of bay and frame. For the vaulted first-floor halls, and perhaps for the fireplaces, there is a more specific possible source. First-floor halls, not unlike those of Pembrokeshire, are depicted on the Bayeux Tapestry. Early in the story Harold is shown feasting in his vaulted first-floor hall at Bosham while fate, in the person of a messenger from the Conqueror, ascends the outside stair and knocks on the door. Most of the houses surviving from the Romanesque period, such as Boothby Pagnell, the 'Jew's House' at Lincoln or the early merchants' houses of Norman Southampton, are first-floor halls, confirming the essential truth of the Tapestry. Although the earliest Pembrokeshire first-floor halls are unlikely to antedate the thirteenth century, it is not unreasonable to ascribe the peculiarly localised concentration of this idea to the conquest and colonisation of the county after 1093. It is likely that the early fireplaces are ultimately tied to the first-floor hall design, and it is noteworthy that the round chimney was known in such houses in Norman England. If, therefore, a father of the Pembrokeshire style has to be found, then surely it is the Duke of Normandy, his heirs and successors.

Peter Smith, *Houses of the Welsh Countryside,* 1975.

V

Holy Places

1. ST GOVAN

St Govan, he built him a cell
By the side of the Pembroke sea,
And there, as the crannied sea-gulls dwell,
In a tiny, secret citadel
He sighed for eternity.

St Govan, he built him a cell
Between the wild sky and the sea,
Where the sunsets redden the rolling swell
And brooding splendour has thrown her spell
On valley and moorland lea.

St Govan still lies in his cell,
But his soul, long since, is free,
And one may wonder — and who can tell —
If good St Govan likes Heaven as well
As his cell by that sounding sea?

A. G. Prys-Jones.

2. *St Govan's*

Upon reaching the cliff-head, we discover a flight of rough steps,
whereof, as the fable goes, no man can tell the number. Descending
the winding way we find ourselves, a few minutes later, before St
Govan's Chapel.

This diminutive structure stands in a narrow chine between wild, tumbled crags. It is rudely constructed of weather-stained blocks of limestone, arched over with a primitive kind of vault, and is lighted by two or three narrow windows. A low doorway in the eastern wall gives access to a cell-like recess, just big enough for a man to turn round in. Here, according to a curious old legend, St Govan sought shelter from his pagan enemies; whereupon the massy rock closed over him and hid him from his pursuers, opening again to release the pious anchorite as soon as the chase was overpassed.

About this queer nook, the popular superstition runs that all who can keep to the self-same wish, while they turn around therein, will obtain their desire before the year is out — a belief that, to judge from the well-worn appearance of the rock face, must be widely entertained.

Upon the western gable rises a small bell-cot, long since bereft of its solitary bell. For it happened, 'once upon a time', that a wicked pirate who chanced to be sailing by became enamoured of its silvery tones, and, landing with his rascally crew, plundered the sanctuary of its treasure. His success, however, was short-lived, for a mighty storm arose and overwhelmed the vessel, so that every soul aboard perished in the raging waves. Meanwhile the bereaved hermit was compensated for his loss with a miraculous stone, which, when struck, gave forth the identical tone of the cherished bell; and credulous folk to this day affirm that the neighbouring rocks ring, upon being struck, with surprising alacrity.

H. Thornhill Timmins, *Nooks and Corners of Pembrokeshire*, 1895.

3.   *St Govan's Bell*

In the chapel was a silver bell, which was stolen one summer evening by pirates, but no sooner had the boat put to sea than it was wrecked. The silver bell was carried by sea-nymphs to the brink of a well, and whenever the stone of that well is struck the bell is heard to moan.

Brewer's Dictionary of Phrase and Fable.

4. *Ecclesiastical Architecture*

The churches are of two main types; the tall-towered churches of Little England and the towerless, bellcoted churches of the North. The tall towers which usually have a pronounced batter (i.e. they taper upwards) and corbelled-out parapets, were intended as refuges, lookouts, beacons, or all three. They are a great feature in the South and their drab grey surfaces are often splashed and mottled with white lichen in exposed places or with rich yellow lichen, moss, ferns and penny-royal in the valleys and sheltered places. Very often, the tower is the only unrestored, or unrebuilt, part of the church. There are also two main types of interior. The first, usual in the North, has a nave and a small chancel, vestry and porch, whitewashed or primrose-yellow-washed, with dark stained pews and furniture and thin dark rafters. Sometimes there is a window by Kempe or a follower; most of the glass is clear and diamond-paned. The church will have been restored or rebuilt in the 1860s or 1870s by one of the architects who became fashionable in these parts — Penson, Lingen, Barker, Withers or Dolby. The other type, characteristic of the south of the county, is an irregular character-full rectangle, usually under two gables, with a wide (often square) transept or aisle tacked on to enlarge it. Medieval bits — corbels, fonts, arcades, built-in crosses — remain, in spite of extensive restoration by one of the above. Enormous squints, sometimes amounting to passages, are a common feature. The building looks as if it could belong to almost any time between the twelfth and the eighteenth centuries, and has of course had attention at many times. Medieval woodwork, except at St David's, is rare; later furnishing of interest, such as box pews and unusual liturgical arrangements, rare; medieval stained glass is almost non-existent, though Tenby has a fragment and there is eighteenth-century clear glass at Manordeifi and elsewhere. Box pews, mostly of late-ish date, remain at Loveston, Manordeifi, Redberth and Yerbeston.

Sometimes the best building in the village is the Nonconformist chapel — serviceable, symmetrical and inventive in ornament and decoration, within the strict Classical or Gothic conventions. At its simplest it is a featureless gabled box; at its most elaborate it can be very showy indeed, especially in the North. Some chapels glow with colour inside as well as out, as do the Congregational Tabernacle in Haverfordwest and the Baptist chapel in Fishguard.

Vyvyan Rees, *South-West Wales,* A Shell Guide, 1963.

5. *Llanwnda*

Llanwnda church is a rough building in a churchyard. There has been a church here since at least the 9th century. Asser, friend and biographer of King Alfred, was educated here. In the 13th century Giraldus Cambrensis was rector and went from here to Rome to demand the bishopric of St David's, to which he had been elected but which the archbishop would not allow him to assume. The church stands on the headland with nothing between it and the busy drop to the sea and there are splendid views from the churchyard. The church has a south porch and aisle and at the west end is a double bellcote. Outside on the east wall of the south aisle is a rectangular stone with a pattern of lines and a face inscribed on it, and nearby on the chancel wall is a stone with a double-line cross. The interior has been restored, but a few old timbers remain in the roof and on the window-sills are old carved stones. The font is crude Norman and the piscina a rough stone bowl set in the wall.

Sean Jennett, *South-west Wales,* 1967.

6. *Cathedral and Bishop's Palace*

You see little of it till you are almost on top of it. The pinnacles on the top stage of the tower (added in the sixteenth century when danger from raiders was over) are all that can be seen even across the open country to the north-west.

To the medieval Englishman this was the end of the world. Two pilgrimages to St David's equalled one to Rome. It was a great effort indeed to get here at all. . .

Standing in the Tower Gate — the main entrance to the Cathedral close and part of an immense fortified wall — you look down on the roofs of the Cathedral and on to the quadrangle of the Bishop's Palace. Palace and wall were built by Bishop Gower in the fourteenth century. The impressive arcaded parapet of the Palace, of many open arches of alternate purple and yellow stone, and the archway and rose window of the Great Hall make a rich display and catch all eyes beside the plain exterior of the Cathedral, especially the cold west front that faces them. John Nash rebuilt this front in 1789 when it was about to collapse from the outward pressure of the Norman arches. Sir Gilbert Scott rebuilt it again in 1863, from drawings of the original — so watered down, it is bound to look cold.

But if the exterior is plain, the interior is rich in colour, mood and detail. The first impression is of the velvety lilac-coloured bloom of the elaborate late Norman arcades, six bays ornamented with chevron and other ornament, clerestory and triforium; and of the sixteenth-century Irish oak ceiling of the nave, with pendants — 'of almost Arabian gorgeousness', as *Murray's Handbook* remarks. There is a general effect of stonework and woodwork combining in a light and handsome setting. There is a violent slope upwards from west to east — a difference of fourteen feet between the west door and the High Altar — which gives a strange rustic personality to this highly-wrought interior, a feeling that the strong and wild outside landscape has possessed the building. An enclosed passage leads through the double walls of the fourteenth-century stone screen to the choir, with its fine late fifteenth-century choir stalls. The transepts were rebuilt after the fall of the tower in 1220. Twenty-eight years later there was an earthquake, which caused further damage. Three Early English windows over the High Altar are elaborately carved, and have Salviati mosaics inserted in them. They were repaired with lighter-coloured stone after the earth-quake shock. The most delicate feature of the whole building is the sixteenth-century fan-vaulted ceiling in Cotswold stone of the Holy Trinity chapel. There is glass of the nineteenth and twentieth centuries — the best of it earlyish, and by Hardman. Butterfield as well as Scott was a restorer. The place has a strong and individual atmosphere, and you feel as if you have come here more as a pilgrim than as a sightseer.

Vyvian Rees, *South-West Wales,* A Shell Guide, 1963.

7. *St David's Cathedral*

People throughout the Middle Ages, kings and commoners alike, streamed down the long road to St David's in pious pilgrimage. Not that St David's will fill you with awe as a greater cathedral might. In fact you will pass right through the village ('Britain's smallest city') and see no sign of the cathedral nor even the top of its tower. Then suddenly there it is below you in a hollow called Glyn Rhosyn, a long, squat, cruciform church with a severe-looking tower. Yet, though so plain and unimposing, it looks perfectly right for its setting in this frequently gale-swept place only a mile from the wild sea cliffs that were the source of its violet stones. Inside it is beautiful. It is much lighter than many cathedrals and churches and you can savour all the nuances of colour in the stones and woodwork. The nave has perfect proportions, a fine clerestory and a richly carved oak roof of the fifteenth century. But it is the arcades on either side that take the eye for they lean outwards and you give their builders full marks for achieving an intriguing perspective until you learn that it is more likely that the arcades were originally upright and have only leaned by accident. The three centuries of medieval work in this cathedral produced a happy blending of styles. Particularly good are the fan-vaulted roof of the chapel of Bishop Vaughan; the stone screens; the bishops' throne; the presbytery screen and other oak screenwork; the rare wooden sedilia; and the stalls with their amusing misericords. There are ancient stones carved with crosses; and tombs and effigies of long-dead priests and bishops. Greatest temporal figure buried here is Edmund Tudor, father of Henry VII. The bells are hung not in the tower but in the gatehouse between the cathedral and the city. You leave the cathedral and cross a trout-darting streamlet to the honey-coloured shell of the palace. Here, where jackdaws now chatter and collared doves coo, the bishops lived in evident splendour. The palace, largely built about 1340, contined in use for several hundred years but has been derelict since the eighteenth century. Elegantly arcaded, it survives as one of the most attractive of Welsh medieval ruins.

William Condry, *Exploring Wales,* 1970.

8. *A Royal Pilgrim.*

On the second day of Easter, the king embarked at sunrise on board a vessel in the outward port of Wexford, and, with a south wind, landed about noon in the harbour of Menevia. Proceeding towards the shrine of St David, habited like a pilgrim, and leaning on a staff, he met at the white gate a procession of the canons of the church coming forth to receive him with due honour and reverence . . .

The king then entering the church founded in honour of St Andrew and St David, devoutly offered up his prayers, and heard mass performed by a chaplain, whom alone, out of so large a body of priests, Providence seems to have kept fasting till that hour, for this very purpose . . .

It appears very remarkable to me, that in our days, when David II presided over the see, the river should have flowed with wine, and that the spring, called Pistyll Dewi, or the *Pipe* of David, from its flowing through a pipe into the eastern side of the churchyard, should have run with milk. The birds also of that place, called jackdaws, from being so long unmolested by the clergy of the church, were grown so tame and domesticated, as not to be afraid of persons dressed in black. In clear weather the mountains of Ireland are visible from hence, and the passage over the Irish sea may be performed in one short day; on which account William, the son of William the Bastard, and the second of the Norman kings in England, who was called Rufus, and who had penetrated far into Wales, on seeing Ireland from these rocks, is reported to have said, 'I will summon hither all the ships of my realm, and with them make a bridge to attack that country'. Which speech being related to Murchard, prince of Leinster, he paused awhile, and answered, 'Did the king add to this mighty threat, if God please?' and being informed that he had made no mention of God in his speech, rejoicing in such prognostic, he replied, 'Since that man trusts in human, not divine power, I fear not his coming.'

Giraldus Cambrensis, *The Itinerary through Wales,* 1188.

9.   *The Church with the Longest Memory*

When the evening sun falls over St David's Cathedral, gilding the old stone, shining on the gentle green hills, the white twisting roads and the little farms, the smallest 'city' in the kingdom lies lost in its mighty memories. The sea wind drops, the smoke rises upward from the chimneys, and a man looking at the church in the hollow knows it to possess the longest memory in Britain.

H. V. Morton, *In Search of Wales,* 1932.

10. *St Mary's on the Hill, Haverfordwest*

St Mary's church dominates the top of the hill. The church has a Norman foundation but it was evidently largely rebuilt and extended in the 13th century; and in the 15th century a number of alterations in the Perpendicular style were made, including most of the windows. The building is essentially rectangular, with a tower included within the rectangle at the north-west corner. The exterior details are of interest, especially the Early English windows with plate tracery at the east and west ends and on the south side of the chancel.

The interior is spacious and fine and justifies the claim that this is one of the finest churches in South Wales. The nave arcades and the chancel arch are Early English, with deep mouldings, rising from clustered columns on which is a series of delightful capitals. Many of these capitals have flower or lead ornament, but among them notice near the font a woman sticking out her tongue; on the next capital is an ape playing a harp and a pig playing the Welsh version of the fiddle, the *crwth*. Another has a lamb biting the head of a serpent. Notice the beautiful 15th century oak roof of the nave, with its 'winged' bosses and carved arched braces; the braces rise from corbels carved on the north side as women's heads and on the south as men's. The west end of the nave rises by seven steps to a platform, on which is an extraordinary font, very slender, which was perhaps originally a holy water stoup. In the south-west corner is an unusual recess, perhaps a confessional box. Near it is a battered 15th century effigy of a pilgrim whose scrip or bag with three scallop shells shows that he had been to Compostella in Spain. At the east end of the nave, by the pulpit, is the mayor's pew, with two ancient carved bench-ends, probably 15th century.

The chancel also has a fine 15th century roof and beautiful arcades and capitals; one of the capitals shows a despondent monk holding a tankard upside down; his left hand has the thumb on the wrong side. The 13th century window of three lancets has plate tracery. On the left side of the window is a monument to Hessy Jones, with an inscription worth reading. On the north side of the chancel is a handsome monument to Sir John Philipps, and opposite is one of the few brasses in Wales, very late (1651).

Sean Jennett, *South-west Wales,* 1967.

11.   *The Lovely Hessy Jones*

Dutiful, pliable & engaging;
Meek, unelated & humble, tho' of
uncommon Beauty & improv'd Talents
nobly rising above the temptations of
a world mading after pleasures holding
all its dazling fashionable follies in
detestation; sham'd neither by scoffs nor railery
from singularly devoting to her God
the bloom of her Youth;
supported in sickness by an assuring Faith;
thanking God for calling her when others were left;
& facing Death, the King of Terrors; without fear.
– Thus liv'd the lovely HESSY JONES,
peculiarly marked by God for his own,
& having made haste to keep his Commandments,
finish'd her task at 16, full of Grace & ripe for Glory,
the hope, pride, delight & the admiration also
of her sorrowing friends,
to whom she continues a Blessing even in Death
by lessening their attachment to Earth
& quickening their longing for Heaven.
O Grave! thy Victory is over the unbury'd,
O Death! thy sting is to the living.
Ob. 19 Jan 1771 fil. nat. max:
JOs. JONES, M:B:

Memorial in St Mary's Church, Haverfordwest.

12.   *In Memory of Lord Nelson*

Amongst the **MEMORIALS** to Lord Nelson in the Church is the
'Truck' of the Mainmast of the *L'Orient*. The following is the
inscription on the tablet:—

'The truck of the mainmast *L'Orient*, CXX Guns, blown up in
action with the Vanguard, LXXIV Guns, was a legacy of Lord
Nelson to Emma, Lady Hamilton, who placed it here as a record of
the Battle of the Nile and of the institution of its anniversary at
Milford, 1st of August, MDCCCI., on which day Lord Nelson and

Sir William and Lady Hamilton were welcomed by the County of Pembroke on their arrival from Sicily. The first stone of St Katharine's Church was laid in the above month by Lord Nelson'.

For many years it was thought that this interesting relic of Lord Nelson had been removed from the Church. Somebody suggested that the small portion of the masthead of the *L'Orient* now in the custody of the Royal United Service Institution was the relic which was given by Lady Hamilton to Milford Church, and that it had been removed from Milford to its present home. There is absolutely no ground for such a supposition. The inscription on the tablet in the Church refers to the 'Truck' of the Masthead, and not the Masthead itself. While for years efforts were made to reclaim for Milford the supposed lost relic from London, experts tell us that the 'Truck' has been with us all the time, but sadly neglected, alas! For years it found a place of rest amidst the lumber of the almost disused belfry in the tower. Since the restoration it has been restored to its place of honour, and is the first object seen on entering the Church. In connection with this relic there is a most interesting legend. The *Illustrated London News* of August 27th, 1864, quotes a story given in the *Haverfordwest and Milford Haven Telegraph.* It refers to an old and strange prophecy noticed by the latter journal a few years previously. 'The prediction or legend was found in the latter half of the last century in an old draw-well in Pill Priory, and the Latin rhyme, which was inscribed in lead, was deciphered by some tourists, amongst them a Mr Holford, who gave it publicity in one of a series of letters entitled "A Gentleman in Search of a Pedigree". It was predicted that when "the highest part of the East" should be elevated in the House of God a great town should be built, to which, with every wind and every tide, merchants from every clime should come likes bees to the flowers. Years after that "the highest part of the East", *viz.,* the Truck of the *L'Orient* blown up at Aboukir, was placed across the roof of the Chancel of the new Church at Milford'.

To the superstitious mind the disappearance of the 'Truck', as it lay for so many years in what was practically a dustheap, coinciding with the terrible depression of trade in the town in those years, may be taken as a case of cause and effect. It is no part of our business to try and explain this, but to note with thankfulness that the 'Truck' has once more been restored to its place of honour, and never in the history of our little town has trade been so prosperous as at the present time.

The Rev. E. J. Howells, *The Centenary of Milford Haven Parish Church,* 1908.

13.   CWM YR EGLWYS

Lonely as your pine from another sea,
your west door a frame
for emptiness, your altar
frontalled far under weed,

sea-walled a faithless age too late, your rood
eroded, your roof wood
only to be guessed at now,
your once saint an unknown ghost.

Car park two shillings a day, radios,
romantic girls, the flowers
of fuchsia, un unfished sea;
for mass the guided missile,

for vespers a call of cars departing,
for priest a white-cowled gull,
for congregation sea-wrack
and soft mist for vestments.

Your simple bell will not resume its call
cold now from the long drowning
unclanged, its dome till Domesday
seal-visited, lit by sea blooms.

But your harvest of graves will rest with you
past touring and rotting,
past all oil soiling your sand,
past our day our declining.

Gwyn Williams, in *Poetry Wales,* 1969.

VI

Saints

1. *Birth of David*

Sanctus, king of the people of Ceredigion, went to Dyfed, and whilst passing through it, there met him a maiden called Nonita, exceedingly beautiful, a modest virgin. Her the king, inflamed with desire, violated, who neither before nor after this occasion had any intercourse with any man, but continued in chastity of mind and body, leading a most faithful life; for from this very time of her conceiving, she lived on bread and water only. There, in that very place where she was violated, and where she conceived, lay a small meadow, pleasing to the eye, and by divine favour, laden with heavenly dew. In that meadow, too, at the time of her conception, two large stones, which had not been seen there before, appeared, one at her head, and one at her feet; for the earth rejoicing in the conceiving, opened its bosom, both in order to preserve the maid's modesty, and also to declare beforehand the significance of her offspring.

Driven by the approaching time of the birth, the mother sought the predicted place. But on that selfsame day, so great a turbulence of the atmosphere sprang up, with such vivid flashes of lightning, such terrifying peals of thunder, and so excessive a downpour of hail and rain, that no one could even go out of doors. But the place where the mother lay groaning in labour shone with so brilliant a light, that it glistened in God's presence, as if lit by the sun, though it was obscured by clouds. The mother, in her travail, had near her a certain stone, on which she leaned with her hands when hard pressed by her pains; whereby the marks of her hands, as though impressed on wax, have identified that stone for those who have gazed upon it: it broke in half in sympathy with the mother in her agony. On that spot a church has been built, in the foundations of which this stone lies concealed.

Rhigyfarch's Life of St David, translated by J. W. James, 1967.

2.   *The Death of David*

And after he had bestowed his blessing on all, he (Saint David) spoke these words: 'Noble brothers and sisters, be glad, and guard your faith and religion, and do the little things which you have heard from me, and which I have shown you. And I shall go the way which our fathers go. And fare you well', said David, 'and may your conduct be steadfast on the earth. For we shall never meet here again'. And then was heard a cry arising from all, a wail and lamentation and weeping, and people exclaiming 'Woe to us that the earth does not swallow us, that fire does not burn us, would that God would raise the sea over the land, and cause the mountains to fall on us', and almost all that were present were near unto death. From the Sunday to the Wednesday after David's death they took no meat or drink, but prayed piteously. And Tuesday night, close on cock-crow, lo, a host of angels filled the city, and all places in the city were filled with song and joy. And in the morning hour, behold, Jesus Christ came, accompanied by the nine orders of heavenly beings, as when He is surrounded by them in majesty. And the brilliant sun shone over the whole host. And that Tuesday the first day of March, Jesus Christ bore away David's soul in great triumph and gladness and honour. After his hunger, his thirst, and cold, and his labours, his abstinence and his acts of charity, and his weariness, and his tribulation, and his afflictions, and his anxiety for the world, the angels received his soul, and they bore it to a place where the light does not fail, and there is rest without labour, and joy without sadness, an abundance of all good things, and victory, and brilliance, and beauty; where Christ's champions are commended, and the undeserving rich are ignored, where there is health without sickness, youth without old age, peace without dissension, glory without vain ostentation, songs that do not pall, and rewards without end.

The Book of the Anchorite of Llanddewibrefi, 1346.

3.   *Collect for St David's Day*

O God, who by the teaching of Thy Blessed Servant, Saint David, didst cause the light of the Gospel to shine in this our land; Grant, we beseech Thee, that having his life and his labours in remembrance, we may shew forth our thankfulness unto Thee for the same, by following the example of his zeal and patience, through Jesus Christ our Lord. Amen.

4. *St David's Shrine*

The shrine of St David is on the north side of the chancel; the single stone which composed it is now broken into many pieces. In the side are four recesses, into which the notaries dropped their offerings, and the monks removed them through doors behind. Our kings frequently made pilgrimages to this shrine, where they paid their devotions to the saint, then in the highest repute. In the year 1080 William the Conqueror invaded Wales with a large army, proceeding in a hostile manner till he came as far as St David's; but there he laid aside the warrior for the votary, and reconciled the princes of the land to the homage he exacted, by the splendour of his offerings, and the humility of his deportment. This was in the time of Bishop Sulien, whose fame for sanctity contributed much to keep alive in the public mind the veneration of this primitive altar. After having held it five years, so great his love of retirement, that he resigned his office to Abraham. On his death, Sulien was compelled by the general voice to resume his charge, which he again relinquished a very short time after King William's visit. He died in the year 1089, with the reputation of the best and wisest man in all Wales. In the year 1170 Henry the Second paid his offerings at this shrine, was entertained at dinner by Bishop David Fitzgerald, Rees ap Gruffyth's cousin, and returned to Pembroke in the evening. The offerings made at all the other chapels were brought hither, and divided every Saturday among the priests; the quantity of money is said to have been so great, that instead of being counted, it was measured out in dishes. Nearly as long as popery lasted this church exceeded every other in celebrity, though since the reformation has extinguished the merit of pilgrimages, it has fallen, I may almost say, into a state of unfeeling desertion. It was said of old, that there was as much merit in going twice to St David's as once to Rome. There was also a superstitious idea, highly expressive of veneration for the place, that every man must go to St David's once, either dead or alive.

Benjamin Heath Malkin, *The Scenery, Antiquities and Biography of South Wales,* 1804.

5.   *The Feast of St David*

In 1398, Archbishop Arundel ordered that the Festival of St David be kept on 1st March, the anniversary of his death, throughout the Province of Canterbury, of which Wales then formed a part, and in 1415 Archbishop Chichele, who had previously been a Bishop of St David's, ordained the festival should be kept with special pomp, including the delivery of nine sermons on that day. The Welsh have faithfully kept the festival ever since, even during the Commonwealth, when there was a ban on Saints' Days. When the Tudors came to the throne, the privy purse expenses show they gave many gifts to Welshmen on St David's Day, and during the Hanoverian period, when the scandal of political appointments to Welsh bishoprics reached its height, and absentee bishops and clergy were the rule rather than the exception, the Welsh eagerly formed Societies to promote the celebration of St David's Day, some of which are still in existence.

Maxwell Fraser, *Introducing West Wales,* 1956.

6.   *St Teilo's Well*

This strong spring rises close to Mr Melchior's farm-house, and within a couple of hundred yards from the ruined church of Llandilo. The well empties itself into a pond; there are so far as I could see no remains of early masonry round the well.

These waters had formerly a wide-spread reputation for the healing of pulmonary complaints. The last cure that created any sensation took place about sixty years ago. A gentleman living in the Gower peninsula had a son, far advanced in phthisis; all known remedies had been tried in vain. Some friend recommended St Teilo's waters as a last resource. The Glamorganshire gentleman, in despair, put his poor lad into a postchaise and drove him over execrable roads up to Llandilo at the foot of Precelly.

The boy drank the waters, and then returned to Glamorgan none the better.

'But', said the friend, 'did your son drink from the Saint's skull?'.

'No! from the well'.

'Ah! that is no good at all, the water must be drunk out of St Teilo's skull'.

So a second time the unhappy father and son performed the pilgrimage. This time the skull was brought out. From it the son drank the healing waters, and was duly cured of his complaint.

A skull is still preserved in Mr Melchior's house.

The story goes that when St Teilo was dying (A.D. 566) he bade a female servant take his skull from Llandilo in Carmarthenshire, to Llandilo in Pembrokeshire, and prophesied that if this was done God would be glorified and man benefitted.

The skull, as now preserved, is imperfect, only the brain pan now remaining. It is evidently a very old piece of bone, coloured like ancient ivory, and polished from constant handling. The open sutures prove it must have been the head of a young person, and as St Teilo is said to have died in extreme old age, it could not very well have belonged to him, besides a part of one superciliary ridge remains, and this is of such slight elevation, that it seems almost certain this is part of a woman's head. There appears no reason to doubt that it is a genuine pre-Reformation relic.

'E.L.', *Pembrokeshire Antiquities,* 1897.

7. *St Caradoc*

During the childhood of Richard [Fitz Tankard], a holy man, named Caradoc, led a pious and recluse life at St Ismael, in the province of Ros, to whom the boy was often sent by his parents with provisions, and he so ingratiated himself in the eyes of the good man, that he very often promised him, together with his blessing, the portion of all his brothers, and the paternal inheritance. It happened that Richard, being overtaken by a violent storm of rain, turned aside to the hermit's cell; and being unable to get his hounds near him, either by calling, coaxing, or by offering them food, the holy man smiled; and making a gentle motion with his hand, brought them all to him immediately. In process of time, when Caradoc had happily completed the course of his existence, Tankard, father of Richard, violently detained his body, which by his last will he had bequeathed to the church of St David; but being suddenly seized with a severe illness be revoked his command. When this had happened to him a second and a third time, and the corpse at last was suffered to be conveyed away, and was proceeding over the sands of Niwegal towards St David's, a prodigious fall of rain inundated the whole country; but the conductors of the sacred burthen, on coming forth from their shelter, found the silken pall, with which the bier was covered, dry and uninjured by the storm; and thus the miraculous body of Caradoc was brought into the church of St Andrew and St David, and with due solemnity deposited in the left aisle, near the altar of the holy proto-martyr Stephen.

Giraldus Cambrensis, *The Itinerary through Wales,* 1188.

8.   *St Botolph's*

Budig, a noble Armorican, put to sea with a fleet and landed in Milford Haven. A chapel was erected to his honour and called by the natives St Buttock's; this was not considered euphonious, so when a mansion was built it was rechristened St Botolph's.

Edward Laws, *The History of Little England Beyond Wales,* 1888.

9.   *St Wrw*

The church is dedicated to St Wrw whose festival is held on the third of November, a saint of whom legend is totally silent . . . In the reign of Queen Elizabeth, there was a sort of chantry chapel in the church-yard, wherein on the south side was shewn the tomb of the saint in hewn stone. The parishioners never buried in the chapel, from a superstitious belief that corpses there interred would in the night-time be ejected; wherefore 'they hold opinion that their holy saint would not have any bedfellow.'

Richard Fenton, *A Historical Tour through Pembrokeshire,* 1811.

Volcanic Folds, St Ann's Head. (Photo: Studio Jon)

Carew Castle, engraved by Paul Sandby (1977).
The incident depicted may be a personal anecdote.

Carew Castle. (Crown Copyright).

Pembroke Castle and part of the Town engraved by Charles Norris (1820).

St David's Cathedral (Photo: Leonard & Marjorie Gayton.)

Detail from miserichord choir at St David's Cathedral

View of Fishguard from Goodwick Sands. W. Daniel aquatint (1813).

A Fishguard Fencible. Artist unknown.

Llawhaden Castle. Wood engraving by H. Hughes 'The Welsh Bewick' (1810).

St Dogmael's Priory. Wood engraving by H. Hughes (1810).

Pembroke Castle. Aquatint by Paul Sandby (1812).

Pentre Ifan Cromlech. (Crown Copyright).

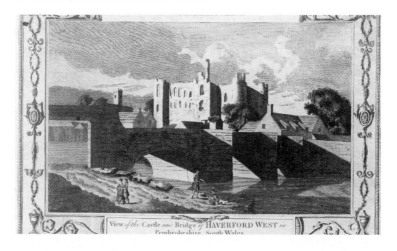

Haverfordwest Castle & Bridge. Line engraving by Morris (1789?)

Benton Castle. Aquatint by Paul Sandby (1775).

Cemais Head. Daniel uncoloured line engraving (1815).

St David's Head from 'Miscellaneous British Scenery'
drawn and engraved by Walmsley & Haven.

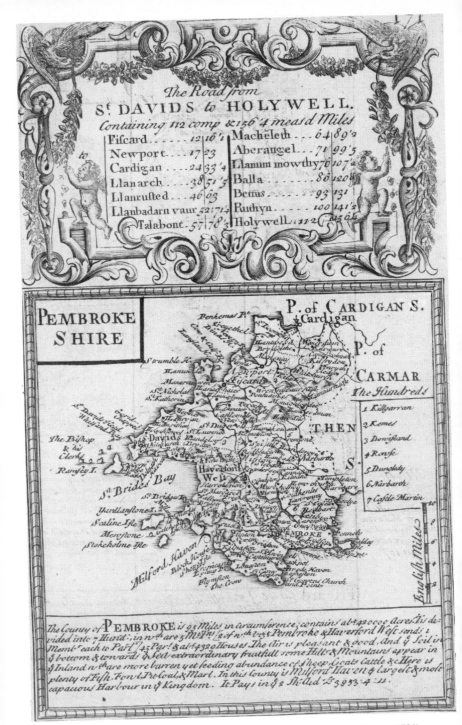

The road from St David's to Holywell. Map drawn by Owen and Bowen (1720).

General Sir Thomas Picton
Engraved by R. Cooper from an original by M. A. Shee, R.A. (1815).

Cilgerran Castle. Wood engraving by H. Hughes (1810).

Carew Castle. Wood engraving by H. Hughes (1810).

St Govan's Church. (Crown Copyright).

Puffins. (Photo: Roger Worsley).

Tenby Daffodils. (Photo: Roger Worsley).

Razorbill. (Photo: Roger Worsley).

Pembroke Castle. Wood engraving H. Hughes (1810).

St David's.

Solva Harbour. (Studio Jon).

Keeston Rath. (Crown Copyright).

Lamphey Castle. Aquatint by Paul Sandby (1775).

VII

Men of Pembroke

1. Tutor to King Alfred

Asser (d.909), bishop and scholar, is known almost entirely from what he tells us of himself in his life of King Alfred. He belonged to the clerical community of St David's, where he was brought up and educated, being a relative of bishop Nobis, who died in 873. In due course, he succeeded to the see and therewith acquired a reputation for scholarship, which spread beyond the borders of Wales. Thus it came about that in or around 884 Alfred, in his zeal for his own education and that of his people, enlisted him in the royal service. Asser was not easily detached from his episcopal responsibilities, but, after a delay partly due to a long illness at Caerwent on his way home, he agreed to divide his year between the court and St David's. Welsh politics provided one reason for his acquiescence. The see was much exposed to the attacks of the local prince, king Hyfaidd of Dyfed (d.892), and it was hoped that the bishop's friendship with Hyfaidd's overlord, the powerful ruler of Wessex, would put an end to this trouble. Alfred found his new tutor indispensable; he heaped favours upon him, which culminated in the episcopal care of Devon and Cornwall, then part of the great diocese of Sherborne. All this is recounted in the life; it can only be added that later he became bishop of Sherborne and d. in 909.

Sir J. E. Lloyd in *The Dictionary of Welsh Biography*, 1959.

2.   *Princess Nesta*

Then he saw his daughter come, unhurried, out of the pool, shaking her yellow-red hair and walking, straight legged, to her grazing mount across whose neck she had flung her clothing. For a moment, she was still one with the water, all her movements liquid; then a flash of white linen covered the gold of her small body from shoulder to knee. Wet feet, high arched, shuffled into sandals. The clasp of a chain girdle clicked over dark blue velvet. There! The Princess Nesta was dressed, except for her jewellery. Bare arms were lifted for the careful arrangement of a coiled golden wire around the left one, wrist to elbow; this ornament had once been a part of the King's magnificent collar — the oldest part, the torc of Irish gold on to which a craftsman of later centuries had hooked the half-foot-deep circle of gem-studded metal. At Nesta's birth, Rhys had withdrawn the torc from the collar and wound it twice around her infant waist. Today, it was a bracelet. Tomorrow, it might be a necklace or a fillet. It was supple and sinuous as a serpent. And she wore it always, in one shape or another, just as her father was never seen without his own barbaric ornament encircling his muscular neck, where it served as armour above the low-cut leather tunic. An arrow had bounced off that collar at the battle of Mynydd Carn, since when he was superstitiously grateful to it for protecting him and never let it out of his sight. Giving Nesta the torc had been like binding her to him for ever, or to whatever destiny lay hidden in the words of the Irish chieftain who had bestowed it upon him when he was in exile in that country:

'I give you the ancient treasure of our house for friendship, that it may bring you back to us who have loved you. For know you that this relic always returns to its own place . . .'

If that were true, and Nesta wore part of the collar always, then he could never lose her completely; she was his most beloved child for whom he had a rare and precious passion — perhaps because his queen had died to give her the gift of life. Nesta had been born for love; she was accustomed to it; she received it graciously but without surprise. And, occasionally, she returned the feeling with a vehemence that could be overwhelming, a generosity that was royal in its openhandedness.

She looked across at her father now with a curious unblinking intensity that was almost an entry into the mind, and he returned her stare. Their eyes were exactly alike, a greyish green as of marble with glinting amber flecks. She saw his rage and his relief. She saw the steel bands of his personal discipline bite into the tenderness he felt for her and Gruffydd and Hywel.

Eleanor Fairburn, *The Golden Hive*, 1966.

3. *Henry Tudor*

The future Henry VII is said to have been born in one of the rooms above the portcullis chamber. His father, Edmund Tudor, eldest son of Owain Tudor and Queen Katherine, the widow of Henry V, had been created Earl of Richmond, and Jasper Tudor, second son of Owain Tudor and Queen Katherine, was created Earl of Pembroke, by their half-brother, Henry VI. Owain Tudor was descended from a family seated at Penmynydd in Anglesey, which traced its descent back to Cadwaladr, the seventh-century Welsh prince who created an heroic tradition in the face of hopeless odds, and ranked with Arthur in the estimation of Welsh bards in later ages.

Henry VII's mother, Margaret Beaufort, was descended from Edward III through John of Gaunt, and was not quite fourteen years old when her son was born, and as his father had died two months before, Henry was Earl of Richmond from the moment of his birth. He was brought up by his uncle at Pembroke Castle, imbibing Welsh traditions — and probably the Welsh language — from his Welsh nurse, to whom he showed his affection in later years by granting her a generous pension. When he was ten years old, however, his uncle became fearful for his safety and sent him first to Harlech, and then to other places of refuge, until he finally escaped with him to Tenby and took ship to Brittany, where the young Earl of Richmond spent the next fourteen years. During his exile, the Welsh centred all their hopes on him, and the bards kept the Welsh people in a constant ferment of expectation, so that they flocked to the young Earl's support when he landed in Milford Haven on 1st August, 1485.

Henry marched to Bosworth Field at the head of an army almost entirely composed of Welshmen, under the Dragon flag of his ancestor, Cadwaladr, under which he later entered London as victor. On the field of battle, after the death of Richard III, he established the famous Yeomen of the Guard — popularly known as Beefeaters — as his personal bodyguard, its first members being men who had shared his exile in Brittany and fought with him in the battle. The Yeomen of the Guard, whose Tudor costume is a 'feature' of the Tower of London today, is the oldest existing body of the kind, and has an unbroken record from 1485.

After his coronation, Henry VII went out of his way to emphasize his Welsh connexions and to reward his Welsh allies. He made the Welsh Dragon one of the supporters of the royal arms, where it remained all through the Tudor period, although eventually displaced by the Unicorn of the Stuarts. Henry VII also established the office of Rouge Dragon Pursuivant in the College of Heralds to commemorate the triumph of the Red Dragon of Cadwaladr. The Venetian ambassador reported to his Government: 'The Welsh may now be said to have recovered their former independence, for the most wise and fortunate Henry VII is a Welshman'.

Maxwell Fraser, *Introducing West Wales*, 1956.

4.   ELEGY FOR RHYS GRYG (Rhys the hoarse) d. 1234

Many a tear flows on its way
Profusely for Rhys, fortress a grave,
Helm of Dinefwr, man of fine children,
Lion of combat, her rank and lord.

Lordly Rhys, king of a realm,
Raven-feeder, leader of battle,
Prime hawk of nimble hawks:
For a lost dragon, we are lost.

I'm lost to sorrow, a slave of grief,
A lord we've lost, red-bladed lion:
Spoiler of Rhos, Rhys is gone,
His end in Mynyw's a tomb of stone.

Near Mynyw a lord, lion of Haverford,
I have seen Rhys, stormer of Rhos,
High prince in battle, of a great myriad,
Armed with iron, a prince was fair.

Fair court of Rhys, Rhos in thrall,
Chieftain, while he lived, of many,
Proud hoarse-talking, sword cruelly notched,
Passionate anger, harsh in battle.

Battle-wager, blade-plunging lion,
Quick fury had Rhys, red spear on slant,
Prince Gryg, of bright golden meadhorns —
A treasure was his hand to hosts!

Y Prydydd Bychan in *The Penguin Book of Welsh Verse*, 1967, trans.
Anthony Conran.

5. *Roger Barlow, Maritime Geographer*

The first Welsh contribution to maritime geography was the
translation of [Enisco's] the *Suma de Geographia* by Roger Barlow of
Slebech. This manuscript now known as *A Brief Sumne of
Geographie,* still remains the only complete English translation of the
Spanish book and the translation was made probably during the
winter of 1540 to 1541 whilst Barlow was in Pembrokeshire. The
manuscript included considerable additional material drawn from
Barlow's own personal experiences gained by sailing with Sebastian
Cabot on his second voyage of discovery in April 1526. His
manuscript which contains the earliest account of the New World in
English lay neglected for nearly four hundred years until it was
published by the Hakluyt Society in 1931. Barlow's manuscript
included a section of the *Geographie* contained parts of the British
Isles and in particular the Bristol Channel and South Wales. This
included Milford Haven, Ramsey, and St David's, but the rest of
Wales is dismissed as follows:

*And upon this costs be many propre townes with smal havens as
fyskard, newport, cardigan and Aberistwith. To aberistwith ther cometh
a river called rrydol and his begynnyng is in the mountaunes of
Snowden.* Barlow left half a folio blank presumably to enable further
details to be added relating to the coast between Wales and Scotland.
The considerable financial assistance given by the Englishmen,
Robert and Nicholas Thorne, friends of Barlow, to the Sebastian
Cabot voyage of discovery in April 1526, together with his own

contribution, enabled Roger Barlow to sail on the Flagship as one of the super-cargoes and he appears to have assisted the Treasurer. In October 1528 Roger Barlow returned to Lisbon in *The Trinidad* to seek further financial help and fresh supplies for Cabot but these were not forthcoming. He also travelled extensively to the Canaries, the Portuguese Azores, and probably as far as the modern Agadir. Professor E. G. R. Taylor thought it was no coincidence that the first English Barbary voyage of 1551 organised by Cabot and Henry Ostrich sailed to the particular port of which Barlow could give them a first-hand account.

At the time of the dissolution of the Monasteries 1539-40 the estate of the Order of St John in Jerusalem at Slebech was leased to Roger Barlow at an annual rental of £125 15s 10½. In June 1546 Slebech was bought for a sum of £523 2s 6d by Roger Barlow and Thomas Barlow of Catford. In February 1543 the Mayor of Pembroke and Vice-Admiral of the coast was suspected of embezzling some of the gold from a Spanish ship forced to shelter in Milford Haven and Roger Barlow was employed by the Privy Council to investigate the matter. In November 1549 the Earl of Warwick (formerly Admiral Lord Lisle) appointed Roger Barlow Vice-Admiral of the coast of Pembrokeshire. Roger Barlow died in February 1554 having founded one of the most important Catholic families of Wales.

Olwen Caradoc Evans, *Marine Plans and Charts of Wales*, 1969.

6. *Father of Mathematics*

Robert Recorde, the mathematician, was born in Tenby about 1510. Fuller said of him, 'His soul did not live in the lane of a single science, but traversed the latitude of learning; witness his works'. Though the greater part of his time was spent in the mathematical science, he is said to have been deeply skilled in rhetoric, philosophy, polite literature, history, cosmography, astrology, astronomy, physic, music, mineralogy, and every branch of natural history. He was also conversant with all matters relating to the coinage, had a good knowledge of Saxon, was no mean divine, and was acquainted with the law. He was also a zealous antiquary, and made a large collection of historical and other ancient manuscripts.

He was probably the first in this country to adopt the Copernican system and was practically the founder of the English school of mathematical writers, and his teaching of arithmetic and mathematics 'rendered (them) clear to all capacities to an extent wholly unprecedented'. He introduced algebra into England, and was the first to use the symbols —; +; and =. Among numerous poetical passages in his prefaces is a beautiful and dignified hymn in the *Castle of Knowledge*, a treatise on Astronomy. His famous *The Whetstone of Witte, or the second Part of Arithmetike, 1557*, on Algebra, is mentioned by Scott in *The Fortunes of Nigel*, and has been acclaimed as 'an oasis in an age deficient in science'.

Maxwell Fraser, *Introducing West Wales*, 1956.

7.   *Archbishop of York*

Young, Thomas (1507-68), archbishop of York; b. at Hodgeston, Pembs. He entered Broadgates Hall, Oxford, graduating B.A. June 14, 1529, M.A. March 19 1553, B.C.L. Feb 17 1538, and D.C.L. Feb 13 1566, and becoming head of his hall, 1542-6. He became vicar of Llanfihangel Castell Gwallter (Llanfihangel-genau'r-glyn), Cards, in 1541, rector of Hodgeston and of Nash, 1542, prebendary of Trallong, 1545, and of Tregaron, 1560. Elected precentor of St David's in 1542, he took up residence in 1547, and became a leader of the faction opposed to bishop Robert Ferrar. Said to have fled abroad in Mary's reign, no trace of his exile remains in Continental archives. In 1559, he was one of the royal visitors of the Welsh dioceses, and was elected bishop of St David's, 6 Dec 1559. On Parker's recommendation, he was elected archbishop of York, 27 Jan 1561. As archbishop and president of the council of the North, he was active in forwarding the Elizabethan settlement, though he incurred censure for his misuse of the temporalities of his see. He d. 26 June 1568, and was buried in York Minster.

Professor Glanmor Williams in *The Dictionary of Welsh Biography*, 1959.

8.   *Virgil at Cilgerran*

Kilgerran is still further distinguished by having been the residence, and affording rest to the remains of an early literary character.

Doctor Thomas Phayer is said, by Fuller and Wood, to have been a native of Wales, but this is contradicted by a note in the Cambrian Register, which represents him as the first of his family, who settled in Pembrokeshire. He was well versed in the common law, and wrote a book on the nature of writs. It appears, however, that he disliked the law; and therefore changed his profession to physic, in which he proceeded to his doctor's degree. It is as a physician, and not as a lawyer, that he is mentioned in old biographical memoirs; and this may perhaps warrant the supposition, that he prescribed with more success than he pleaded. He seems to have been an inveterate author; for he translated several medical books out of the French. Writing may be thought to have been more to his taste than the exercise of a profession; for he withdrew himself to the banks of this romantic river, and translated Virgil, marking at the end of each book the date when finished, and the time employed about it. The three first books of the *Æneid* were completed at Kilgerran, in the year 1555; the fourth at the same place, in 1556; the fifth in 1557, after an escape from some very great danger or calamity, while on a visit to his wife's family at Caermarthen; the sixth and seventh were finished at home, in the same year; the eighth in 1558; and the ninth in April 1560. The tenth was begun, but left incomplete.

Benjamin Heath Malkin, *The Scenery, Antiquities and Biography of South Wales*, 1804.

9. *Owen of Henllys*

The early Tudor period saw Rhys ab Owain Fychan consolidating the Henllys estate, and by 1497 he was already designated a 'gentleman'. His son, William Owen, had a legal training at the Middle Temple in London and settled in Pembroke, where he held a number of offices. At various times he was mayor of Pembroke, joint steward and receiver of the shire of Pembroke and controller of the ports of Pembroke, Haverfordwest and Tenby. The most significant of Owen's achievements, however, was to become lord of Cemais. The previous lord had got himself deeply in debt, mortgaging his Cemais lands to Owen. Eventually, Owen acquired these lands outright and, given the good sense and judgement which was notably lacking in his predecessor, his own and his family's fortunes were assured; but

William Owen did not rest there. The process of estate building in Tudor Wales was sometimes spectacular, as when large portions of monastic or Crown land were acquired by major families; but normally it was a gradual, continuous process of land accumulation on a small scale. To this end Owen bought out as many of his freehold neighbours as he could. He married well. His second wife was Elizabeth, niece of the earl of Pembroke and daughter of Sir George Herbert of Swansea. William Owen's social standing was yet more secure as a result; and another important link between gentry families was forged.

George Owen [his son] was in many ways typical of that top layer of Welsh gentry who were so vital to the government and administration of their county and country. He inherited status and a large estate; but he made the best of his advantages. In B. G. Charles's words, 'He was industrious, thrifty, ambitious and far-sighted . . . the process of building up a freehold estate around Henllys, begun by his father, was vigorously pursued'. From his writings we know of his progressive methods of farming. He preached and practised enclosure. He used fertilisers — limestone, marl and seaweed; he discussed their merits at length in his writings.

He too married well. His first wife was that most coveted of women, an heiress — the daughter of William Philipps of Picton. George's fortune and social standing were greatly enhanced by this alliance with one of the leading Pembrokeshire families. It also helped to cement Owen's allegiance in the politics of Elizabethan Pembrokeshire. Both Philipps and Owen were leaders of a group of families who opposed that most influential of the county gentry, Sir John Perrot. The implications of this power struggle in Pembrokeshire were far-reaching because of the clashes which resulted. One of the most interesting has been recounted in detail by B. G. Charles. A market day in Haverfordwest provided the occasion for a possible riot between armed retainers of the two factions. As it turned out there was no clash, but the sheriff, who was pro-Perrot, ordered the arrest of two of George Owen's men. Rees Jenkin Awbrey of Newport, 'by repute . . . a card-player, a frequenter of taverns and an associate of a thieving woman', was clapped in gaol. Rees Gwyneth of Nevern, 'a one-eyed North Walian with something of a reputation for horse-stealing, even of murder', managed to escape to the house of an Owen supporter.

The sheriff's men pursued him up the stairs and at the top of the second flight were confronted by William Philipps himself, his strongest adherent John Barlow of Slebech who had a long-lasting feud against Perrot . . . and George Owen. Alban Stepney arrived shortly afterwards. When told that they had no right to arrest the man within the town liberties, the sheriff's officers had to retire with their tails between their legs. But a crowd had gathered outside; only a spark of temper was needed to start a row. To avoid trouble the mayor was summoned to the scene and, being a partisan of the anti-Perrot faction, he was only too ready to put the under-sheriff in the town gaol for infringing the rights of the borough. If either of the parties scored over the other that day, it was not Perrot's. Owen and his men trudged home through the snows of Prescely without great loss of prestige.

It is surprising to recall at the end of this story that George Owen played a prominent part in government and peacekeeping in his county; it is certainly paradoxical that he applied himself seriously as a J.P. from about 1584, as sheriff of the county twice, deputy-lieutenant for several years and deputy vice-admiral. As J.P. he applied his probing mind to the problem of sheep-stealing; and he got the Council in the Marches to accept his suggestions for regulating and registering sheep ear-markings. He was deputy-lieutenant in a county with which the central government was particularly concerned because of the threat of invasion through Milford Haven. Although the deputy-lieutenants were not always at hand to perform their duties properly, there is no doubt that Owen and his fellows put a lot of effort into organising the military defences of Pembrokeshire. They were also responsible for raising money for armour and caring for it. Often it was kept in gentry houses, but one of Owen's proud achievements was to build an armoury house to serve that part of the county for which he was particularly responsible. He also played his part in interrogating Spanish sailors whose ships were wrecked off the west coast of Wales and in caring for wounded sailors returning from the Irish wars.

When we add George Owen's literary achievements to those of estate manager and public servant, we realise how wide-ranging were his activities and talents. He was a man of considerable intellect and ability. But he was also a child of his age and therefore not untypical of that class which was presented with economic, administrative and educational opportunities of immense potential in Elizabethan Wales.

Gareth Jones, *The Gentry and the Elizabethan State*, 1977.

10. *Lord Deputy of Ireland*

Perrot, Sir John (1530-92), Elizabethan statesman and Lord Deputy of Ireland, 1584-8. He was popularly believed to be an illegitimate son of Henry VIII and Mary Berkeley, one of the royal ladies-in-waiting who married Sir Thomas Perrot of Haroldston. Henry knighted Sir Thomas on his marriage. Sir John was born, probably, at Haroldston, in 1530 and, according to his own statement, was educated at St David's. Later, at the age of 18, he entered the household of the marquis of Winchester, after the custom of the times. He possessed great stature and physical strength, but he had an arbitrary temper and a brawling nature. With the Tudors he enjoyed great popularity; Henry VIII offered him preferment but died before he could grant it; Edward VI valued him as a friend and made him a Knight of the Bath; Mary did not, at first, take exception to his strong Protestantism, but, later, after he had been denounced by one Catherne, a countryman of his, for harbouring heretics at his house in Wales, for which he was imprisoned for a short time in the Fleet, he deemed it more politic to spend the rest of her reign abroad, serving in France under his friend the earl of Pembroke. He returned to this country only a few months before Mary's death. Under Elizabeth he enjoyed great favour and was one of four appointed to carry the canopy of state at her coronation. In 1562 he was appointed vice-admiral of the coast in South Wales and keeper of the gaol at Haverfordwest, while in the following year he was returned to Parliament as member for Pembrokeshire. He now rapidly became the most powerful personality in the county, but his numerous lawsuits and intense love of litigation as a means of embarrassing his enemies made him very unpopular among his powerful neighbours. In 1570 he became mayor of Haverfordwest, after a period during which the mayor and corporation had been bitterly anti-Perrot.

In 1573 he returned to Wales (after a sojourn in Ireland as president of Munster) in poor health and determined, as he told Burghley, to live a countryman's life and stay out of debt. For the next ten years his 'countryman's life' became one of intense litigation and attempts to enlarge his lands. He again took part in Haverfordwest affairs, but his relations with the mayor and corporation now appear to have improved considerably, he himself becoming mayor for the second time in 1575. The previous year he had been appointed a member of the Council in the Marches of Wales and he became actively interested in the suppression of piracy along the south coasts. When, in 1575, the Privy Council set up a commission to suppress piracy in Pembrokeshire, he was made chief commissioner, but the following year, when a similar commission was appointed for Glamorgan and Monmouthshire, he declined to accept charge of it on the plea of ill-health. His anti-piracy activities are chiefly of interest because of the bitter feud which they created between him and Richard Vaughan, deputy-admiral in Wales and chief commissioner for piracy in Carmarthenshire, who deeply resented Perrot's interference in what he regarded as his sphere of influence.

In Sept. 1579 Perrot was given command of a squadron of five ships with orders to cruise off the west coast of Ireland and intercept any Spanish shipping that might attempt a landing there. Apart from sighting one pirate ship, the 'Derifold', which Perrot chased and caught, the expedition was an uneventful one, though, on the return to the Thames, Perrot's ship ran aground on the Kentish Downs. When finally the squadron reached the Thames in safety, he found that his enemies had used this incident, and the uneventfulness of the expedition, to discredit him at Court. He was able, nevertheless, to clear himself completely.

It must have been with great relief that many of Perrot's Welsh neighbours heard of his appointment as lord deputy of Ireland, a post which he held from 1584 till 1588. The queen had held his Munster service in high esteem. She had asked his advice, too, in 1581, about Irish problems and had been much impressed with a 'Discourse' he had written in answer, in which he outlined courses of action to be taken in that country. Again, he was a man of considerable financial means, well likely to be able to bear the expense of such an important office under the parsimonious queen. His four years as lord-deputy were not happy ones and, thwarted by the English officials of his council, a victim of his own unbridled tongue and temper, irritated beyond measure by the enmity of Adam Loftus, archbishop of Dublin, and others, he begged to be recalled. He returned to England in 1588, bitter and disillusioned, suffering from gallstone and kidney trouble, but able, nevertheless, to boast to his successor, Sir William Fitzwilliam, that he had left Ireland in a state of profound peace.

In 1589 he was made a member of the Privy Council but it was not long before rumours of treasonable activity were current about him. These had been instigated in the first instance by Philip Williams, his secretary in Ireland, and Adam Loftus had taken care they should reach the right quarter. They became the subject of investigation by the Privy Council and, in March 1591, Perrot was removed to the

Tower. He was tried for treason in April 1592 and was sentenced to death. He died in the Tower in June 1592, before sentence could be carried out. There seems little reason to doubt that he was innocent of treasonable activity but guilty of indiscreet words concerning the queen's person, a fault of his hasty temper. He was more a victim to the animosity of his many enemies, not the least among whom was Sir Christopher Hatton, whose daughter Elizabeth he had seduced, and who had been stung by Perrot's taunt that he had found his way to royal favour by means of the galliard. In spite of his attainder, his estates were soon granted to his son, Sir Thomas Perrot.

He married (1) Ann, daughter of Sir Thomas Cheyney, by whom he had a son, Sir Thomas Perrot, who married Dorothy, daughter of Walter Devereux, earl of Essex, and (2) Jane, daughter of Sir Lewis Pollard, by whom he had a son William (d. 1597) and two daughters Lettice, who married (1) Roland Lacharn of S. Bride's, (2) Walter Vaughan of S. Bride's, and (3) Arthur Chichester, baron Chichester of Belfast and later lord-deputy of Ireland, and Ann, who married John Philips. Besides these he had a number of illegitimate children of whom the most important were Sir James Perrot, by Sibil Jones of Radnorshire, Elizabeth, daughter of Elizabeth Hatton, and a daughter who married David Morgan, gent.

In 1580 he donated lands and properties of the yearly value of £30, free of all charges, to the town of Haverfordwest, and these became known as 'The Perrot Trust'. Through the centuries many have been alienated, but the Trust still yields approximately £400 annually.

P. C. C. Evans in *The Dictionary of Welsh Biography*, 1959.

11.   *Callice Unbeknown*

Those of the inhabitants of South Wales (and they were many) who were inclined to regard the spoliation of other people's goods on the high seas with equanimity, must have found much to admire in the recklessness and good fortune of a Monmouthshire gentleman named John Callice. Born at Tintern, he left home at the early age of eleven, and had been placed in the care of a London alderman, who discovered a natural aptitude for seamanship in the boy and encouraged it by sending him on trading voyages to various continental countries. There came a day in 1573 when Callice did not return to London. He appeared instead at Penarth on board a Portuguese vessel which he had captured near the Azores, and in the happy possession of a valuable cargo of sugar. It was evident that he had decided to abandon legitimate commerce for piracy, and both the Government and the receivers of those goods, which evaded the Queen's customs houses along the South Wales coast, made their respective arrangements to deal with him . . .

Callice sold his sugar, and with the proceeds he purchased a stout ship, the *Olyphant,* in which he began to chase every category of merchant vessel from Dover to the Azores, and from Ireland to France. Not even the alarming experience of being blown as far west as Newfoundland convinced him of the errors of his course, and, in fact, he took advantage of his un-announced visit to raid the French fishing fleet and to ballast the *Olyphant* with their catches of cod.

There was hardly a Vice-admiral or Crown official in South Wales who did not receive at some time or other an urgent order for the arrest of Callice, but the proposition was wholly impracticable. The 'mainetayners and aiders' of the pirate were to be found everywhere and belonged to all classes.

Then came the news that he had brazenly landed in Milford, had lodged comfortably in Haverfordwest, and then returned to his ship without the slightest attempt being made to apprehend him. Shocked by the indifference of the local Justices of the Peace to their express demands, the irate Council wrote to Sir John Perrot, the Vice-admiral of Pembrokeshire, that,

> 'they do not a letill mervell at the negligence of suche as are Justices in those parts that, knowing the said Callice to be so notable and (*sic*) offendour and spoiler of suche her Majesties neighbors as are in good league and amytie with her, a matter greatlye touching her Highnes in honor, woulde suffer him to departe in that order and not apprehend him.'

Sir John, the Council directed, should investigate this dereliction of duty and take immediate steps to arrest Callice. Sir John obeyed to the extent of making some routine enquiries in Haverfordwest, but when the mayor of that town protested that he had not even been aware of Callice's presence there, it was plainly a waste of time to pursue the matter any further.

G. Dyfnallt Owen, *Elizabethan Wales*, 1964.

12. *Mistress or Queen?*

Walter, Lucy (1630?-58), mistress of king Charles II, had connections with some of the leading county families in West Wales. Her father, William Walter of Roch Castle, Pembs, was the grandson of William Walter, who had purchased the manor of Roch from the de Longuevilles c. 1601. He had married Jane, daughter of Francis Laugharne of St Brides, and Janet, daughter of John Philipps of Picton Castle. Her mother was Elizabeth Prothero, daughter of John Prothero of Hawksbrook (Nantyrhebog), Carms., and Eleanor, daughter of Walter Vaughan of Golden Grove, and thus a niece of John Vaughan, 1st earl of Carbery. Lucy's parents were involved in a long and acrimonious dispute. In May 1641 her mother complained that William Walter had deserted her and she obtained a sequestration order on his estate. This was ultimately revoked in 1647 when he was given charge of the children, of whom there were three, Richard, Lucy and Justus. Roch castle was garrisoned for the king by Richard Vaughan, 2nd earl of Carbery, in 1643. It was taken by Rowland Laugharne after his defeat of the Royalists at Pill (in Milford Haven) in Feb. 1644, but again seized for the king in the following June by Sir Charles Gerard. William Walter alleged that his losses there amounted to £3,000 and that he had been forced to flee to London. There is no doubt that the family spent much time in London in pursuance of the dispute which has already been mentioned. How the young Prince of Wales came to meet Lucy Walter is not known. She was with the exiled court at the Hague in the summer of 1648, and subsequently in Paris. Their son, James, was born at Rotterdam on 9 April 1649. Lucy also had a daughter, Mary, born at the Hague on 6 May 1651. In 1656 she returned to London and was arrested as a suspected spy and lodged, with her maid Anne Hill, in the Tower. Her defence was that she had come to collect a legacy of £1,500 left her by her mother, who had recently died. She was discharged and ordered to be deported. Charles II, who acknowledged the paternity of James, got possession of the child and handed him to the care of his mother, queen Henrietta Maria. After the Restoration he was created duke of Monmouth and was later married to Anne Scott, in her own right countess of Buccleuch. At the time of the Exclusion Bill agitation (1679-81) the story that Charles had married Lucy Walter and that, therefore, Monmouth was the rightful heir to the throne was put out and widely credited. Lucy herself died in Paris in 1658.

Sir Frederick Rees in *The Dictionary of Welsh Biography*, 1959.

13. *Apricot Sponge with a Sage*

I was down in West Wales doing a travel piece for a magazine when I decided to call on the Sage (a well-known philosopher-poet who had retired to the back of beyond) to find out something about the meaning of life. Usually I had been disappointed when I called on philosopher-poets to ask them this question. They invariably looked embarrassed, shifted about uneasily, and never looked me straight in the eye. They were stoics, unwilling to entertain such questions.

I needed to get an answer that day because my luck and post office savings were running out, I was having practical problems with my woman friend, and the landscape was particularly depressing. If forty-nine others had been down there with me, feeling as I did, the Samaritans would have had a field-day.

It was the end of summer, and along this bit of coast there were the usual tatty ice-cream shacks and junk stalls, a clutter of caravan sites and frail, ramshackle chalets that looked as if they had been made out of packing cases and old tea chests. Paper chip-bags and the odd used Durex littered the grass. Small herds of flea-bitten ponies were strung out on the dunes, trotting up cliff paths or wandering about in gardens, like the mangey sheep back in the valleys. The wind blew like a cutlass and penetrated my thin coat. It howled dramatically on the high ground.

I looked at the seaside mess around me: it was nearer to what George Orwell described before the war than to the jolly childhood excursions of Dylan Thomas. People had brought their dung here, and it stuck. I couldn't help envying the Cistercian monks across the water in their chosen isolation in a monastery on Caldy, away from the thump and crunch. Somebody told me they lived only on potatoes, parsnips, swedes and cabbage while they meditated and made their perfume. But a local grocer who supplied them denied this and said the brothers lived well on red meat and plenty of fruit. Anyway, Caldy looked tempting in the afternoon lemon light, the cold sun sitting flat on the roofs of the long, white house. You could have written the Great Welsh Novel there in perfect peace.

I had to hoof it inland to the Sage's place, and should have brought a compass because it was at the end of nowhere. After an hour's trudge through drab coastal country, with not a soul in sight, I came to the silent, shuttered hamlet — like something out of Mauriac — where the great man lived. I bought a box of chocolates for his wife in a smelly little shop, and a cigar for him. The woman in the shop had a twitch, and her scruffy Welsh terrier kept scratching himself.

When I knocked on the door of the Sage's wooden cottage, he appeared in a sagging corduroy suit and beckoned me in. He looked like King Lear gone to seed. I gave him the cigar. In the small front-room there were those three awful china flying ducks on one wall, and the Mona Lisa, Chinese Horse and Laughing Cavalier on the others. Some poor philistine woman's touch was everywhere, but the Sage didn't seem to mind. He was sucking a Polo mint, bringing it to the point of his tongue from time to time, and didn't say anything. There were only three books in the room — a Bible, Spinoza, and a cookery book.

The wife came in, or rather crept in. The old man must have led her a cat's life, she was so scrawny, nervous and subdued. She nearly vanished into the carpet. She had scraped in his long shadow for fifty years and had not experienced much kissing, by the look of it. When I put the chocolates on a table, she gave a little cry, scuttled almost sideways across the room without looking up, and snatched the box. 'Thank you, oh thank you,' she whispered. 'Diolch yn fawr.' Then she retreated to wherever she had come from.

This was my moment. I didn't hesitate. 'What's the meaning of life?' I asked the Sage, suddenly, like a dagger.

But he had already switched on an obsolete television set and was watching a Western. 'I remember this one,' he said. 'They're just getting to the bit where the Indians come in.'

'No, they're not,' I said, trying to put him off. 'This is one of those intellectual Westerns where they just talk.'

'The Indians were the finest light cavalry in the world,' he said.

We both stared at the tiny screen for an hour until my eyes ached. Later the wife padded in with food and we sat down to eat. We had oxtail soup, a big mixed grill with kidneys and mushrooms, and excellent apricot sponge soaked in sherry, followed by Gaelic coffee stiff with whiskey and cream, and two bottles of cheap but potent Portuguese rosé. No one spoke. I was full as a frog at the end of the feast and collapsed in a shattered armchair. They might be a pretty crummy pair, I thought, but they knew how to eat and drink.

Exhausted, I fell asleep, and when I woke up about two hours later the Sage was still watching the box, and the wife had disappeared again.

He switched off with a sigh. 'No Tom and Jerry tonight,' he said. 'Time to go. I'm going to bed now.' It was about eight in the evening.

'All right,' I said.

I was closing the front door and wondering how I would get back to civilization when I heard the great man shout:
'What's the meaning of apricot sponge?'

John Tripp, 'Apricot Sponge with a Sage' in
The Old Man of the Mist and Other Stories, ed. Lynn Hughes, 1974.

13.   *The Execution of John Poyer*

A military court sat from April 4th to April 12th 1649 and, after a full hearing of parties and witnesses, condemned Laugharne, Poyer and Powell to death. Their relatives hastened to petition for mercy towards them: Elizabeth Poyer for her husband; Maud, Mary and Elizabeth Powell for their brother; while Mrs Laugharne pathetically urged that her husband's one ill-advised act 'might not cause all his former eminent services to be forgotten'.

The Council of State having decided that the death of one man would satisfy the ends of justice, Fairfax instructed the prisoners to draw lots for their lives, and three pieces of paper were prepared; two of which bore the words 'Life given of God', while the third was blank. They were unwilling to choose for themselves. A child therefore drew the lots, and the blank paper announced Poyer's fate. 'It is observable,' a contemporary remarked, 'that the lot should fall on him who was the first beginner of the second war'.

Poyer's execution, originally appointed for April 24th, but for some undisclosed reason postponed to the following day, took place at Covent Garden. Early in the morning of April 25th two ministers, Mr Knight and Mr Walter Cradock, the latter of whom had known Poyer in Pembroke, visited him at Whitehall and accompanied him to the place of execution, riding in a coach guarded by two troops of horse and three companies of foot.

The site of Covent Garden Market was then a large open space bordered on the north by a row of fashionable houses and closed on the west by St Paul's church, while the garden wall of Bedford House ran along its southern side. After the procession had marched round the great space Poyer was placed between two 'Bulges' of the wall to await his fate. He prayed for a short time, and added —

I confess that I have lived very loosely . . . though I was once low yet I became very high . . . but now I must leave all . . . although my fortune changed my affections to the Parliament did not alter . . . I was always honest with them until an unhappy disaster which hath brought this misery to me.

Then, raising his hand, he died, as Clarendon testified, 'with singular courage'.

Arthur L. Leach, *The History of the Civil War (1642-1649) in Pembrokeshire*, 1937.

14.   *Pirate Captain, 'Barti Ddu'*

Roberts, Bartholomew [originally John] (1682?-1722), pirate; b. in Pembrokeshire. In 1718, when he was second mate on the *Princess*, his ship was captured by the Welsh pirate, Howel Davis, and he was forced to serve under his captor. When Davis was killed, Roberts, who in six weeks had shown great courage and resourcefulness, was elected captain. He accepted, saying that since he had dipped his hands in muddy water it was better to be commander than a common man. Notoriety came speedily. He sailed into a fleet of forty-two Portuguese ships, ascertained which was the richest, boarded, and sailed off with her. Soon he struck terror everywhere. When he entered a harbour in Newfoundland, their crews abandoned the twenty-two ships there. After successes, the pirates went ashore at places like Surinam and Sierra Leone, indulging in wild debauchery until their resources were exhausted. Not that success was unbroken; once at least they were long in extremities for want of provisions and water. One of their finest captures was a frigate built ship of the Royal African Company. Roberts renamed her the *Royal Fortune*. Captain Chaloner Ogle, R.N., managed to bring her to battle off Cape Lopez; Roberts was killed (5 Feb. 1722), and his body, in all its pirate finery, thrown overboard, as he had previously requested. His crew then surrendered. Bold as pirate captains were, Roberts's calculated daring was exceptional. In a drink-sodden and blood-stained community he was comparatively temperate and humane.

W. J. Thomas in *The Dictionary of Welsh Biography*, 1959.

15.   *Friend of Dr Johnson*

Only a dovecote remains of the Great House of Rosemarket, which belonged to the Walter family, who also owned Roch Castle, in which Lucy Walter was probably born, although it is sometimes claimed she was born in Rosemarket. A very different type of woman was born at Rosemarket in the following century — Anna Williams, the poetess, who was befriended by Dr Johnson and his wife. Boswell, in his *Life of Dr Johnson*, says Lady Knight told him:

> 'She was a person extremely interesting; she had uncommon firmness of mind, a boundless curiosity, retentive memory and strong judgement; she had various powers of pleasing. Her personal afflictions and slender fortune she seemed to forget when she had the power of doing an act of kindness. She was social, cheerful, and active, in a state of body that was truly deplorable.'

Richard Fenton, who met her in London, confirmed Lady Knight's account of her, and adds the touching detail:

> 'She had all the nationality of her country, tor finding I was a Welshman, she increased her attentions; but when she had traced me to Pembrokeshire, she drew her chair closer, took me familiarly by the hand, as if kindred blood tingled at her fingers ends, talked of past times, and dwelt with rapture on Rose Market.'

Maxwell Fraser, *Introducing West Wales*, 1956.

16.   *The First Welsh Lord Mayor of London*

Lewes, Sir Watkin (1740-1821), Lord Mayor of London; second son of Watkin Lewes, Penybenglog, Melinau, and Ann Williams of Ambleston, Pembs. His father was rector of Melinau (1735-59) and of Newport, Pembs, (1759-70). The son was educated at Shrewsbury school and Magdalene College, Cambridge, where he graduated in 1763. He entered the Middle Temple (1760), and was called to the (Chancery) Bar in 1766. He married Rebecca Eleanora, eldest daughter and co-heir of Thomas Popkin of Fforest, near Swansea, who brought him considerable estates in Glamorgan, and Rudbaxton in Pembs. Having contested Worcester unsuccessfully in four elections, he sought civic and parliamentary honours in the City of London. His rise was rapid; in 1772 he was made sheriff and also alderman of Lime Street Ward, was knighted in 1773, and in 1780 became Lord Mayor. In 1771 he had presented addresses in the Tower from the counties of Pembroke, Carmarthen, and Cardigan to the political prisoners, John Wilkes, the Lord Mayor Crosby, and alderman Oliver. In 1780 he was elected one of the four MPs for the City of London, which seat he retained until 1796. He took an active interest in Welsh literature and music, and was at one time Treasurer of the Society of Ancient Britons; [he was the second president of the Cymmrodorion, in succession to Richard Morris]. The last part of his life was clouded by financial difficulties; he was arrested for debt and ended his days (13 July 1821) in the London Coffee House on Ludgate Hill within the rules of the Fleet prison.

J. J. Evans in *The Dictionary of Welsh Biography*, 1959.

17.   *Ioan Siencyn, Heir to an Ancient Discipline*

During the wars of Napoleon there was a country squire of the name Lloyd living in the old house of Cwmgloyn, inland a little from Trefdraeth (or Newport in the English maps) on the north coast of Pembrokeshire. He was a justice of the peace. His father had been high sheriff of the county in 1771. The family had been much concerned with the sea, and squire Lloyd had ships built for him at Trefdraeth and at Aberystwyth. One of these, the *Hawk*, was a fifty ton schooner made from his own woods at Trefdraeth, partly for trade, partly for his pleasure voyages. It was later sunk by the French. At its launching a local poet, one Ioan Siencyn, wrote a poem to greet it and its captain, and its squire-owner. After a finely-imaged description of the *Hawk* breasting the sea, the poet visualises squire Lloyd on board, travelling to England and Ireland, but especially visiting his friends in North and South Wales. There the gentry and local poets come to meet him and one verse describes their welcome to him:

> Around their tables laden with steaming dishes,
> He shall hear histories of those good men, our ancestors,
> And cywydd and englyn and odes of Taliesin,
> And he shall drink his fill of golden barley beer.

That poem was written close to the beginning of the nineteenth century. It speaks simply and naturally of odes of Taliesin and *cywydd* and *englyn* as part of the pertinent welcome to squire Lloyd of Cwmgloyn. Taliesin was a poet of the sixth century. *Cywydd* and *englyn* were metrical forms of the Welsh Middle Ages. But for Ioan Siencyn at the very end of the eighteenth century they were all necessary for the proper entertainment of the Welsh squire in any Welsh country house. Poetry was part of the tradition of hospitality . .

Now will you imagine with me that a poet of the fifteenth century, some great figure such as Tudur Aled, had been released to revisit Pembrokeshire at the launching of the *Hawk*, and had listened to the reading of Ioan Siencyn's verses to squire Lloyd? What would our fifteenth century master have thought or said? He would note with warm approval the occasion of the poem. Just such an event, the completion of a new house or a new ship, had in his time also been the appropriate moment for a complimentary poem to the head of a family. And Tudur Aled would have relished Ioan Siencyn's development of the image of the *Hawk* as it was launched on the water:

> Spread now your wings, forget the green woodlands,
> Learn to live mid the mouthing of seas.

When Siencyn calls on Neptune and Triton to protect the schooner, Tudur Aled would remember that he, in the early sixteenth century, was beginning to learn the use of those Greek gods from his friends in the circle of Cardinal Wolsey; and that when the poet returns to his bird-schooner and describes the *Hawk*:

> Your wings playing high as the clouds,
> Your breasts cleaving the salt billows,
> Let your beak pierce the waves, your belly furrow them,
> Your rudder scatter them in spray-suds . . .

the fifteenth-century poet would have recognised it as just that serious playing with image that was part of the technique of poems inspired by manual craft in his own day. And as the poem grew to the final eulogy of squire Lloyd and his society, to the reference to Taliesin and talk of the deeds of his forefathers storied over the yellow beer on the laden dining table, Tudur Aled might well exclaim: "My art still survives in this last decade of the eighteenth century and the great technique and the old mastery are not all forgotten. This country poet, this Ioan Siencyn, is truly an heir of our ancient discipline; he also sings the immemorial ideals and the pattern of behaviour of the leaders of the Welsh people, and I recognise him as a poet of the long line that began with Taliesin in the North'.

There, I think, we capture something essential in the progress of Welsh poesy. We call it the literary tradition of Wales. It means you cannot pluck a flower of song off a headland of Dyfed in the late eighteenth century without stirring a great Northern star of the sixth century. And all the intermediaries are involved. The fourteenth century gave the technique of *dyfalu* or image-making, the sixteenth century brought in the Virgilian echoes, the seventeenth gave the measure. The whole body of Welsh poetry from the sixth century onward has contributed directly to Ioan Siencyn's verses. And mark you, the poem I am discussing is an obscure piece of work by a little known poet whose name is in no history of Welsh literature nor in any anthology. It was last published in a forgotten volume at Aberystwyth in 1842. Why do I use it as a peg for this talk? Because it reveals the nature and continuity of the Welsh poetic tradition and because it reveals its quality and creative virtue: for the virtue of that tradition is that it may enable a quite minor poet to write a major poem.

Saunders Lewis in *The Essence of Welsh poetry*

18. *The Revivalist*

13 July 1739. Newgale, Pembrokeshire. Toward St David's. Caerfarchell. To my great surprise I find God metling the people, notwithstanding my vileness. Discoursed to 12. Many seemed pricked through, then toward Bridaeth or Bready (Brawdy), there discoursed through the rain. The Lord I hope was with us, then toward Wolff's Castle past 6 through all the rain, and the Lord was never better. Thrown from the horse and broke my hand, but the Lord had so ordered it that I was just by one of His servant's house that took care of me. I fainted. Slept past 11.

Howell Harris in *Howell Harris's Visits to Pembrokeshire (1739-1752)*, transcribed by Tom Beynon, 1966.

19.   *John Wesley in Pembrokeshire*

Sunday, 29 [August, 1764]. The minister of St Mary's [Pembroke] sent me word he was very willing I should preach in his church, but before the service began the mayor sent to forbid it, so he preached a very useful sermon himself. The mayor's behaviour so disgusted many of the gentry that they resolved to hear where they could, and accordingly flocked together in the evening from all parts of the town.

*   *   *

Tuesday, 20 [August 1771]. I rode to Haverfordwest and in the evening preached in St Martin's churchyard to a numerous and deeply attentive congregation. The next evening I strongly applied the story of Dives and Lazarus, and many were almost persuaded to be Christians.

I rode on Thursday the 22nd to Dale, a little village at the mouth of Milford Haven. It seemed to me that our preachers had bestowed here much pains to little purpose. The people, one and all, seemed as dead as stones — perfectly quiet and perfectly unconcerned. I told them just what I thought. It went as a sword to their hearts. They *felt* the truth and wept bitterly. I know not where we have found more of the presence of God. Shall we at last have fruit here also?

*   *   *

Monday, 14 [July 1777]. I reached Llwyn-gwair about noon. In the evening Mr Pugh read prayers and I preached at Newport. This is the only town in Wales which I had then observed to increase. In riding along on the side of Newport bay I observed on the ground a large quantity of turfs. These are found by removing the sand above high-water mark, under which there is a continued bed of turf with the roots of trees, leaves, nuts and various kinds of vegetables. So that it is plain the sea is an intruder here and now covers what was once dry land. Such probably was the whole bay a few centuries ago. Nay, it is not at all improbable that formerly it was dry land from Aberystwyth to St David's Point.

Wednesday, 16. About nine I preached again in Newport church and found much liberty among that poor simple people. We dined with Admiral Vaughan at Trecwn, one of the most delightful spots that can be imagined. Thence we rode to Haverfordwest, but the heat and dust were as much as I could bear, I was faint for a while, but it was all gone as soon as I came into the congregation, and after preaching and meeting the society I was as fresh as at six in the morning.

Thursday, 17. I preached at Roch and took a view of the old castle, built on a steep rock. A gentleman wisely asked Mr S*: 'Pray, is this natural or artificial?' He gravely replied: 'Artificial to be sure; I imported it from the north of Ireland.'

*   *   *

Tuesday, 1 May [1781]. I rode to St David's, seventeen measured miles from Haverfordwest. I was surprised to find all the land for the last nine or ten mile so fruitful and well cultivated. What a difference is there between the westernmost parts of England and the western-most parts of Wales! The former (the west of Cornwall) so barren and wild, the latter so fruitful and well improved! But the town itself is a melancholy spectacle. I saw but one tolerable good house in it; the rest were miserable huts indeed. I do not remember so mean a town even in Ireland. The cathedral has been a large and stately fabric, far superior to any other in Wales, but a great part of it is fallen down already and the rest is hastening into ruin — one blessed fruit (among many) of bishops residing at a distance from their see. Here are the tombs and effigies of many ancient worthies, Owen [recté Edmund] Tudor in particular. But the zealous Cromwellians broke off their noses, hands and feet and defaced them as much as possible. But what had the Tudors done to them? Why, they were progenitors of kings.

A. H. Williams, *John Wesley in Wales*, 1971.

20.   *O'er those gloomy hills*

O'er those gloomy hills of darkness
    Look, my soul; be still, and gaze;
All the promises do travail
    With a glorious day of grace:
        Blessed Jubil
Let thy glorious morning dawn.

---

* John Rees Stokes of Cuffern.

Kingdoms wide that sit in darkness,
  Let them have the glorious light;
And from eastern coast to western
  May the morning chase the night.
    And redemption,
Freely purchased win the day.

Lord, I long to see that morning,
  When Thy Gospel shall abound,
And Thy grace get full possession
  Of the happy promised ground;
    All the borders
Of the great Immanuel's land.

Fly abroad, eternal gospel,
  Win and conquer, never cease;
May the lasting wide dominions
  Multiply and still increase;
    May thy sceptre
Sway the enlightened world around.

William Williams, Pantycelyn, 1761-91
(said to have been composed during a visit to Llwyngwair.)

21.   *Rebecca?*

Rees, Thomas ('Twm Carnabwth'; 1806?-76), pugilist; b. at
Carnábwth, Mynachlog-ddu, Pembs. He was one of the 'Rebecca
rioters', but his part in that affair has been greatly exaggerated. He
won great fame as a pugilist, but in 1847, in a fight (when drunk) with
a man named Gabriel Davies, he lost one eye. This sobered him, and
he became a member of Bethel Baptist church at Mynachlog-ddu.

R. T. Jenkins in *The Dictionary of Welsh Biography*, 1959.

22.   *The Rebecca Riots*

In the meantime yet a third riot had taken place at Efail-wen. On
Wednesday afternoon, 17 July, a large crowd assembled, again

with blackened faces and in women's clothes, but this time in broad daylight. The constables who were guarding the chain took to their heels, except a lame man who failed to get away and was severely manhandled. On this occasion the leader was addressed as Becca, and the name 'the Rebecca Riots' thereby came into use. Local tradition has always identified him with Thomas Rees, a pugilist who farmed the little homestead of Carnabwth nearby, in the parish of Mynachlog-ddu. It is said that there had been difficulty in finding women's clothes large enough to fit him until he succeeded in borrowing those of Big Rebecca, who lived in the neighbouring parish of Llangolman. From that day to this the name of Twm Carnabwth has been inseparably associated with the Rebecca Riots in popular tradition, but the truth is that he played no further part whatsoever in them, nor did any subsequent riot take place within eight miles of Efail-wen.

David Williams, *The Rebecca Riots,* 1955.

23.   *General Sir Thomas Picton*

Young Thomas was determined from his earliest childhood to be a soldier, and actually received his ensign's commission in the 13th Foot when he was only thirteen! He studied at a military academy for two years before joining his regiment at Gibraltar, but in 1783 his regiment was disbanded, and he returned to Pembrokeshire on half-pay at the age of twenty-five. Twelve years later he went to the West Indies and did such good service there against the enemy that the Governors of Caraccas and Guiana offered a reward of 20,000 dollars for his head — and he wrote each of them a humorous letter, regretting his head was not better worth the money!

He was appointed Governor of Trinidad in 1797, and soon showed his fine abilities as an administrator, giving the island peace and prosperity, and transforming the roads from the worst to the finest in the West Indies. It was mainly due to him that Trinidad remained a British possession, and when he was accused in the King's Bench in 1806 with having permitted a native to be ill-treated, the islanders subscribed £40,000 towards his legal expenses. Picton, however, returned the whole amount to the island for the relief of sufferers from a disastrous fire in Port of Spain.

Picton went to Portugal in 1810, where he quickly became the

Duke of Wellington's 'right-hand man'. Over six feet in height, and strongly built, with piercing brown eyes, he was a warm friend and formidable enemy. Stern, and even ruthless at times, he spared none — least of all himself — and the most typical story told of him is his retort to a Spanish commissary who made difficulties about supplying much-needed rations for his men. Picton pointed out a tree and said, 'If my men's rations are not delivered by twelve noon tomorrow, I will hang you on that tree'. The commissary hurried off to complain to the Duke of Wellington, who commented calmly, 'If Picton said that, he will certainly keep his word' — with the natural result Picton's men got their rations on time!

Absorbed as he was by his profession, he was a very unconventional general, and had no use for the 'spit-and-polish' of his day — it is said he even went into some of his battles carrying an umbrella, and fought at Waterloo in a shabby great-coat, and a top hat which can be seen to this day in the United Services Museum in Whitehall. Surprisingly enough, he was equally indifferent how his soldiers looked, saying that he did not care how they dressed as long as they minded their fighting. As he was equally ready to share their hardships and dangers, there is small wonder they were ready to follow wherever he led.

When the Peninsular War ended, he returned to his estate at Iscoed, near Ferryside, but when Napoleon escaped from Elba, Wellington sent for him and he was posted to London, spending his last night in Wales with his brother, Richard Picton Turbervill, at Ewenny Priory in Glamorganshire. He was badly wounded at Quatre Bras, but although his ribs were broken, he kept it secret, and two days later fell in repulsing one of the most serious attacks of the day at Waterloo. General Gascoyne said that after his death, men who saw the wound he had received at Quatre Bras marvelled how he could have endured the agony in secret, and Sir William Fraser told how the commission appointing Picton commander-in-chief, in the event of Wellington being disabled or killed, was found in his breast pocket. His body was brought back to England and buried in the family vault in St George's, Hanover Square, and a memorial set up to him in St Paul's Cathedral.

Maxwell Fraser, *Introducing West Wales*, 1956.

24. *Charles Norris*

Charles Norris was born in 1779 at Hughenden Manor, near Beaconsfield, Bucks. He was the second son of John Norris, a wealthy London merchant, who had married Catherine, the divorced wife of Henry Knight of Newton Nottage, Glamorgan. She was the daughter of Dr John Lynch, Dean of Canterbury and grand-daughter of Archbishop Wake. The bulk of the property of an old Warwickshire family, of which Charles Savage was the head, had been transferred to the Norrises, who represented the younger branch. Elizabeth, daughter of Charles Savage, married Dr Walter Landor and thus became mother of a famous son, Walter Savage Landor, author of the 'Imaginary Conversations'. Charles Norris and Walter Savage Landor were therefore related, but not closely, the latter being the son of Norris's first cousin.

Charles Norris's parents, who died when he was very young, had made adequate provision for his education and in due course he went to Eton and Oxford (Christ Church College), but he left the university without taking a degree and soon obtained a commission in the King's Dragoon Guards. Any inclination he had felt for a soldier's life ended when, marching through Coventry with his regiment, he caught sight of pretty Sarah Saunders, daughter of a Norwich Congregational Minister . . .

Perhaps a clue to Norris's selection of Tenby as a place of residence may be found in his connection with Walter Savage Landor. The young men had certainly met some years before Norris left Clifton; for Landor, writing from Paris to his sister Elizabeth in 1802, said of the Emperor Napoleon, 'his figure and complexion are nearly like those of Charles Norris'. Landor had visited Tenby in 1795 and again in 1796 at the time of his affair with 'golden-haired Nancy Jones'.

Arthur L. Leach, *Charles Norris 1779-1858*, 1949.

25. *'Y Mochyn Du'*

Owen, John (1836-1915), Calvinistic Methodist minister and author of the popular ballad 'Cân y Mochyn Du' ('The Ballad of the Black Pig'). Born 1 April 1836, the son of Simon and Rachel Owen, Blaenpencelli, Eglwyswrw, Pembs. He received his early education at the Sunday school held at Ebenezer Baptist chapel. Before he was 12 years of age, he was engaged as a shepherd boy at Henllys, the former home of the 16th century historian, George Owen, and after serving thus for a period of two years, he took leave for eight weeks in order to attend the day school held at Eglwyswrw. His knowledge of English and his proficiency in music and Welsh shorthand he obtained by self-tuition.

He wrote his famous ballad 'Y Mochyn Du' about 1854. He was then in the service of Mr and Mrs Thomas James, of Felin Wrdan (Jordan's Mill), Eglwyswrw, and it is believed that the ballad was published by Mrs James at a later date, without the author's knoweldge. The characters referred to in the ballad were all drawn from life, and the tragedy recorded befell one David Thomas, of Parc-y-maes, Brynberian. The ballad was sung at local fairs by the well-known ballad-monger Levi Gibbon, who also added some of the verses. Soon it became one of the most popular of Welsh ballads, sung not only throughout Wales, but in all quarters of the globe where Welshmen gathered. Its author, however, remained deeply ashamed of his composition to the end of his days. He forbade its further publication and could not tolerate its strains. There is but one brief mention of the work in his manuscript autobiography: 'During this period (i.e. 1850-57) I wrote "Y Mochyn Du", now so well known throughout the land; a song that will continue to corrupt the tastes of our young people when the tongue that first sang it will have long been silent in the grave. Forgive, O Lord, the sins of my youth!'

Dillwyn Miles in *The Dictionary of Welsh Biography*, 1959.

26. *The Lloyd George Connection*

Mr William George was the eldest son of Mr David George, of Trecoed, in the parish of Jordanston, near Fishguard. He was of a literary turn of mind, and although pressed to stay at home and manage the farm, he would not do so. He was articled to Dr Brown, of Haverfordwest, with the view of becoming a doctor. His bent, however, was for literature, in the pursuit of which he spent so much midnight oil that Dr Brown, realising that his inclinations were not for physic, advised his parents to let him pursue his literary studies. Mr George accordingly took up the position of tutor in London.

Whilst there, he became acquainted with Messrs Murray (the well known publishers). He had access to the libraries and lectures, and thus acquired a profound knowledge of literature in its widest aspect. After remaining in London for about ten years, reasons of health compelled him to return home, and for a few years he pursued his studies in his more congenial native air. He then opened a private school at Llysronen, Granston, near Mathry . . . Among Mr William George's pupils were the late Mr T. M. Phillips, chemist, Castle Square; Mr Edwin W. John, solicitor, (father of the world-renowned artist, Mr Augustus John); Mr David Morris, the well known Pembrokeshire auctioneer; Mr Edwin A. John, stationer, and many others whose names are forgotten.

During this time Mr William George became acquainted with a Miss Huntley who, with her companion, Miss Legge, then resided in Haverfordwest. The acquaintance ripened into friendship, and ultimately into something stronger, and they afterwards married. Mrs George, however, died a year or two after her marriage. She was buried in St Thomas' Churchyard, Haverfordwest.

Mr George then took up a scholastic appointment in North Wales, where he became acquainted with and afterwards married a Miss Lloyd, of Caernarvon. After residing there for a few years, he became tutor at a college in Manchester, where Mr D. Lloyd George was born. Whilst there, Mr William George made the acquaintance of Dr Martineau, the well-known literateur, with whom he became closely associated in the various branches of his work. Unfortunately, Mr George's health again gave way, and he was advised to return to Pembrokeshire to take up some agricultural pursuit. He accordingly took a lease of the farm of Bullford, near Johnston, where he resided for two years prior to his death. His remains were taken for burial to his own native parish. Under the auspices of Mr William Davies, solicitor, the farming effects and furniture were sold by auction, and the widow and three children went to reside with her uncle, Mr Richard Lloyd, at Criccieth, in Carnarvonshire.

I recall the sale held at Bullford about the year 1865, if I remember rightly. The auctioneer at the sale was the late Mr Henry Davies, of the Old Bridge Haverfordwest, and my fellow clerk, the late Mr J. M. Martin, managed and booked the sale. Having business in the neighbourhood, and passing from Tiers Cross to Johnston, I looked in at the sale to see how things were going. A short time before his death Mr Martin and I recalled our memories of the sale. I remember him remarking to me at the time, 'Do you see that little chap swinging on the gate? He's a little terror. There was one lot being taken away just now, for which he evidently had a strong attachment, for he fiercely resisted it being taken away by the purchaser.' As I passed out through the lawn gate, the boy referred to (Mr D. Lloyd George) was swinging on it with intense energy, and he returned my look at him defiantly. The next time I saw this lad, after the lapse of considerably more than half a century, he was in the Castle Square, Haverfordwest, beaming with smiles. The little chap I saw swinging on the gate at Bullford had then become a grey-headed man, and become the most notable statesman of his time.

W. D. Phillips, *Old Haverfordwest*, 1935.

27.   *Twm Waunbwll*

He used to come into Cardigan on market day by train, with a sack into which he put all the provisions for the week; meat, fish, tea, sugar being dumped together unceremoniously to be carried on his shoulder down to the station. One Saturday he arrived without his trousers. Apparently he had sat on an ant-hill, and in the train he began to itch. To get rid of the ants he took his trousers off, but while he was shaking them vigorously outside the window they filled with air and were wrenched from his grasp. Undeterred he carried out his shopping clad in his huge Welsh woollen long underpants with black longitudinal stripes.

He was an old bachelor, though his mother once tried to teach him the first steps of courtship. 'Now Twm,' she said, 'I'll go upstairs; you go outside, and throw up some gravel at the bedroom window.' So out he went, and threw up the gravel. His mother opened the window saying coyly, 'Who is there?' 'O dammo Mam!' he retorted, 'you know its me, for you only sent me out about a minute ago!'

When his mother died he insisted she be buried just inside the gate of the churchyard, for as he told the minister, 'There'll be one hell of a rush to get out once the resurrection trumpet blows.'

James Williams, *Give Me Yesterday*, 1971.

28.   *Augustus John*

Soon after the death of my mother, when I was five or six, my father made the great decision of his life. He left Haverfordwest with all its old associations, its family traditions such as they were, with all his professional and social links, and moved to Tenby. (It was here, as a matter of fact that I was born, during a former sojourn of my parents at this town.) I think the superior gentility of Tenby attracted him.

On market day at Haverfordwest the streets and squares were full of life and movement. Noise too, with the continual lowing of cattle, the screaming of pigs, and the loud vociferation of the drovers. Among the crowd were to be seen the women of Langum, in their distinctive and admirable costume, carrying creels of the famous oysters on their backs. Tramps, looking like peripatetic philosophers of the school of Diogenes, would congregate idly at the street-corners. Perhaps they had passed a night on the lime-kilns where sometimes, it was said, the unwary among them, seeking warmth, would fall asleep upon the upper stones, till, sinking gradually, they would soon be asphyxiated and reduced to ashes by the morning.

Gypsies arrived on the scene with their horses and light carts. These people interested me greatly. Those sardonic faces, those lustrous oriental eyes, even then did cast their spell upon me. We were taught to beware of the Gypsies; their habit of kidnapping children was notorious; yet they seemed to have plenty of their own. Aloof, arrogant, and in their ragged finery somehow superior to the common run of natives, they could be recognised a mile off. I was destined to know these people better in time to come . . .

Another resort of ours was Begelly. Left to ourselves in the big house overlooking a wide infertile common, disdained by the land-grabbers, and populated only by a few cattle, geese and gypsies, we ran happily wild. But the messages of earth and changing sky, our observation of birds and beasts, and the example of the nomads in their caravans below, our desultory but voracious reading and unfettered day-dreams — all conspired to stir up discontent and longing for a wider, freer world than that symbolically enclosed by Tenby's town walls; we craved for Art, Liberty, Life, perhaps Love!

Augustus John, *Chiaroscuro*, 1952.

29. *Dylan Thomas at Fishguard*

Dylan had met Richard Hughes, the novelist, during an earlier return visit and they had taken a liking to one another. The National Eisteddfod, that Welsh convention of late eighteenth-century origin at which druids preside and bards are honoured, was being held that year (1936) at Fishguard. There was also a painting competition, for which Fred Janes had entered a picture and which Augustus John was to judge. Fred, who was also at home in Swansea, suggested to Dylan that they borrow Fred's father's car and drive to Fishguard for the judging. Dylan improved on this, with the proposal that they ask if they might call on Richard and Frances Hughes, at Laugharne Castle, on the way. Hughes replied, inviting them to lunch. Dylan probably knew that Augustus, an old friend of the Hugheses, and with him Caitlin, would be staying at Laugharne. It would seem probable that she had told him so. It also seems likely that she had not informed Augustus of this.

The account of this meeting, as given by Augustus John in his auto-biography, is quite misleading. He speaks of finding Dylan seated alone by the roadside and introducing him to Caitlin and to Richard Hughes, both for the first time, and tells how Dylan and Caitlin fell into one another's arms in the back of his motor-car. The real story of that day, for most of which Fred Janes was present, is rather different.

After lunch with the Hugheses in their pretty pink Georgian house which is called the Castle because it abuts on the ruins, Augustus and Caitlin set off for Fishguard in Augustus's large and very fast car, a six-cylinder Wolseley. Dylan and Fred followed in Fred's father's car, an older, slower and smaller machine. The judging took place, a lot was drunk, and in the evening the four of them set off for Carmarthen, where they proposed to dine, travelling as before. Augustus was driving even faster now over the bad Welsh roads, and in St Clear's Fred's car broke down. Dylan was transferred to Augustus's car, while Fred remained in St Clear's to see about having his father's repaired. Later he returned to Laugharne, dined at the Castle with Richard and Frances Hughes, and slept at Brown's Hotel.

Dylan and Augustus and Caitlin had dined, though that may well be a euphemism, in Carmarthen. Then Dylan insisted that Augustus take him, too, back to Laugharne, but this the old painter refused to do. He was by now thoroughly annoyed by Dylan's and Caitlin's public love-making. Was he jealous? It is possible. Did he know about Dylan's illness? It is probable, as so many people in Soho did. Thus it seems likely that mingled with normal jealousy there was an element of paternal responsibility towards the young girl as well. In the event tempers rose, and eventually it came to a fight in the car park. Dylan was often pugnacious, but he was quite useless with his fists and mostly got the worst of it. Augustus, though some forty years his senior, had little trouble in knocking Dylan down. Then he and Caitlin got into his large motor-car and drove away.

Constantine FitzGibbon, *The Life of Dylan Thomas*, 1965.

30. *Graham Sutherland comes to Pembrokeshire*

It was in 1934 that I first visited Pembrokeshire. I was visiting a country, a part of which, at least, spoke a foreign tongue, and it certainly seemed very foreign to me, though sufficiently accessible for me to feel that I could claim it as my own.

After a good deal of wandering about, I came upon two very remarkable passages of country situated in the arms of land which embrace the great area of St Bride's Bay. The arm towards the north is like an isosceles triangle on its side, the narrowest angle forming St David's Head to the west. One approaches across a wide plain from the north, its emptiness relieved by the interlocking of tightly-packed strips of field and their bounding walls of turf-covered rocks. One soon notices an irregularity of contour on the horizon which resolves itself into what appears to be two mountains. As one approaches still closer one sees that these masses of rock scarcely attain a height of more than seven hundred feet. But so classically perfect is their form, and so majestic is their command of the smoothly-rising ground below, that the mind comfortably corrects the measurement of the eye, and holds their essential mountainous significance. A rocky path leads round the slopes of the nearer mountain, where, to the west, the escarpment precipitates itself to a rock-strewn strip of marsh, marked out with the crazy calligraphy of the foundations of primitive hut dwellings; from here the ground rises to a vast congregation of rocks, fallen cromlechs, and goats' caves, which continue their undulating and bewildering disorder, until they plunge, in the terraces of St David's Head, into the table of the sea. The southern slopes yield to the plain again; but here the land, gradually sloping to the sea, is studded with rocky cairns of every size. Between these are fields, each with a spear of rock at its centre. It is as if the solid rock foundation of the earth had thrown up these spears to transfix and hold the scanty earth of the fields upon it. Farms and cottages — glistening white, pink, and blue-grey — give scale and quicken by their implications our apprehension of the scene.

In this direction, nearer the sea, the earth is comparatively flat, but this flatness is deceiving and makes the discovery of little steep valleys more surprising. These valleys possess a bud-like intricacy of form and contain streams, often of indescribable beauty, which run to the sea. The astonishing fertility of these valleys and the complexity of the roads running through them is a delight to the eye. The roads form strong and mysterious arabesques as they rise in terraces, in sight, hidden, turning and splitting as they finally disappear into the sky. To see a solitary human figure descending such a road at the solemn moment of sunset is to realize the enveloping quality of the earth, which can create, as it does here, a mysterious space limit — a womb-like enclosure — which gives the human form an extraordinary focus and significance.

At the risk of talking like a guide-book, I must tell you of the area to the south. I shall never forget my first visit. We approached by a flat winding road and had slipped into one of the little valleys such as I have attempted to describe. To the left this opened out to reveal what appeared to be a watery inlet narrowing to its upper end. As the road progressed we caught further glimpses of this and curiosity was roused. We had intended making for a village called Dale, marked on the map as lying to the north side of the mouth of Milford Haven. Fortunately, we missed the road and found ourselves descending a green lane buried in trees, which, quite unexpectedly, lead to a little cove and beach by the banks of a narrow estuary.

Here is a hamlet — three cottages and an inn crouch under the low cliffs. A man is burning brushwood cut from a tree, bleached and washed by the sea. The flame looks incandescent in the evening light. The tide in the estuary (or pill, as such inlets are called here) is out, and we walk across the sandy bed of the opening and look down its winding length to the place where it narrows to the upper end.

I wish I could give you some idea of the exultant strangeness of this place — for strange it certainly is, many people whom I know hate it, and I cannot but admit that it possesses an element of disquiet. The left bank as we see it is all dark — an impenetrable damp green gloom of woods which run down to the edge of low blackish moss-covered cliffs — it is all dark, save where the mossy lanes (two each side) which dive down to the opening, admit the sun, hinged, as it were, to the top of the trees, from where its rays, precipitating new colours, turn the red cliffs of the right-hand bank to tones of fire. Do you remember the rocks in Blake's 'Newton' drawing? The form and scale of the rocks here, and the miutiæ on them, is very similar.

The whole setting is one of exuberance — of darkness and light —

of decay and life. Rarely have I been so conscious of the contrasting of these elements in so small a compass.

The right bank has field above the cliff, some covered with ripe corn, others with rough gorse-clad pasture. The life-giving sound of the mechanical reaper is heard. Cattle crouch among the dark gorse. The mind wanders from contemplation of the living cattle to their ghosts. It is no uncommon sight to see a horse's skull or horns of cattle lying bleached on the sand. Neither do we feel that the black-green ribs of half-buried wrecks and the phantom tree roots, bleached and washed by the waves, exist but to emphasize the extraordinary completeness of the scene. Complete, too, is the life of the few inhabitants — almost biblical in its sober dignity. The people in this part appear quite incurious of the activities of a foreigner. The immense soft-voiced innkeeper and his wife, small as he is big, sit, when they are not working, bolt upright, on a hard bench in the cool gloom of the parlour which forms the only 'bar' of the inn, or they sit — for he is ferry-man and fisherman, as well as innkeeper — gazing across the ferry.

The quality of light here is magical and transforming — as indeed it is in all this country. Watching from the gloom as the sun's rays strike the further bank, one has the sensation of the after tranquillity of an *explosion* of light; or as if one had looked into the sun and had turned suddenly away.

Herons gather. They fly majestically towards the sea. Most moving is the sound of snipe which flicker in their lightning dash down the inlet, to and from the sea.

These and other things have delighted me. The twisted gorse on the cliff edge, such as suggested the picture 'Gorse on Sea Wall' — twigs, like snakes, lying on the path, the bare rock, worn, and showing through the path, heath fires, gorse burnt and blackened after fire, a tin school in an exuberant landscape, the high overhanging hedges by the steep roads which pinch the setting sun, mantling clouds against a black sky and the thunder, the flowers and damp hollows, the farmer galloping on his horse down the estuary, the deep green valleys and the rounded hills and the whole structure, simple and complex.

It was in this country that I began to learn painting. It seemed impossible here for me to sit down and make finished paintings 'from nature'. Indeed, there were no 'ready made' subjects to paint. The spaces and concentrations of this clearly constructed land were stuff for storing in the mind. Their essence was intellectual and emotional, if I may say so. I found that I could express what I felt only by paraphrasing what I saw. Moreover, such country did not seem to make man appear little as does some country of the grander sort. I felt just as much part of the earth as my features were part of me. I did not feel that my imagination was in conflict with the real, but that reality was a dispersed and disintegrated form of imagination.

At first I attempted to make pictures on the spot. But soon I gave this up. It became my habit to walk through, and soak myself in the country. At times I would make small sketches of ideas on the backs of envelopes and in a small sketch book, or I would make drawings from nature of forms which interested me and which I might otherwise forget. The latter practice helped to nourish my ideas and to keep me on good terms with nature. Sometimes, through sheer laziness, I would lie on the warm shore until my eye, becoming riveted to some sea-eroded rocks, would notice that they were precisely reproducing, in miniature, the forms of the inland hills. At all events, I never forced myself here, or consciously looked for subjects. I found it better to visit this country because I liked it — and ideas seemed to come gradually and naturally.

Graham Sutherland, 'Welsh Sketch Book' in *Horizon*, V, 28, 1942.

VIII

The Quality

1. Shrieval Intrigue

As the maintenance of the office was an expensive business, only landowners, and a few burgesses like the Canon family of Haverfordwest, could accept the appointment with any confidence. In neighbouring Carmarthenshire, for instance, it cost the Sheriff in 1625 as much as £1,000 for his year, a very considerable sum at that time, and there is no reason to believe that it cost any less in Pembrokeshire. So important was the financial element that it could be used to harass certain men who, for one reason or another, had incurred the displeasure of their fellows. Early in the reign of Charles I, Henry Lort of Stackpole Court had sold large quantities of grain to other parts of Britain during years when an 'extraordinary dearth' obtained in Pembrokeshire, with the result that he was reported to the authorities; two years later he was accused of converting arable lands into pasture, resulting in depopulation of the countryside, and was brought before the Court of Star Chamber where he was fined the sum of £2,500, which proved a severe financial body-blow. His enemies found another way to increase his embarrassment. Although he had been High Sheriff in 1619, they caused his name to be submitted for another year of office, for either Pembrokeshire or Carmarthenshire, and through influence in high places ensured that Henry Lort's name was placed first in the list to be submitted to the king which made it a certainty that he would be 'pricked' for the year 1639-40, and at a time when his finances were under severe strain. His son, Sampson, who happened to be in London at the time, discovered what was afoot, and immediately wrote to the Lord Chancellor, outlining reasons why his father should not be 'pricked'. A revealing letter, it reads as follows:

'I humblie make boulde to entreate your Lordshipp's assistance by way of letter to a friend at Court or some other shure course, if your Lordshipp cannot be heere in person, to keepe my father from being Shirriff either of Carmarthen or Pembrooke shire for this next yeare. It is an office of much trouble and expense and will doe him more harme this yeare than it could doe at anie other tyme in respect of those greate somes of monie which he is to pay the kinge for fine of depopulacon, and in regard of his monie troubles not yet ended. I perceve our adversaries doth use what meanes they can to have him pricked for this yeare, and I verily beleeve they will prevayle unlesse by your Lordshipp's meanes it may be prevented. The usuall day for that business your Lordshipp may please to remember is Sunday next, and it is in your Lordshipp's goodness that we only relie conserninge this particular. I beseech your Lordshipp excuse my unmannerly bouldness herein, and presentinge my humble service to your honor I take leave and rest your Lordshipp's most humble servante, Sampson Lort, London, this 31st of October 1639.'

To make certain that his Lordship should have no worry about finding a suitable substitute, Sampson obligingly enclosed a list of 'Names of sufficient gentlemen to be shirriff of Pembrooke shire: Lewis Barelow of Criswell, George Carew of Carew, George Heaward [of Fletherhill], James Phillipps of Benteba [Pentypark], Hugh Bowen of Upton, Nicholas Lewis of Hencastle, all Esquires. The like names for Carmarthenshire: John Lewis of Llangeler, Henry Jones of Llangadock, John Vaughan of Llanelthy, Phillipp Lloyd of Llanfehangell, Henry Middleton of Llanarthney, John Harris of Llandilovawer, George Vaughan of Penbre, David Lloyd of Llanegwad, all Esquires.'

Sampson's letter did the trick, and in 1639 Thomas Warren of Trewern was 'pricked' for Pembrokeshire, and Henry Jones for Carmarthenshire. In such wise are matters quietly and genteelly arranged.

Francis Jones, in Foreword to *The Sheriffs of the County of Pembroke,* 1976, by Dillwyn Miles.

2.   *The London Season*

A few of the wealthier Pembrokeshire gentry went on their travels to the continent, to France, Germany, Holland, Switzerland and Italy. In 1740 Mr Erasmus Philipps of Picton, a man of culture and refinement, visited Italy, where, in the fashion of his day, he bought works of art, including a St Sebastian by Guido Reni, which went home as his distinctive contribution to the family treasures. John Campbell, created Baron Cawdor in 1796, spent much of his time in Italy and purchased works of art to embellish his stately mansion at Stackpole Court. In 1791 Mrs Morgan observed that at the approach of this mansion there stood 'two inimitable antique statues of Marius and Sylla, brought from Rome by Mr Campbell, when on his travels'.

During the winter months some of the more substantial Pembrokeshire gentry joined in the London season, that 'brilliant society which made up the world of politics and fashion'. The London season was the great social occasion of the year and the cause of financial burdens on many country estates. Money was spent on drinking, gambling, and the gay round of social amusements, including balls, plays, coffee houses, pleasure gardens, cock fights, prize fights and dog fights. Yet, with all its extravagance, the London season was an essential element in the lives of the landed classes, and could be dropped only at the expense of loss of prestige and influence.

Journeys to and from the capital were made in the family coach. While staying in London the normal practice was to rent a house for the season as did Mrs Owen of Orielton in the winter of 1791, her half year's rent amounting to £90. The diary of Sir John Philipps for the winter months of 1757 shows him caught up in the social whirl of dinner engagements, the opera, concerts and playing whist. His entry for 11 November reads 'Went with David Thomas from Norbiton Place (rented by Sir John) to London, din'd at Coco Tree 5s. 6d., Chocolate 6d., Pamphlet 6d., Play 5s., Chair and Coach 3s.'

The season was especially attractive to the wives and daughters of the gentry, both for its social amenities and its expensive clothes and jewellery which only London could offer. In 1742 Mrs Campbell of Stackpole Court wrote elatedly to her son Pryce of her being 'at Court on the occasion of the King's Birthday and at the Ball given at night at Court where the King spoke very kindly to me'. The opportunity for purchasing clothes and jewellery was taken by Anne Owen of Orielton in 1790 when, for instance, on 29 March she paid £5 15s. 6d. for a gold necklace and on 7 April £5 14s. 3d. for a silk gown. Later, in

1811, it was reported of Charlotte Owen 'we understand that the beautiful and accomplished Mrs Owen of Orileton is among the present leaders of fashion in the gay metropolis, and that Owen bonnets, Owen scarfs, and Owen caps are all the rage'.

David Howell, 'Landed Society in Pembrokeshire, c. 1680-1830, in
The Pembrokeshire Historian, No. 3, 1971.

3.   *The Last Jester*

Some of the happiest years of my youth were spent at my mother's old home, Clawddcam in the parish of Llanrheithan. My grandmother's family had been associated with the parish for many generations, and one of her ancestors had been collector of rates and taxes for Llanrheithan a few years after the accession of King George II. My visits to Clawddcam were made all the more pleasant by my grandmother's expertise in the art of story-telling. Possessing a phenomenal memory and an undoubted talent as a raconteur, she was a veritable storehouse of traditions, legends and anecdotes, and it was from her that I first heard of the cavortings of Mr Laugharne, sometime squire of the parish. It seems that he dissipated a fair estate, that Llanrheithan House was guarded by armed retainers, that the squire found a crock of gold beneath the hearthstone and had used it to support the Jacobites during the rising of the Forty-Five. I learned that he was the last of the Pembrokeshire gentry to maintain a jester — 'Ffŵl Llanrheithan' — whose antics endeared him to his master, but proved a sore trial to guests and visitors. She did not know where Mr Laugharne had died, but it was said that during the twilight his ghost haunted the footbridge over the stream hard by his old home.

Francis Jones, 'Llanrheithan' in *The Pembrokeshire Historian,* No. 3, 1971.

4.   *The 1831 Election*

Catherine Barlow of Colby (near Haverfordwest) brought to her husband, Sir William Hamilton, an estate said to have been worth £8,000 a year. He is chiefly remembered because of his second wife, Emma, Nelson's mistress, but his wealth came from his first marriage. His sister had married Francis Greville, first earl of

Warwick (of a new creation), and her son, Charles Francis Greville, succeeded in 1803 to a life interest in the Pembrokeshire estate, to develop which he had already obtained an act of parliament for the foundation of the new town of Milford. When he died, six years later, his interests passed to his brother, Robert Fulke Greville, equerry to George III, who had married Louisa, countess of Mansfield, *suo jure,* and in turn in 1824 to their son, also named Robert Fulke Greville, who was to dissipate much of the estate in the Pembrokeshire elections of 1831.

As the poll entered its second week, obstruction became more outrageous. The bribery oath was administered in several instances to respectable men. Many were asked if they were excise officers, or held any other Government post, when everyone knew they did not. Worse still, frivolous questions were asked, partly in jest but with the intent of causing delay: 'Are you the Pope of Rome?'; 'Are you one of the Cardinals?'; 'Are you the Prime Minister?'; 'Are you the Lord Chancellor?'; 'Are you a peer of the realm?'; as well as 'Are you a pauper?' and even 'Are you an idiot?' The sub-sheriffs did not try to restrain the agents from wasting time, and the assessor claimed that he had no authority to intervene. Altercations in the booths therefore became increasingly violent.

Conditions had also become tumultuous in the streets of Haverfordwest which were packed with Orange (Tory) partisans and their Blue (Whig) opponents. Sir John's headquarters were at the Castle Hotel and Greville's at the Mariners. They were the only 'tolerable' inns in the town; there were a great number of others, and all had laid in a remarkable stock of provisions. Landlords eagerly solicited the patronage of the two sides and both candidates 'opened' inns for their supporters, Sir John (Owen), who was experienced in these matters, confined himself to a few inns, and from the start adopted a system of tickets, thereby giving offence to some voters. Greville was much more lavish. The rumour had spread that he had deposited £30,000 with Messrs Morris, the Carmarthen bankers, to meet the cost of the election. The innkeepers were jubilant, for no less than thirty-one houses were 'opened' for Greville. They received their instructions from a member of Greville's Committee, Major Arthur Bowen, of Great Hook in the parish of Ambleston, a regular army officer on half-pay who owned considerable property in the neighbourhood, including houses and inns in Prendergast itself. His impulsiveness in taking on this duty was to cost him dear. He placed stewards in the inns to take over all their ale, spirits, and provisions.

But there was so much extravagance and waste that, after two days, the Blues copied their opponents and set up a ticket system. Voters, nominally after they had polled, were sent to an inn where one of Greville's agents directed them where to get refreshment. The system quickly broke down. Voters wished to go the inn of their choice. They objected to being sent backwards and forwards. They demanded refreshment for their wives as well as for themselves. It was difficult enough to keep them together for days on end while they waited their turn, and arrangements had to be made for their lodgings. They threatened to go home unless they could get meals without tickets. And so everyone got refreshment in the Blue inns, including some Orange supporters, and the detailed accounts kept by the stewards grew at an alarming rate. Never had there been so much turmoil in Haverfordwest.

The most noteworthy case was that of Mrs Sarah Williams, licensee of Greville's headquarters, the Mariners. She presented a bill for £1,878 covering all expenses, including provision for Greville's professional gentlemen, and sued Greville for that amount. It included an item of £443 described as 'eating for voters', and another for drink supplied, amounting to £982. This particular item covered an astonishing quantity of drink: 42½ barrels of beer, 67 gallons of brandy, 59 gallons of rum, 1068 bottles of port, and 780 bottles of sherry, as well as other more exotic drinks, all consumed in two weeks.

David Williams, 'The Pembrokeshire Elections of 1831' in *The Welsh History Review*, Vol. 1, No. 1, 1960.

5. *Nelson at Milford*

Later that day with the band of the Pembrokeshire Militia, a troop of the Haverfordwest Cavalry and with the flags of the different companies and societies flying high, the Mayor and Corporation waited upon his Lordship at Captain Foley's House in Goat Street and presented him with the freedom of the 'opulent town of Haverfordwest'; this fashionable 'little Bath' of balls, parties and gambling, Pembrokeshire's social centre of the *élite*. Quite recently one of the writers had the opportunity of rescuing from obscurity the original charter handed to Lord Nelson on this occasion. The document which came up for auction at Sotheby's, London, was purchased and presented to the Mayor of the ancient borough.

At the expanding and flag waving new town of Milford, the

reception was tumultuous as the carriages sped into half completed Front Street between buildings in every state of construction, and came to rest outside the New Hotel, at the end of the first half of a tour which was originally suggested by its developer, Charles Greville, in a brilliant piece of showmanship. The visit had been arranged to coincide with the fourth anniversary of the Battle of the Nile on August 1st. There was to be a regatta, a fair, a cattle show and a boat race and competitions, all arranged to popularise the amenities of the new town.

Greville was delighted to see his uncle again and also no doubt his former mistress Emma, whom the solicitous nephew had packed off many years previously (with her mother and two Greek vases) to Sir William at Naples.

After a sumptuous banquet, Lord Nelson, surrounded by all the nobility and gentry of the county, rose to make a speech which was calculated to put his colleague's brain-child on the charts for all time. He said among other things that he considered Milford Haven in relation to Trincomalee in the East Indies, the two finest harbours he ever beheld. 'The obstacles which had hitherto impeded the employer of so important an appendage as Milford Haven to the Empire, appeared merely artificial. Individual exertion had already proved this by bringing mails to the water side, establishing daily packets to and from Ireland, and nothing was now wanting to make it the only safe sea-port on the West Coast of Great Britain. When it was viewed in relation to the former country, it became the central port of the Empire. The American settlers had already established a Whale Fishery. I applaud the decision to improve naval architecture at Milford and consider it would benefit the service considerably to use timber 'on the sides of the Severn' for the purpose of building ships on the draughts of the ingenious French refugee ship builder Monsieur Jean-Louis Barrallier, who was already busy in the harbour.'

In short he said the port of Milford was adapted to become of the greatest importance to Great Britain in a naval and commercial view, and if only the Government would continue a fair encouragement to the officers and seamen of the county of Pembrokeshire, it could not fail to effect important services to the nation; he was in perfect admiration of this fine neglected port . . .

The foundations for the church which Greville had planned at what was to be the centre of the town, but which it never became, had been hurried on to enable Sir William to lay the first stone during his visit. Contrary to what has been written before, the stone was not laid by Lord Nelson in 1801; his one and only visit to the haven was on the occasion we are recording.

E. C. Freeman & Edward Gill, *The Story of Lord Nelson and Sir William and Lady Hamilton's Tour in Wales,* 1962.

6.   *The 'Widow' of Castle Villa*

At Castle Villa in Brawdy parish lived an heiress, Anne, the daughter of Richard Morris and Katherine Wogan his wife. She was descended from ancient families and was the heiress to one of the largest estates in North Pembrokeshire. She had married William Scourfield of Moat, a scion of a family long settled in the county. William was a great traveller, and one day having taken a fond farewell of his wife he set forth on a voyage to the little known territory of Barbary. The years rolled by with no news of the voyager, and the lady of Castle Villa brooded uneasily over the absence of her lord and master. Not unnaturally she concluded that she was bereaved and decked herself in the dark weeds of a widow. It was about then that Morgan Philipps decided it was high time for him to bring home a bride to the moated castle of his forebears, and after studying his little book of Pembrokeshire pedigrees in conjunction with the extent of Pembrokeshire estates, his choice fell on the young 'widow' of Castle Villa. His suit was accepted and before long the joyous peals of the Slebech bells and the gay bunting from Picton's towers proclaimed that Morgan and Anne were man and wife. They lived together happily and they had one child, a little girl. However, a terrible day arrived, for a bronzed and bearded William Scourfield turned up in his native county. He had been captured off the coast of Barbary by the Moors, and after some five years in their hands contrived to regain his freedom. On his return to Castle Villa, bursting with marvellous tales of mountainous Barbary and turbaned Moors, he found that there was no adoring wife to listen approvingly to his wondrous narratives. No Enoch Arden was our Scourfield, and he immediately demanded his wife's return. Morgan Philipps, being extremely fond of the many-acred Anne, refused, and told him to clear off back to Barbary; whereupon Scourfield sought redress in the courts, with the result that his wife was restored to him.

Francis Jones, 'The Pageantry of Picton' in *The Slebech Story,* ed. B. L. Morris, 1948

7.   *Social Glory*

The Pembrokeshire gentry were in their social intercourse intensely aware of their social standing and there was a ceaseless struggle in their ranks for precedence. This thirst for social glory was openly and hotly contested over the procurement of the richest prize of all, a seat at Westminster. During the seventeenth century we see the start of the control of certain families over the Pembroke county and borough seats leaving the Haverfordwest seat to the lesser county families. The family of Owen of Orielton emerged as the political leaders of the county and only twice between 1660 and 1700 was Pembrokeshire not represented by the family. In the eighteenth century the growing expenses of attending Parliament meant that the Pembrokeshire constituencies, as those elsewhere, drew their representatives from a small and progressively narrowing circle of county families, those whose estates were growing at the expense of the lesser ones at this time. The Owen family continued their control of both county and borough seats well into the latter half of the century. Haverfordwest was by arrangement the shared possession of the families of Philipps of Picton Castle and Edwardes of Johnston, the latter representing this seat in return for supporting Picton Castle in the County. The central theme running right through the electoral history of the county in this century was, therefore, the challenge to the Owen monopoly by the other great houses of the county, mainly by the Campbell family of Stackpole early in the century and exclusively by the Philipps family from the 1760's. By the closing years of the century the triumph of Picton castle over Orielton was complete. The Picton ascendency was successfully challenged by Orielton in 1812 and the seat remained with this house up until the celebrated election of 1831.

From 1688 to 1715, when party strife was raging, the Pembrokeshire gentry, with the notable exception of the Owen family of Orielton, were Tory in outlook, a characteristic common throughout Wales. Major Francis Jones has admirably demonstrated how the majority of the Pembrokeshire gentry in the closing years of the seventeenth century hoped for the return of James II. And at the time of the Jacobite rising in 1715 they forceably broke up loyalist meetings. Jacobite sympathies lingered on in south west Wales and were concentrated in the secret Society of Sea Serjeants which existed from 1726 to 1762.

Evidence of direct intervention in elections for the Pembrokeshire constituencies is lacking but given the secret nature of the organisation is lacking this is by no means proof of inactivity. And it is clear that the Picton Castle electoral hold on Haverfordwest was strengthened in July 1760 when twenty eight Sea Serjeants 'who have deserved well of this Corporation', were created burgesses of the Borough. These gentry families with Jacobite sympathies, then, formed an identifiable band working to some extent at any rate towards the return of candidates of like sympathies. Such candidates, if successful, sat in the House of Commons as independent country gentlemen unambitious for office. They retained their separate identity as Tories in their opposition to the Hanoverian dynasty but their politics, it must be stressed, were indistinguishable from those of the independent country Whigs. After 1760 the 'English' character of the new King, George III, won over the Jacobite families to the alien dynasty. The days of the Sea Serjeants were over and even Sir John Philipps of Picton Castle came into official favour.

David Howell, 'Pembrokeshire Gentry in the Eighteenth Century' in *Carmarthenshire Studies,* ed. T. Barnes & N. Yates.

8. *The Society of Sea-Serjeants*

There are some who venture to trace its origin back so far as to suppose it a leaven of one of those factions that divided the kingdom during the contention of the houses of York and Lancaster, that continuing to ferment in a few families, held them together long after the cause of their first union was lost, creating a kind of free-masonry. Others ascribe it to pure Jacobitism, and an adherence to the family of the abdicated monarch. They had an anniversary meeting which lasted a week, and was held in rotation at the different sea-port towns. Their number was not to exceed twenty-five. They had a president, a secretary, an examiner, and two stewards. When there was a call of serjeants. . . they were to attend in their coifs and proper habit of the order, unless the president should dispense with the same. That a silver star with the figure of a dolphin in the centre was to be worn as a characteristic badge on the coat by every member during the week of meeting. That every member heard to curse or swear during the meeting in the public room incurred a penalty, as did every person the heavy forfeiture of five guineas who should presume to play at dice.

Richard Fenton, *A Historical Tour through Pembrokeshire,* 1811.

9.   *Social Distinction*

Unlike the diminished office of Sheriff, that of Lord Lieutenant and Custos Rotulorum still carried great prestige and it is not surprising, therefore, that it passed back and forth between the two main rival families of Owen and Philipps. The majority of the lesser gentry, excluded from Parliament through lack of fortune and influence, coveted the office of Justice of the Peace as a means to social distinction and power in their neighbourhood. For this reason the magistracy in the eighteenth century increased in numbers 'not in relation to the needs of local government, but to the desires of the gentry'. In 1663 and 1680 there were thirty-five and thirty-nine justices respectively on the Pembrokeshire bench, but by 1727 this figure had almost doubled. By the third decade of the nineteenth century there were two hundred and fifty eight justices in the county commission.

In their judicial capacity at Quarter Sessions the magistrates dealt with cases of theft, assault, slander, the uttering of base coin and absconding servants. Belief in the sanctity of property as the bulwark of a stable society was the abiding ethos of the landowning class. Transgressors like thieves and poachers were consequently punished with a severity that to us today is staggering. At the Pembrokeshire Epiphany Sessions of 1741 the magistrates ordered that Dorothy Rees of Prendergast should be publicly whipped and then transported for seven years for stealing a petticoat worth 6d.

David Howell, 'Pembrokeshire Gentry in the Eighteenth Century' in *Carmarthenshire Studies,* ed. T. Barnes & N. Yates.

10.   *Georgian Gentlemen*

With few exceptions the Georgian gentlemen of Little England ordered their affairs wisely and well. There can be no doubt that they drank a great deal more port wine than was good for them, but that was the custom of the day, and in matters of morality the patriarchal system survived in certain establishments. One gentleman of large estate is known to have given an entertainment to his friends in celebration of the birth of his fiftieth 'love child'. A story is told concerning another squire, who when smitten with the charms of a collier's spouse, sent for the husband and proposed to purchase the lady. After some haggling a bargain was struck, and the woman (nothing loth) was handed over to her new proprietor in exchange for a crown, a gallon of beer, and a calf-skin waistcoat.

Edward Laws, *The History of Little England Beyond Wales,* 1888.

11.   *Mrs Jordan*

Mrs Jordan, celebrated as a comic actress, but better remembered as King William's discarded mistress, is said to have spent some portion of her childish days in a Pembrokeshire parsonage. Towards the middle of the 18th century a gentleman named Bland was vicar of Jordanston, near Pembroke; he had a son who went on the stage, married, and had two daughters; one of these, Dorothy Bland, born at Waterford in 1763, followed her father's profession, and finding it convenient to assume brevet rank as a married woman, took the name of 'Mrs Jordan' from her grandfather's parish.

Edward Laws, *The History of Little England Beyond Wales,* 1888.

12.   *The Baron Meets his Bride*

'Shortly after my arrival at Rome, I dined with Italinsky — Chevalier d'Italinsky the Russian Minister — and Medem — Count Medem (Paul) — asked me after dinner, what I was going to do. I said I was going home to get up Boccacio for my Italien master for tomorrow. Oh, if that is all, said Medem, come with me to a Mrs Phillips, a remarkable handsome English woman, without much English non-sense. She speaks very good French, knows everybody and has a charming daughter who, moreover, is considered the best Pianist in the whole of Rome. It is Mrs Phillips's at home tonight, and we are sure to meet the cream of the beau monde. It was late when we arrived — the rooms were nearly full. Presently there was a simultaneous move — a sort of gentle press towards another room. Miss Phillips was going to play. The instant she touched the Piano, there was a breathless silence, yet no ostentatious prelude, only the favourite Waltz of the day at once; but with such a band-like power and precision and a truely soul stirring expression. The suppressed 'Brava's' were more than an ovation. Had this little Waltz been so plain in Public, all the bouquets would have been at her feet. Miss Phillips was rising, when a very handsome young man, who was sitting by the Piano, shewed her a Cahier of Notes: she looked at them shrugged her shoulders and was going. Being, however, much entreated by this man & some others that were standing round, to play on, she again looked at the Notes, read some parts with marked and visible attention — then looked imploringly & apologetically around and after a short, sharp and appropriate prelude, began the piece, which was one of Rossini's overtures, just come out. At the first turning over, the man that sat by her bungled — at the second, he was evidently by some bars out, and this disconcerting Miss Phillips a good deal, I stepped forward, asked to be allowed to turn over, as the light was very much in that gentleman's face — which, in fact, was the case — and being attentive, of course, got through satisfactorily so that Miss Phillips, when she had done, said to me, 'Oh mille remerciment, je vois que vous êtes musicient'. I said, unfortunately I was not, and a Lady, who, I afterwards learnt was Lady (Countess of) Compton (Northampton) coming up & saying to Miss Phillips, 'Well done Mary', I retired — indeed there was nothing else for it, as every one wished to say his say. . .

Miss Phillips insisted on speaking English as she said she had understood I might pass anywhere for an Englishman. (By way of episode I would say here that) being well aware that no English could surpass though they might equal me in French, and knowing the great importance of a superior knowledge & command of languages & the disadvantage of the contrary, I very reluctantly gave in: besides I had ever made it a rule never to speak English to any one out of England; Miss Phillips, however, made that resolution to the wall.'

And there the Baron's fragment ends. It is a pity that the complete memoir has not survived, but the foregoing tells us clearly where and how the Baron met his future bride . . .

. . . The marriage was blessed with seven children. The Baroness continued to charm her family and friends with her musical talent, and a haunting little melody of her own composition, called 'Slebech Hall' has survived. They lived first at Brighton until 1829 when they moved to Bedford Square, London. By the death of her brother, Edward Augustus Phillips, in 1830, the Baroness and her sister, Lady Anson, became co-heiresses to the estates in Jamaica and Slebech.

In 1830 the De Rutzens came to live at Slebech, to fit into a way of life that differed greatly from that of fashionable European capitals

SLEBECH HALL.

and watering places. The Baron now had to undertake the duties and responsibilities of an English country gentleman. The Slebech estate which had become the property of Mary Dorothea and her husband, comprised over 3,700 acres lying in the parishes of Slebech, Minwear, Newton, Martletwy, Robeston Wathan, Narberth and Lampeter Velfrey. It produced a rental of £5,300 per annum. The estimated value of the extensive woodlands alone amounted to over £70,000.

The house, then known as Slebech Hall, largely if not wholly rebuilt by a former proprietor in the 1770s, was a substantial building in the form of a square with a circular tower at each corner, and a wing containing domestic offices on its north side. The demesne land, nearly 1300 acres in extent, was park-like in character, laid out with trees and plantations, while the river Cleddy, about 300 yards wide, flowed nearby. The river was navigable as far as Blackpool bridge (built by the De Rutzens about 1830), and all craft entering within the bounds of the estate had to pay toll to the owner and to load or discharge cargoes at Backpool Quay. The fishery on the river also belonged to him. The tolls and fishery were let for £40 per annum. Owing to its seclusion the area abounded in wild fowl of all description, and a very large heronry in the wood near the mansion was the only one on the Milford Haven estuary at that time.

The Baron and his wife were Lords of the Manors of Slebech, Minwear, Newton, Narberth and Robeston Wathen, and of the Manors or Reeveships of Lampeter Velfrey and Llandewi Velfrey.

The manorial dues and renders were small, but the mineral rights always had a potential value, while the sporting rights were extremely valuable and immediately available. The Baron insisted on these perquisites, and had to have recourse to law to enforce some of them. In the town of Narberth he built a hotel, 'The De Rutzen Arms', and also a market house, and enjoyed tolls of the weekly market and of the fairs held in that town.

The Baron shared a passion for the chase with his Pembrokeshire neighbours, and was a noted performer with rod and gun. He preserved game on a big scale, and in 1835 added to them by importing black fowl from Russia. Some of his activities were influenced by his continental background, sometimes to the discomfiture of his tenants. To add to his pleasures he imported animals that had long been extinct in England. Among these were wild boars. In November 1834 he arranged for the Duke of Brunswick to send him two wild boars, aged $1\frac{1}{2}$ and 2 years, in a cage via Hamburg. The boars were let loose in the Canaston woodlands and provided good sport for the Baron, but their presence was deeply resented by the farmers and tenants, and as a result of their hostility, the Baron, much to his disgust, had to discontinue importing them. He agreed to destroy them all provided he could do so in his own way — by more intensive hunting. It seemed to the farmers, however, that they took 'an unconscionable time a-dying', and the baron enjoyed several more years of exciting sport before the last boar was bowled over. At one time he even toyed with the idea of importing *wolves*!

Francis Jones, 'Some Further Slebech Notes', in *The National Library of Wales Journal,* 1966.

IX

Everyday Life

1. *A Happy Peasantry: 'huggling'*

The early eighteenth century saw a general effort being made to improve agriculture. These efforts, largely unco-ordinated, represented only a small section of the farming community. However, from about 1750 there was a genuine awakening and a determined effort made by landowners and farmers to improve the condition of the land and stock. Societies were formed, rewards were offered for crops and cattle, and the Royal Society encouraged husbandry by offering premiums for good works. The results were often noted by travellers, such as Warner (*Walks in Wales,* 1798, pp. 339-342), who describes the conditions in North Pembrokeshire in 1798. He writes:—

'Our object was Eglwyswrw, a small village in Pembrokeshire, about six miles from Kilgerran, where we had already bespoken accomodations for the night. The road to this place carried us through a rich country, which, unlike any thing we had hitherto seen in Wales (excepting in the vale of Clwyd), exhibited a general system of good husbandry. We observed with much satisfaction the admirable effects of this system in the appearance of the lands, and the heaviness of the crops, but were still more gratified by the comfort and decency amongst the little farmers and labouring poor.

'Perhaps, throughout the whole British empire, there is no spot where the peasantry exhibit more happiness than in the northern parts of Pembrokeshire. Their families, on an average, consists of five people, provided for in the following manner:— The father is generally employed through the whole year by the same farmer, who allows him during the eight summer months four pence per day, and for the remaining four months three-pence per day. He eats, however, his meals, breakfast, dinner and supper, at the farmers', and is usually allowed beside a jug of skimmed milk. The mother employs all the time not dedicated to domestic labours in knitting, or more commonly in making pieces of flannel, to be disposed of at some of the neighbouring fairs, of which there are several annual ones in every Welsh town; out of the profits of this, the rent of the cottage is usually paid. No increase of wages to the labourer takes place in general, at harvest, as he expects to be recompensed in another way. But this is optional on his part; and if he choose money, the farmer gives him eight pence per day during that season. If not, he is paid by what the people in this country call an huggling, a practice of the following singular nature:— At Christmas, the farmer pays off any little debt which his labourer may have contracted at the millers' and presents him with three large coarse loaves, and two large wheaten loaves (each about two gallons) together with a quarter of good mutton. Thus assisted, the Pembrokeshire peasant partakes, in some little degree, of those gifts of a bountiful Providence, which the higher classes of society in other countries monopolize entirely to themselves. He sees himself brought to something like a rational level with his fellow creatures, perceives that he has a state in society and feels that the practice of certain duties results from this situation, all which convictions operate upon him as powerful motives to decency and integrity, to cheerfulness and content. The cottages of this part of Pembrokeshire generally let at fifteen or eighteen shillings per annum each, having a small plot of ground attached to them which enables the tenant commonly to keep a pig and very often a cow.'

Francis Jones, 'Some Farmers of Bygone Pembrokeshire' in *The Transactions of Honourable Society of Cymmrodorion*, 1943-44.

2. *Rural Life: 'bundling'*

In those days the labourer dwelt in a cottage usually built of clom (i.e., clay mixed with chopped straw), which is strange, seeing that in many neighbourhoods stones are apparently more plentiful than soil; but clom being the cheaper material to work, of that the peasant's dwelling was generally constructed. It frequently consisted of but one apartment, never I think of more than two: at one end stood a huge round stone-built chimney, in which a culm fire used to burn summer and winter; the house was lighted (save the mark), by tiny windows, which were not made to open; sometimes these consisted of a single small pane (such as one existed a short time back in the village of St Florence). The floor was of beaten clay, the roof of unceiled thatch. Though the pig had a house of his own he was accustomed to wander over the establishment at pleasure, and fed on much the same food as his master, which they ate from the same iron pot. Of course from feelings of delicacy on rare occasions when 'liggy's' deceased relatives provided the feast, he was not invited to partake. Usually the contents of the iron pot consisted of broken barley bread, vegetables from the garden, and water thickened with meal. Wheaten flour, tea and butcher's meat were unknown delicacies. Very frequently the wife went barefoot, the children always, though in other respects they were better clothed than their descendants; for in those days men and women alike were clad in brown homespun which kept out the cold and turned off the rain more effectually than fabrics woven from devil's dust, such as we too frequently see in use at present; the women wore a jacket and short petticoat, a close cap with long lappets, and a straw or felt hat; on high days and holidays only was the great churn-shaped Welsh hat produced.

I do not expect these men paid rent for their cottages, or the gardens attached thereto. Very many farmers boarded and lodged their labourers (as indeed they do to the present day in the northern districts of Pembrokeshire), an arrangement which led to that extremly objectionable form of love-making known as 'bundling'. When the young peasant had fixed his affections on some buxom lass, he naturally objected to pay court in the farm kitchen before his giggling comrades. Green fields and hollow lanes were well enough during summer, but in wild wintry weather apt to chill love's ardour; so the courtship was carried on in the girl's apartment after the young woman had gone to bed, which she did pretty early. As may be supposed this method of love-making was not conducive to morality.

Edward Laws, *The History of Little England beyond Wales,* 1888.

3. *Marloes Folk*

The Sandy lane, meandering beside a streamlet, lands us right abreast of the church at the entrance to the village. The little edifice makes a pleasant picture, with a handful of low thatched cottages grouped around. Inside we find the small pointed chancel arch with projecting wings, characteristic of the churches in this locality.

There are some curious features here, notably an old bronze sanctus bell, and a modern baptistery sunk in a corner of the floor, to meet the predilections of the Welsh churchman, who does not apparently consider the ceremony of baptism complete unless he can 'goo throw the watter.'

Dwelling apart from the busier haunts of men, the good folk of this remote parish have kept pretty much to themselves, and have acquired the reputation of being a simple-minded, superstitious race — 'Marloes gulls,' as the saying is. In order to save the long Saturday's tramp to Haverford market, a Marloes man hit upon the ingenious device of walking *half* the distance on Friday, then returning home he would complete the *rest of the walk* the next day!

In the 'good old times,' if tales be true, these Marloes people were notorious wreckers. On dark tempestuous nights they would hitch a lanthorn to a horse's tail, and drive the animal around the seaward cliffs; then woe betide the hapless mariner who should set his course by this Fata Morgana! There is a story of the parson who, when the news of a wreck got abroad in church one Sunday morning, broke off his discourse and exclaimed, 'Wait a moment, my brethren, and give your pastor a fair start!'

H. Thornhill Timmins, *Nooks and Corners of Pembrokeshire*, 1895.

4. *Stock and Crops*

At the commencement of the century, as now, breeding black Castle-martin cattle was the staple industry of the county. The pure bred Welsh sheep, with straight goat-like horns, had retreated to the Kymric end of the county; in the southern half, the mountaineer had been crossed with English breeds. Ewes were milked, and 'cheese made with a proportion of their milk gave it a peculiar tartness preferred by the peasantry to the milder sort'. Swine were reared in great numbers — huge gaunt brutes, nearly as high as a small donkey, with flapping ears like newspapers. The horses were of galloway type, measuring about 14 to $14\frac{1}{2}$ hands and excellent; when the mares were served by thorough-bred stallions they frequently produced really valuable stock. Every farmer grew more or less grain. The best in the county. St David's and Caldey Island were celebrated for their barley; oats of various values were grown through the length and breadth of the land. Flimstone Downs produced rye, and Mr Mirehouse of

Brownslade grew coleseed in Castlemartin Corse, which he had lately reclaimed.

Potatoes were a common field crop. Not so turnips, as the latter required too much attention to suit our slovenly agriculturalists. The ploughs were terrible instruments, with a great blunt wedge for a share, an awkward colter and, in place of a moulboard a simple stake, the consequence being that the furrow often fell back into the place from which it had been cut. These clumsy contrivances were mostly drawn by oxen. The carts, too, were generally hauled by a mixed team, two oxen being yoked abreast with a long pole between, preceded by a pair of horses also abreast.*

Edward Laws, *The History of Little England beyond Wales,* 1888.

5. *An 'affaire' with God*

I remember how William Breit, an old man who earned his living hauling with a little donkey cart, walked in his clogs at night to Fishguard from Cilgerran, a distance of twenty miles, stayed for the 10.00 a.m., 2.00 p.m. and 6.00 p.m. services, to listen to a total of six or seven sermons, then walked back on Sunday night discussing the merits of each sermon with his fellow travellers. The nearest comparison to this knowledgeable discussion of a sermon is a crowd of Welshmen in a pub discussing an international rugger match they have witnessed, or a few nostalgic old men talking about Percy Bush or Bancroft — the very persons who would switch later that evening to a talk beginning, 'I remember hearing Roberts Llwynhendy at So and So, preaching on the Judgement to come, etc.' It is no disrespect to mix rugger with sermons in Wales — they are both most respectable Welsh passions. There were two brothers in North Pembrokeshire, Glasnant and Jubilee Young, both preachers of considerable power. I would travel quite a distance to listen to a sermon by someone of the calibre of Jubilee Young. His melodious voice in the 'hwyl' was cumulative magic; he was a wonderful performer, and a great showman. In his day he was the Garrick of the Welsh Baptist circuit, a polished practitioner of the ancient art of oratory. His audiences

---

* The writer well remembers a retailer of culm who used a cow to drag his fuel up and down the streets of Pembroke. He also traded in milk, and when the latter was required by a customer it was straightway obtained from the beast of burden.

knew their Bible, and he was preaching to congregations willing, even fervently desiring to be moved, to be hypnotised, to be laid spiritually. At a certain moment, his sense of timing impeccable, he would subtly modulate his voice, and there he was embarking on the 'hwyl'. The voice changed to a sing-song tone, the delivery became cadenced, and the content of the sermon assumed harmonious poetic periods, free-ranging, but highly charged with emotion. Preacher and congregation became possessed and the mouth of the preacher was not a trumpet whence issued ecstasy; it had become the authentic voice of God speaking to his chosen people. It was the voice of a Father who was angry, forgiving, loving, kind, an understanding Father who rewarded repentance with salvation, with an everlasting life among the saints. The anguish endured by the preacher was evident to all, for the veins of his neck and temples stood out, while streamlets of sweat made furrows down his face. His collar and tie became sodden, proof that he was wrestling mightily on their behalf. He was on a 'hot' line to God. Then, when the climax, or the pinnacle of the 'hwyl' had been reached there was a *rallentando,* a coasting down from the climax to the relaxed tempo of normal life, a steady descent from the high mountain peak in the rarefied air, to the plain below. Throughout the sixty to seventy-five minutes of the sermon the congregation had suspended all judgement, abandoned all doubts. Blasted with ecstasy they were indulging in an 'affaire' with God. This fiskery of the spirit was most joyful, and it was legitimate. When it ended, the congregation awoke out of their trance and felt cleansed. Men like Jubilee Young or Roberts, Llwynhendy, were the folk heroes of Wales, who created the Welsh Nonconformist Conscience, and then became its custodians.

James Williams, *Give Me Yesterday,* 1971.

6. *Municipal Authority*

Municipal authority resided in a compact hierarchy of officials, composed of a mayor, aldermen and bailiffs, supported by a common council. These dignitaries were chosen annually by the burgesses or, where the corporation was a close, co-optive oligarchy, selected by members of that body from amongst themselves. The method of choosing burgesses also varied from town to town, but most of them were drawn from the more reputable and wealthier class of tradesmen and freeholders. Occasionally they represented a mere minority of the townspeople, a situation which often fomented internal discord and an estrangement between the privileged and non-enfranchised citizens.

The juridictional powers exercised by the mayor and his officials were quite extensive, and there was a variety of municipal courts to deal with offences committed within the town liberties, and to enforce the fulfilment of civic duties by burgesses and other classes. At Haverfordwest, for instance, the mayor was empowered to hold two ordinary courts every fortnight, and a third — the 'Pie-Powder Court' on special occasions to supervise the activities of strangers and to control transactions whenever fairs were held in the town.

G. Dyfnallt Owen, *Elizabethan Wales,* 1964.

7.   *Courts Baron and Courts Leet*

Two courts were held in the borough: (1) The Court Leet and View of Frankpledge, (2) the fortnightly Hundred Court.

(1) The title used in the rolls for the first court is the 'Court of the View of Frankpledge' and in the later rolls the 'Court Leet and View of Frankpledge'. It was held at Newport twice a year, soon after Michaelmas (Sept., Oct. or early November) and about Easter (April or May). In the early part of the seventeenth century the place of meeting was the Guildhall but from about 1625 the court was held at the house of the bailiff of the borough, probably because the old Guildhall was falling into ruins. The court was held before the reeve (*prepositus*) of the borough or his deputy. Burgesses and freeholders, inhabiting within or without the borough, owed suit of court, and for each default they were amerced 7s . . .

At the Court Leet and View of Frankpledge a 'grand inquisition' consisting of from fifteen to nineteen jurors (sixteen was the normal number) were elected by the reeve (mayor) from amongst the suitors to the court and it was their duty to make presentments and amerce offenders. . .

Early in the proceedings of the court would come the calling of the roll of suitors. Defaulters, both freeholders and burgesses, were presented and amerced 7s. each, a sum which was later mitigated by the affeerors. It has been noticed that generally speaking the persons who absented themselves regularly were men of standing — the 'esquires' and gentlemen'.

The jury then made their presentments on oath. The following extracts from the rolls will give a good idea of this aspect of the business of the View of Frankpledge:

James Perrott, knight, Walter Rees, knight, Cicil, daughter of James Perrott, Owen Picton, gent, John Kiblewhite and Rowland Thomas Yong the younger, freehold tenants of the town, because they did not appear at the Court of View of Frankpledge but defaulted, are amerced 7s. each (3 May 1604).

That Jenet John, widow, kept her pigs unringed to the damage of her neighbours, in mercy 2s 6d.

That Caria Tanner, widow, broke the assise of ale, selling small measure in illegal measures, therefore she is in mercy 12d. . .

That James William Lloyd and Hugh John, smith, kept playing cards and other illicit games in their houses, in mercy 2s. 6d. each (31 Dec 1604 — ? adjourned leet).

That Richard ap Ievan, tailor, and ten others kept taverns in their houses and sold ale without licence (25 Aug 1606) . . .

That William Melchior encroached on the common of the burgesses of Newport and erected a stone hedge on the common west of his mansion house and north towards Carnengly to the damage of the burgesses. On 8 June the court ordered him to remove the hedge before the next court under penalty of £5 to the lord (4 May 1612). For not complying with the order of the court he was later deprived of his right of being a burgess (12 Oct 1612).

That David Thomas and Thomas Hughe caught small salmon in the river Nevern near the bridge of the town, in mercy—

The jury present William Anthony, Katherine James, John Lloyd, clerk, and Trevor Hugh, clerk, for keeping mangy horses contrary to the Statute, amerced 7s. each.

Because Thomas Owen Smith did take tobacco in open court he was amerced 3s 6d. (25 Feb 1655).

The jury present the stocks and whipping post to be out of repair (20 Oct 1720).

(2) The other court which was held within the borough of Newport was a court of record. In early times it was called the Hundred Court 'holden before the mayor or portreeve every fifteen days there, which Court holdeth plea of any action personal or mixed of what sum soever and to the said Court are all freeholders by tenure of their land and the burgesses by reason of their freedom bound to do suit and service' . . .

In some eighteenth century rolls it is described as the 'Court Baron' . . .

To illustrate the work of the court the following excerpts (summarised from the Latin of the originals) have been taken from the rolls at random. Some of the Clerk's annotations are summarised in the square brackets.

Owen John of the parish of Newport complains against James Lewis of the town of Newport in a plea of trespass, 10s. Defendant on 1 Nov 1610 promised to find five fishing nets for herring-fishing in the fishing season of 1610 and to place them in the boat of Rees Lloyd, gent, in which they would fish together (5 Aug 1611).

Thomas Bowen, gent, complains against Owen Hugh of Newport in a plea of debt 15s 6d. in respect of 1½ meizes of herrings and 30 herrings sold to defendant. (11 Nov 1611) . . .

Owen John David complains against Griffith ap Ievan Gall in a plea of trespass 20s. Defendant 1 Sept 1611, demised 35 sheep to plaintiff to enjoy their milk and half their wool while in his care, but defendant on 1 May took the sheep without permission to his own house to the damage of plaintiff of all the milk and half of the wool from 1 May to 31 Oct. (11 May 1612).

Nicholas David, mason, and Margaret his wife complain against William Thomas Penry in a plea of trespass to the damage of plaintiffs £20 for scandalous words spoken by defendant about the said Margaret, viz. Ty di (i.e. Margaret) a rhegaist fy nha ag y ma fynghosin n waeth nag y by or hanner oi dy achos di [20 July defendant pleaded not guilty. 3 Aug 1612 the jurors found he was guilty and assessed damages at 3d.] (20 July 1612).

Robert Llewelyn of Fishguard complains against Henry William in a plea of trespass; damage £100. Defendant at the high cross on 29 May 1614 spoke those scandalous words against the plaintiff: Lleydr wyti a mab y Leidr, a whiw leidr,

nyw gadawaist ti ddim erioed heb ddwyn ond y fae ry-drwm neu
ry-boeth, ond torri tai A mab y Leidr ysyn torri Llongau ac yn
dwyn keffyle ac yn ei kuddio yn r Eithin (31 July 1615).

B. G. Charles, 'The Records of the Borough of Newport in Pembrokeshire' in *The National Library of Wales Journal,* VII, 1, 1951.

8.   *Mayor and Admiral of the Port*

During the early medieval period the townsfolk quickly acquired a
measure of self-government, and as the years went by their privileges
and powers increased, the overlordship of the magnates became
minimal, and the burgesses achieved a remarkable measure of
independence, as witnessed by charters granted by the Crown and by
the Earls of Pembroke. Between 1154 and 1702, twenty-one charters
and confirmations were granted to Haverfordwest. The first was
made by King Henry II (1154-89) and from that time until 1479 the
chief citizen who presided over the affairs of the town was usually
known as the 'prepositus'. It is to a Prince of Wales that Haverfordwest owes its Mayor. On 30 April 1479 the young Edward, by his title
of 'Prince of Wales and Lord of Haverford' granted a charter which
decreed that henceforth the town should be incorporated, ruled by a
mayor, sheriff, and bailiffs, together 'twenty-four of the honestest
men of the town of Haverford, and furthermore that the Mayor
should also be a Justice of the Peace, Coroner, Admiral, and Clerk of
the Market'. Since that day Haverfordwest has never been without its
Mayor and Admiral of the Port (whose jurisdiction, incidentally,
extended to the Port of Milford).

Francis Jones, *Town and County of Haverfordwest, 1479-1974.*

9.   *Tenby Council Decisions*

October 17, 1780. — It having been made to appear to the Mayor and
Common Council of this Borough that many avaricious persons have
in a great measure destroyed the Oyster Fishery on Caldey bed, owing
to their taking Oysters of too small a size, for Pickling, by which

means they destroy the brood thereof. In order to remedy the same, We, the Mayor and Council aforesaid, do unanimously agree, that if in future any dredging-boat shall presume in taking any small oysters on the said bed, without throwing the same overboard (excepting a quarter of a hundred each man), shall be fined, i.e., the master of each boat not under five shillings for each offence; also that the said fishing-boats shall not sell any of the said small oysters to any vessel under the like penalty.

March 30, 1784. — 'Tis observed by the Mayor and Council that great numbers of pigs are suffered to go about the streets of this Borough, which is become an insufferable nuisance to the inhabitants thereof, 'tis therefore thought necessary to appoint Thomas Harris and Abraham Richards, two constables, to impound all pigs that shall be found going about the streets and environs of this Borough in the common pound, and for their so doing they shall be entitled to one shilling for each pig from the proprietors of the said pigs over and above the poundage money to the keeper of the said pound.

Edward Laws, *The History of Little England beyond Wales,* 1888.

10.   *The Royal National Eisteddfod*

The Eisteddfod came to Pembrokeshire for the first time in 1936, when it was held at Fishguard. It was opened on the Monday morning by the Lord Lieutenant, Sir Evan D. Jones, Bart., supported by the Member of Parliament for the county, Major Gwilym Lloyd George, Eisteddfod officials and local dignitaries. On the Tuesday morning, before eight o'clock, the Gorsedd procession assembled on Fishguard Square and, led by the mounted figure of Sieffre o Gyfarthfa (Captain Geoffrey Crawshay, the Herald Bard,) proceeded to the Gorsedd Circle erected on Penslade, overlooking Fishguard Bay. At this ceremony, J. J. Williams (J.J.), the winner of the chair at Caernarfon in 1906 for his *awdl* to *Y Lloer* (The Moon), and at Llangollen in 1908 for a poem in memory of *Ceiriog,* was installed Archdruid in the place of Gwili (J. Gwili Jenkins: 1872-1936) who had died the previous May.

The programme of the day at Fishguard contained an explanatory note on the procedure to be followed during the crowning ceremony:

The Ceremony of Crowning the Bard will be according to the rites of the Bards of the Isle of Britain. He will be proclaimed by sound of Trumpet; the Gorsedd Recorder will call the Muster of the Bards; the Adjudication will be delivered; the successful Bard will be escorted to the platform by two of the Principal Bards. The Victor will be duly invested as Crowned Bard of the National Eisteddfod of 1936. The Bards will deliver their addresses, and Madam Margaret Thomas will sing the Crowning Song. The whole ceremony will be under the direction of the Gorsedd of Bards.

SPECIAL NOTICE. No person whatsoever other than:—

(a) Members of the Gorsedd in their Official Robes; or

(b) Official Representatives of the Eisteddfod Committee in the capacity of Adjudicator, or otherwise officially engaged in the Ceremony of Investiture, can be allowed to take part in the Ceremony of Crowning the Bard on the Eisteddfod Platform. The whole of these proceedings will be under the sole control of the Gorsedd, exercised through the Recorder, and the Herald Bard as Master of the Ceremonies.

Dillwyn Miles, *The Royal National Eisteddfod of Wales,* 1978.

11. *Road-Side Hostelrie, Robeston Wathen*

I arrived in the afternoon at the village of Robeston Wathen, in the neat inn of which place, as the rain had begun to fall in torrents, I determined on taking up my quarters during the night. For a road-side hostelrie I found in it more appliances of comfort than I had expected, and mine host was active in his civilities. But it had other and more intellectual claims upon my notice; for in travelling, whether far or near, I quite agree with one of the most delightful writers of our age, that 'we multiply events, and that innocently. We set out, as it were, on our adventures; and many are those that occur to us, morning, noon and night. The day we come to a place which we have long heard and read of, is an era in our lives; and from that moment the very name calls up a picture'. And so it was with me. I met in 'the inn's best room' an agreeable and intellectual companion — one whose profession was connected with all that is refined and liberal. He was a painter. He had followed the same wild coast-path as myself. He had seen the winged watchers on the Stacks, and stood on the bold jutting promontory of St Govan, looking out upon that broad ocean, whose ever-rolling waves fitly suggest the idea of eternity. He had, like me, struck off from the stormy scenes of savage nature, with her stern rocks and foaming billows, to luxuriate in her peaceful smiles, as she hushed and cradled the winds in the rich glens and valleys of this picturesque county. We compared our pictures, not our graphic or caligraphic ones, but those original paintings traced on the clear fluid of the vision, and then transferred in all their richness to the memory, as their receding lines vanished before the advancing forms of another and yet another, still more sublime and lovely than the first. It was but an instantaneous mental act to summon from their secret store-house picture after picture, and to expatiate again and again upon their surpassing beauties and sub-limities; revelling in this interchange of thought and fancy, with emotions as fresh and rich as those with which they were first seen. This was an evening in my changeful life that I shall long remember.

Thomas Roscoe, *Wanderings and Excursions in South Wales,* 1820.

X

Living Things

1. *The Last of the Beavers*

The Teivi has another singular particularity, being the only river in Wales, or even in England, which has beavers; in Scotland they are said to be found in one river, but are very scarce. I think it not a useless labour, to insert a few remarks respecting the nature of these animals; the manner in which they bring their materials from the woods to the water, and with what skill they connect them in the construction of their dwellings in the midst of rivers; their means of defence on the eastern and western sides against hunters; and also concerning their fish-like tails.

The beavers, in order to construct their castles in the middle of rivers, make use of the animals of their own species instead of carts, who, by a wonderful mode of carriage, convey the timber from the woods to the rivers. Some of them, obeying the dictates of nature, receive on their bellies the logs of wood cut off by their associates, which they hold tight with their feet, and thus with transverse pieces placed in their mouths, are drawn along backwards, with their cargo, by other beavers, who fasten themselves with their teeth to the raft. The moles use a similar artifice in clearing out the dirt from the cavities they form by scraping. In some deep and still corner of the river, the beavers use such skill in the construction of their habitations, that not a drop of water can penetrate, or the force of storms shake them; nor do they fear any violence but that of mankind, nor even that, unless well armed. They entwine the branches of willows with other wood, and different kinds of leaves, to the usual height of the water, and having made within-side a communication from floor to floor, they elevate a kind of stage, or scaffold, from which they may observe and watch the rising of the waters. In the course of time, their habitations bear the appearance of a grove of willow trees, rude and natural without, but artfully constructed within. This animal can remain in or under water at its pleasure, like the frog or seal, who shew, by the smoothness or roughness of their skins, the flux and reflux of the sea. These three animals, therefore, live indifferently under the water, or in the air, and have short legs, broad bodies, stubbed tails, and resemble the mole in their corporal shape. It is worthy of remark, that the beaver has but four teeth, two above, and two below, which being broad and sharp, cut like a carpenter's axe, and as such he uses them. They make excavations and dry hiding places in the banks near their dwellings, and when they hear the stroke of the hunter, who with sharp poles endeavours to penetrate them, they fly as soon as possible to the defence of their castle, having first blown out the water from the entrance of the hole, and rendered it foul and muddy by scraping the earth, in order thus artfully to elude the stratagems of the well-armed hunter, who is watching them the opposite banks of the river. When the beaver finds he cannot save himself from the pursuit of the dogs who follow him, that he may ransom his body by the sacrifice of a part, he throws away that, which by natural instinct he knows to be the object sought for, and in the sight of the hunter castrates himself, from which circumstance he has gained the name of Castor; and if by chance the dogs should chase an animal which had been previously castrated, he has the sagacity to run to an elevated spot, and there lifting up his leg, shews the hunter that the object of his pursuit is gone. Cicero speaking of them says, 'They ransom themselves by that part of the body, for which they are chiefly sought'. . .

Thus, therefore, in order to preserve his skin, which is sought after in the west, and the medicinal part of his body, which is coveted in the east, although he cannot save himself entirely, yet, by a wonderful instinct and sagacity, he endeavours to avoid the stratagems of his pursuers. The beavers have broad, short tails, thick, like the palm of a hand, which they use as a rudder in swimming; and although the rest of their body is hairy, this part, like that of seals, is without hair, and smooth; upon which account, in Germany and the arctic regions, where beavers abound, great and religious persons, in times of fasting eat the tails of this fish-like animal, as having both the taste and colour of fish.

Giraldus Cambrensis, *The Itinerary through Wales,* 1188.

2. *The Pembrokeshire Corgi*

Not until 1934 was the Pembrokeshire Corgi officially recognized by the Kennel Club as a pure breed in his own rights and given the necessary separate classification from his cousin, the Cardiganshire Corgi . . . thus you *could* say the Pembrokeshire Corgi is less than a score years old. Most of us know, however, that he is much older than that: he almost certainly dates back to the early twelfth century and quite probably to the reign of Hywel Dda, King of Wales, in the early tenth century. Moreover I do not think he has changed a great deal in physical and mental make-up during the last 1,000 years.

In 1933 H.M. the King (then Duke of York) became interested in the Corgi and bought a little red puppy as a pet for his elder daughter, the Princess Elizabeth. This dog was registered as 'Rozavel Golden Eagle' (by Ch. 'Crymmych President' out of Ch. 'Golden Girl') but soon became famous as one of the pets of the Royal Family — with lay reporters of the national Press (as they usually do) tripping over the breed name and describing him as a Welsh Terrier more often than not.

Whether this reporters' error resulted in an increase in demand for Welsh Terriers I do not yet know but it is absolutely certain that the wide interest taken in the Corgi from that time onwards was due to the right Royal fillip thus given the breed. Princess Elizabeth's pet Pembrokeshire was usually known as 'Dookie', and he fairly captivated the hearts of our Royal Family, genuine dog lovers all as they are. It is not surprising then that in due course another Pembrokeshire, a bitch registered as 'Rozavel Lady Jane' was bought from Mrs Gray. 'Jane' became the dam of the Royal favourites 'Crackers' and 'Carol' (they were born at Christmastide) and so it all started . . . with two of H.R.H. the Princess Elizabeth's present Corgi pets, 'Susan' and 'Sugar', the Pembrokeshire has indeed been well represented by the Royal Family.

The early *Corgwn* owned by our Princesses were much photographed and I always think one of the most delightful series of studies of them with their owners (then known and loved by us as the Princesses 'Lilybets' and Margaret Rose) was that made in and about the little thatched house that was presented to Princess Elizabeth by the people of Wales on her sixth birthday, and which was called 'Y Bwthyn Bach'.

Clifford L. Hubbard, *The Pembrokeshire Corgi Handbook,* 1952.

3. *The Sealyham Terrier*

Captain John Edwardes was an eccentric sporting gentleman of noble birth, and resided at Sealyham, an attractive country mansion situate between Haverfordwest and Fishguard, and which is now in the occupation of Mr and Mrs Victor Higgon, the latter a well-known breeder and judge, and chairman of the Sealyham Terrier Club since its formation in January, 1908. The Terrier is called after the residence of its founder.

Captain Edwardes, as I have just stated, was a great sportsman, and he conceived the idea that the mongrel dog of sixty or more years ago which he was obliged to use in his numerous sporting excusions, was not quite the kind of animal for bolting the fox and otter or digging out the badger, which he wished for. There seems little doubt that the Terrier of that date was more or less a nondescript kind of creature, with no pretension to beauty or breeding, nor with the least claim to uniformity of type. It will, therefore, be apparent that to evolve a short-legged, smart, workmanlike Terrier, which above all other considerations, must be dead game, was a problem not easy of solution, and only a man possessed of indomitable courage and tenacity would have persevered in his efforts to realise an ideal which repeated failures must sometimes have indicated was incapable of accomplishment. But Captain Edwardes, in his lonely country mansion, plodded on, and by careful selection and judicious breeding eventually established a short-legged, rough-haired Terrier capable of facing any vermin then prevalent in the county. At this period the polecat was fairly plentiful in the dense woods abounding in the vicinity of the Captain's residence, and the old gent made it a *sine qua non* that no dog should be given lodging at Sealyham which would not dispose of a full-grown specimen of the *Putorius foetidus;* and anyone who has seen these denizens of the forest will at once realise that the standard of pluck fixed by the gallant Captain was by no means insignificant.

His method of testing the young dogs, which took place when they were about a year old, was as follows:— A live polecat was dragged across a field, and then enclosed in a small pit, roughly a couple of feet deep, with an entrance about the size of an ordinary badger's hole. The quarry was secured with sufficient liberty to enable him to put up a fair and square fight. As the polecat is a notoriously odoriferous animal, the dog, which would previously have done plenty of ratting, usually experienced no difficulty in following the trail and arriving at the spot where the length of its stay in the world was to be decided by the character of the combat which then took place. If the dog 'went in' and killed, all well and good; if he funked the encounter and minced about outside, and declined to tackle his quarry, his doom was sealed, but our old friend was not always wise in his estimate of the character of his dogs. One day a particularly good ratting dog turned craven, and refused to tackle the polecat. Every facility and encouragement were given, but without effect; the verdict was soon pronounced — the coward must die. The man who had walked the dog had become attached to the Terrier, and begged hard that as he was such an excellent ratter, and so useful to him about the farm, he might be allowed to keep him. The reluctant consent was given, and before the dog was a year older he turned out one of the gamest Terriers ever bred at Sealyham, the old Captain subsequently purchasing him from the farmer. The dog lived to a ripe old age, and when he died was mourned as one of the best tykes that ever went to earth.

Fred W. Lewis in *The Sealyham Terrier*, by Theo. Marples, 1921.

4.   *Castlemartin Blacks*

The Castlemartin Black Cattle had long drooping horns, and were known for their hardiness. They were good milkers and produced good beef, and the breed was greatly improved by the efforts of John Mirehouse of Brownslade, Castlemartin, who, like Colonel Johnes of Hafod in Cardiganshire, devoted his wealth towards improving his estate and experimenting and applying the growing scientific knowledge of agriculture to land development and stock-breeding, with excellent results.

Strangely enough, the labours of John Mirehouse seem to be forgotten today, although Colonel Johnes's work is often quoted. Yet Mirehouse was esteemed 'one of the best gentlemen farmers in the kingdom', and won the gold medal of the Society for the Encouragement of Arts, Manufactures and Commerce in 1800, for his work in improving waste moors. It was undoubtedly due to his work that the Castlemartin Blacks had their own herd-book in 1874, but they have since been merged into the Welsh Black variety.

Maxwell Fraser, *Introducing West Wales*, 1956.

5. *A Nightingale Sang*

Even the nightingale, though a *rara avis* in these parts, has, this phenomenal season, been heard in the woods near Cresselly. The following tradition explains how these little songsters came to shun the county of Pembroke. It appears that St David, 'being seriously occupied in the night tyme in his diverse orizons, was soe troubled with the swete tuninges of the Nightingall as that he praied unto th'Almightie that, from that tyme forward, there might never a Nightingall sing within his Dioces; and this was the cause of confininge of the bird out of this countrey. Thus much, ' remarks the chronicler, 'to recreat the reader's spirettes.'

H. Thornhill Timmins, *Nooks and Corners of Pembrokeshire,* 1895.

6.   *This Odious Bird*

Nevarne is the greatest and largest parishe in the Sheere and taketh name of the ryver Nevarne wch runneth well neere throw the myddest of the same.

In welsh it is called *Inhyver* and in old tyme was dedicated to the bryttifhe Saint called *Sainct Burnaghe* whose festifalle day is yet dulie observed within this and dyverse other parishes with noe smale solempnitie the seaventh of April, on wch day yt is wth us said the Cocow first beginneth to tune her laye. I might well here omytt an old report freshe as yet of this odiouse bird that in the old world the parishe priest would not beginne Masse in this parishe untill this bird (called the Citizens ambassador) had first appeared and begann her note upon a stone called Saint Burnaghes stone being a stone curiouslie wrought with sondrie sortes of knottes standing upright in the Churcheyarde of this parishe, and one yere stayeinge verey longue and the priest and people expecting her accustomed cominge (for I accompt this byrd of the feminyne gender) cam at last and lightinge upon the said stone her accustomed preaching place and being scarse able once to sounde the note upon the said stone presentlie fell downe dead. This religiouse tale althoughe yt Concerne in some sorte Churche matters you may eyther beleave or not without perill of damnation.

George Owen, The Second Book of George Owen's Description of Pembrokeshire' in *The National Library of Wales Journal,* 1948 by B. G. Charles.

7. *Seine Fishing*

Although no commercial salmon fishing has been practised in the Nevern estuary in recent years, the present regulations allow the use of draft nets 'between the iron bridge at Newport and an imaginary line drawn straight across the said river from Dinas Head to Penybal at the estuary of Nevern'.

Seine netting was stopped in 1958, despite the fact that the Nevern is regarded as a good salmon river. According to witnesses to the Commissioners appointed to inquire into salmon fisheries in 1861, seine nets as well as coracle nets and weirs were utilised on the Nevern. At Newport, said one witness, four seine nets were in regular use 'and in some seasons', he stated, 'when there has been a great take of fish, I recollect a great many coming from St Dogmaels near Cardigan. I have seen as many as five extra seines come on account of the fishing being so good'. Nevertheless, during the early eighteen-sixties, there was a sharp decline in the use of seine nests in the Nevern, due to overfishing in weirs and 'from the evils resulting from the spear and small meshed nets'. The result was that the number of salmon and sewin caught in the Nevern 'can scarce pay the expenses of a single draught net'. By 1870, however, four draft nets were in regular use in the estuary, while during the first quarter of the present century, three or four teams were engaged in seine netting. According to one informant there were seventeen fishermen at Newport in 1921. One boat was manned by a team of five and used a net 200 yards long, while the other two boats were each manned by teams of six and they used seine nets 320 yards long. As on the Teifi, a Nevern seine net was made up of a number of nets fixed together with twine. Each member of a fishing team was expected to provide a net 50 yards long and each one was carefully tied to the next (a process known as *murio'r rhwydi*), to provide one long net, each section being expected to last for three fishing seasons. Nineteen-foot rowing boats built by David Williams of Aberystwyth were the usual boats used on the Nevern before the last war and in fishing the boat owner or 'captain' was employed on the rudder, two were engaged in rowing and two were concerned with paying out the net on the starboard side in the centre of the boat. The other member of a six-man team was engaged as a shoreman. A fishing session usually began three hours after high tide when a particular stone (*Y Garreg fach*) appeared on the shore, and when one of the stone steps on the quayside was also visible at the same time. Usually, only the morning tide was fished, as night tides were considered.poor. Fishing was carried out in a number of stations in the estuary, the principal ones being *Y Llygad* (the eye) or *Gene'r Afon* (river mouth), *Y Dor* and *Tyn Segur*. The first boat on the first day of the fishing season fished *Y Llygad* while on the second day it went to *Y Dor* and on the third to *Tyn Segur*. A strict rotation was followed throughout the season. On incoming tides, two other fishing stations, *Benet* and *Pen Ucha'r traeth,* were also fished, and whichever boat was fishing at *Y Dor* on the ebb could proceed to *Pen Ucha'r traeth* to fish on the flood tide. The team fishing *Y Llygad* on the ebb proceeded to *Benet* on the flood. *Y Llygad* and *Pen Ucha'r traeth* were considered the most fruitful fishing stations, but only two trawls at the most could be completed on any one flood tide, a single trawl usually taking about 45 minutes.

In the nineteen-twenties the cost of the nets and licence (£2 per 50 yards in 1921) was shared between all members of a fishing team, but the boat was usually the property of the captain of the team. The proceeds were divided equally between all the members, the salmon being sold to a Cardigan merchant.

Occasionally the weather would be unsuitable for seine netting in the estuary of the Nevern and in the sea beyond, and it was customary then for the fishermen to undo the separate sections of the net, to make a series of short 50 yard wade nets. A wade net was known locally as *rhwyd wad,* and it could be used as any time by any of the fishing teams, with the exception of the team that was allocated to *Y Llygad* on a particular day. That particular team was not allowed to go upstream with a wade net and if the weather should be too rough to use a seine at *Y Llygad,* the team allocated to that station could not fish that particular tide.

J. Geraint Jenkins, *Nets and Coracles,* 1974.

8.   *Rare Plants*

A few plants to be found on Pembrokeshire cliffs occur in few other localities in Britain. Prostrate broom (*Sarothamnus scoparius* ssp. *maritimus*) differs from common broom (ssp. *scoparius*) in its spreading or prostrate habit, often with stems tightly pressed to a rock face or the ground. It grows in a number of places between St Ann's and Cemais Heads, most frequently on the Dale and Marloes cliffs, on precipitous rock faces and with gorse and black-thorn on the cliff-top. Hairy greenweed (*Genista pilosa*) occurs at St David's Head and a few other stations in the vicinity and near Strumble Head. It is a dwarf replica of prostrate broom, and both make a striking display in May and early June. Perennial centaury (*Centaurium portense*) is a beautiful little plant which grows in tufts bearing a mass of bright pink flowers from late June to August, often with heather above cliffs but also on dunes. In Britain it is known only near Newport and in west Cornwall. Two species of rock sea lavender each have only one station in Ireland and one in Pembrokeshire: *Limonium paradoxum* grows on basic rock at St David's Head and *L. transwallianum* is plentiful over a limited area at Giltar Point.

The Tenby daffodil (*Narcissus obvallaris*) has aroused interest for more than 150 years on account of the mystery of its origin and the beauty of its flowers, which are out before the end of February. It may well be indigenous in West Wales since legends that it was brought to Pembrokeshire from the Continent are discounted by the fact that it is not known as a native species anywhere in Europe. It was abundant in fields around Tenby until in the nineteenth century it became an object of trade, with the result that the country was scoured for the bulbs. A letter from a local botanist, J. E. Arnett, quoted by C. T. Vachell (*Transactions of the Cardiff Naturalists' Society, 1893-94*), records that up to 1885 there was a steady trade and that 'about half a million bulbs were sent to London in the course of two years'. By 1893 few Tenby daffodils remained. Increasing use of the plough has almost if not quite exterminated any that survived, though there are a few records as recent as the 1950s which may refer to plants still growing in traditional fields. It is, however, to be seen in many places in the National Park on roadside hedge-banks near dwellings or ruins, in pastures close to farmsteads, and in woods near large country houses, with every indication that it is thoroughly naturalised.

T. A. Warren Davis, 'Flora and Vegetation' in *Pembrokeshire Coast National Park Guide,* ed. Dillwyn Miles No. 10 1973.

9. *Grey Seal*

Seals are warm-blooded creatures like ourselves. British seals have calm, soulful eyes, larger than those of man, with which they gaze forwards with a concentrated stare, the rich dark pupil and iris filling the aperture with little white showing. This gives the head a warm, kindly, human look, the long whiskers adding a wise adult touch. It is not at all surprising that their faces and ways have given rise to so many legends and tales of mermaids and mermen.

In fact seals are sentient beings of an advanced order of intelligence not far removed from that of man, ape, dog and dolphin. In one respect they have advanced farther from the ancestor which they share with these mammals. The structure of the skeleton and limbs of the seals shows that they onced lived terrestrially with four articulate limbs able, like the polar bear and otter today, to walk about on dry land. Having become land mammals with man, they are returning, have almost completely returned, to the sea — which may yet be man's not-too-distant fate when the land fails to satisfy his requirements and if he continues to destroy his environment from lack of foresight.

Yet seals are not wholly marine, like the whale and the dolphin. They have not lost their covering of fur like those mammals in which only a few vestigial hairs remain. Seals still like to get out of the water and lie in the wind and sun for long hours, and rest and sleep.

Of the three islands in Pembrokeshire where grey seals might find the safest sanctuary — Skomer, Ramsey and Grassholm, only the first two are used regularly as nursery sites, which are either in caves or upon open beaches, both storm-swept. But Grassholm, uninhabited and difficult of access, seems the safest from both man and storms, as there are good shelving rock platforms where the seals haul out above high tide, and these give access to gradual slopes of grass, ideal — one would have thought — for a safe nursery. But until recently there has been no record of a calf born there. Why, I do not know.

R. M. Lockley, *Grey Seal, Common Seal,* 1966.

XI

Islands

1. *Skokholm*

When I first saw Skokholm, vivid upon the horizon in the windy
sunlight of a May evening, I was warned that it was uninhabited,
unfarmed, almost inaccessible. But as I had long possessed a natural
exhilaration for nature, the sea and solitude, this good news only sang
loud within me, to make me restless to sail there. Even before I set
foot on it, I was losing my heart to this rock in the ocean.

After two days of waiting for the wind to abate, the young fishermen, whose lobster-pots were set about the island, agreed that the
weather might fine off next morning, when they would take friend
Harry and me across.

The talkative fisherman said: 'Thee want to go to Skokum?
Wunnerful islant, rich, beat anywhere for corn and root crops.
Overrun with rabbuts now. Last man to farm it was Bulldog
Edwards. Go and see 'im. Lives at Orlandon, a few steps down the
road. Particular cuss, my uncle, likes to be asked permission — 'e's
still got the lease. Better chat 'im up. Just down the road and over the
bridge.'

In remote Wales the natives never tell you its miles away; that
would be discourteous. Keep you happy as long as possible. Life's too
short . . . 'Just a few steps' proved to be a four mile walk. After all,
distance is relative.

Many local rumours about Bulldog Edwards. A tight man, they
said; and how he had lived obstinately, happily, unconventionally
with a pretty housekeeper on the Island. Robust still, with flowing
white beard, a belligerent eye, wind-wrinkled skin and a voice not
without the singing larks of Skokholm still in its soft drawl. His talk
was old-fashioned and quiet, as with resignation.

'Ah, Skokum! Now that's an islant for thee. Thee'll like 'un if thee likes the burrds. I ought'n never to have left 'un. Peaceful as 'eaven. But the dratted war came. Aye, 'elp thyself — if thee can get there. Come and tell me afterwards.'

R. M. Lockley, *The Island,* 1969.

2. *Summer Days on Skokholm*

We had reached smooth water in the shelter of a little creek in the south-east cliffs of Skokholm. A flight of steps in the red rocks made landing easy.

I find it difficult to tell you how wildly happy I was to be walking up those steps. I had got enough information in the last two days to realise that I might with luck obtain this abandoned island for myself. My mind was already filled with the thoughts of a settler and pioneer as I put my foot on Skokholm for the first time.

On the sea and in the air were thousands of sea-birds. The cliffs were lavishly strewn with wild flowers, wide open to the sunlight. Rabbit-holes seemed to be discreetly draped with tresses of sea-campion, scurvy-grass, and lady's fingers, and at these decorated thresholds stood puffins, singly and in pairs. These small sea-birds have droll white faces. The parrot-like bill with its crimson, blue, and yellow rings is stuck on like a clown's artificial nose. The eye has a lead-coloured badge above and below, like the face, but the rest of the plumage is black, including the cravat under the chin, but excepting a grey patch at the back of the head. The legs and feet are the colour of a blood-orange skin. The whole is like a toy alderman in evening dress who has opened many crackers and adorned his face with the contents.

That day mated puffins were indulging in courtship rites, beak-rubbing and a kind of goose-stepping foxtrot, and they were slow to move from our path. At the last moment they dived into their burrow homes or flew away to sea. It was easy to imagine them possessing human feelings, for the glances they gave us suggested emotions of surprise, fear, indignation, and indifference, according to how near we passed them.

Gulls glided and swooped overhead, resenting visibly this intrusion upon their territory. They had nests here and there in the steep cliff.

Oyster-catchers, red-legged, red-billed, with black-and-white plumage, ran before us trying to conceal the whereabouts of their nests of fine pebbles. When they had lured us far enough these sea-pies would rise, and with loud whickering cries join in the protest of the gulls.

We made our way through sheets of bluebells, among which the new fronds of bracken stood up like bishops' croziers. A meadow-pipit leaped from a cup-nest in the mouth of a rabbit-scrape. In a little hollow there was a walled-in spring of fresh water. As we drank there a sedge-warbler flew out of some dropwort near us and began its clatter of defiance and scolding.

We moved towards the house along a path that curved, as old paths do, without apparent reason — there was nothing to prevent a man walking straight across this meadow to the house. No doubt in the first place, I thought, a man with a yoke and two buckets of water from the well had probably taken the line of least resistance with his burden, avoiding perhaps weeds and little hillocks, and so he had sketched out a crooked route which had ever since been followed.

R. M. Lockley, *In Praise of Islands,* 1957.

3. SKOKHOLM

At dusk great rafts of shearwaters
Rise and fall with the slow tide
And the island's edge and colour
Lose definition. The wide
Fingered buzzard spirals down.
No wind sucks the sun-dried
Grass: the air contracts, still, but alive . . .

Suddenly the mist explodes, the sense
Is bruised by buffeting wings, the night
Is luminous with noise as bird after bird
Comes swinging home. I light
My torch, and catch one spread on the turf
Before its gull-proof hole. It hooks its wings
And slides below, leaving flecks of surf
To trace its track on the yellow grass.

In the iridescent morning air
Below the singing bird-shot sky,
Their sharp wings spread like arms,
The lost shearwaters lie
Eviscerated by the gulls.
Those without deep-shelters die.

John Stuart Williams from *Pembrokeshire Poems,* 1976.

4. SEAL ISLAND

seal-curved sleeping island
grey-skinned under channel wind

from your glistening black trees
bracken giant ferns rise

above the red and white Monastery
nestling in deep skin-folds

surrounded by gulls, you bask
eyes shut, frozen to stone

yet we half expect you to slide
oil-smooth over rocks vanishing
under green Atlantic waves

Alison Bielski from *Pembrokeshire Poems,* 1976.

5. *Gwales in Penfro (Grassholm)*

And then Bendigeidfran commanded his head to be struck off. 'And
take the head,' he said, 'and carry it to the White Mount in London,
and bury it with its face towards France. And you will be a long time
upon the road. In Harddlech you will be feasting seven years, and the
birds of Rhiannon singing unto you. And the head will be as pleasant
company to you as ever it was at best when it was on me. And at

Manorbier Castle. (Photo: Leonard & Marjorie Gayton).

Manorbier Castle. Aquatint by Paul Sandby (1775).

Death of Sir Thomas Picton.
Drawn by J. A. Atkinson; engraved by M. Dubourg (1816).

Angle & Thorn Island. (Photo: Aerofilms Ltd.).

Stack Rock Fort (1852-70). The most complete of the 'Palmerston Follies' around the Haven. A Palliser cannon is still 'on board'. (Photo: Roger Worsley).

St David's. Paul Sandby aquatint (1775).

Pembroke Castle & Town. Drawn & engraved by J. Laporte (1824).

Manorbier Castle. Paul Sandby aquatint (1779).

Owen & Bowen, Map of Pembrokeshire.

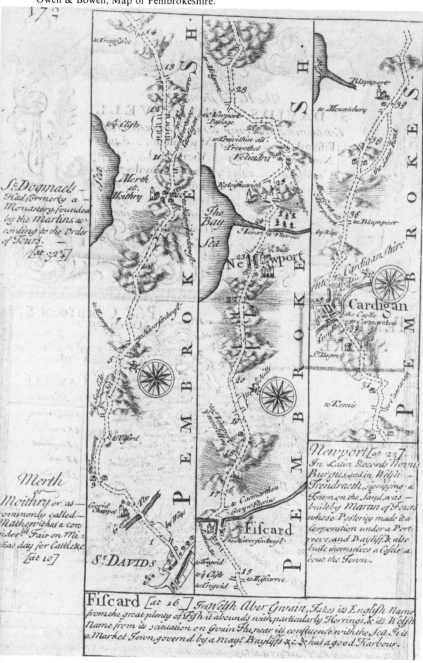

Tudor Merchant's House, Tenby. (Photo: Roger Worsley).

Mediaeval chimney construction characteristic of Pembrokeshire.
(Photo: Roger Worsley).

Milford Haven & Docks

Pembroke Dock showing guard ship *Blenheim*
from a drawing by E. Duncan, engraved by T. A. Prior.

THE SOUTH-EAST VIEW OF KILGARAN-CASTLE, IN THE COUNTY OF PEMBROKE.

Cilgerran Castle drawn & engraved by Samuel & Nathaniel Buck. (1740).

John Speed's Map of Pembrokeshire (1610).

St Dogmael's Priory, drawn & engraved by Samuel & Nathaniel Buck (1740).

Whitesand Bay and Ramsey Island from Carn Llidi, near St David's.
(Photo: Leonard & Marjorie Gayton).

Goodwick Pier
drawn, engraved (and coloured) by the Daniel Brothers (1814).

Solva, drawn engraved and coloured by the Daniel Brothers (1814).

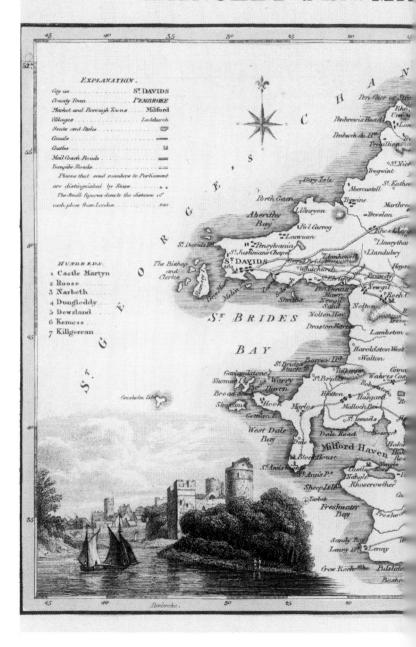

LANGLEY'S new MA

PEMBROKESHIRE.

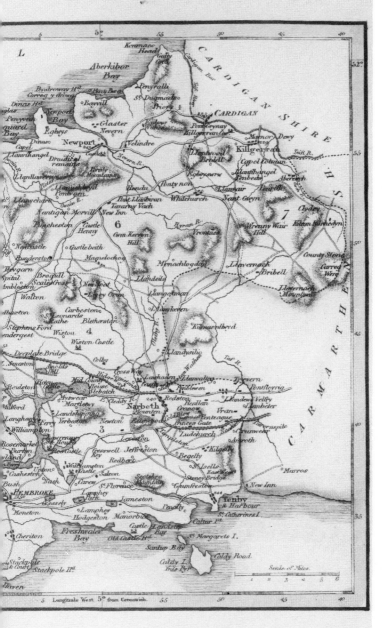

Panegyric to Hessy Jones

Newport Castle engraved by Newton Fielding from Carter Edwards.

Gwales in Penfro you will be fourscore years; and until you open the
door towards Aber Henfelen, the side facing Cornwall, you may bide
there, and the head with you uncorrupted. But from the time you
have opened that door, you may not bide there: make for London to
bury the head .'

And at the end of the seventh year they set out for Gwales in
Penfro. And there was for them there a fair royal place overlooking
the sea, and a great hall it was. And they went into the hall, and two
doors they saw open; the third door was closed, that towards
Cornwall. 'See yonder,' said Manawydan, 'the door we must not
open.' And that night they were there without stint, and were joyful.
And notwithstanding all the sorrows they had seen before their eyes,
and notwithstanding that they had themselves suffered, there came to
them no remembrance either of that or of any sorrow in the world.
And there they passed the fourscore years so that they were not aware
of having ever spent a time more joyous and delightful than that.

This is what Heilyn son of Gwyn did one day. 'Shame on my
beard,' said he, 'if I do not open the door to know if that is true which
is said concerning it.' He opened the door and looked on Cornwall
and Aber Henfelen. And when he looked, they were as conscious of
every loss they had ever sustained, and of every kinsman and friend
they had missed, and of every ill that had come upon them, as if it
were even then it had befallen them; and above all else because of
their lord. And from that same moment they could not rest, save they
set out with the head towards London. However long they were upon
the road, they came to London and buried the head in the White
Mount.

The Mabinogion, trans. Gwyn Jones and Thomas Jones, 1949.

6.   *Harry-Birds*

Over-against Justinian's Chapel, and separated from it by a narrow
Fretum, is Ramsey-Island (call'd formerly Ynis Devanog from a
Chapel there dedicated to that Saint, now swallow'd up by the sea)
which seems by the proverb (Stinan a Devanog dau anwyl gymydog)
to have been once part of the Continent, if I may properly call our
Country so, when I speak of such small insulets. In it there is a small
promontory or neck of land, issuing into the sea, which is call'd Ynis

yr hyrdhod, whence I presume is the name of Ramsey. To this Island, and some rocks adjoyning, call'd by the sea-men The Bishop and his Clerks, do yearly resort about the beginning of April such a number of birds of several sorts, that non but such as have been eye-witnesses can be prevail'd upon to believe it; all which, after breeding here, leave us before August. They come to these rocks, and also leave them, constantly in the night-time: for in the evening not a bird shall appear, and the next morning the rocks shall be full. They also visit us commonly about Christmas, and stay a week or more, and then take their leave till breeding-time. Three sorts of these Migratory birds are called in Welsh, Mora, Poeth-wy, and Pâl; in English, Eligug, Razorbil, and Puffin; to which we may also add the Harry-bird*; though I cannot at present assure you, whether this bird comes and goes off with the rest.

The Eligug lays but one egg; which (as well as those of the Puffin and Razorbill) is as big as a Duck's but longer, and smaller at one end. From this egg she never parts (unless forced) till she hatches it nor then till the young one be able to follow her; being all the while fed by the male. This and the Razorbil breed upon the bare rocks, making no manner of nest; and sometimes in such a place, that being frighten'd thence, the egg or young one (which before was upheld by the breast, upon a narrow shelving rock) tumbles into the sea. The Puffin and Harry-bird breed in holes, either those of Rabbits (wherewith Ramsey is abundantly furnish'd, all black) or such as they dig with their beaks. The Harry-birds are never seen on land, but when taken; and the manner of taking these and the Puffins, is commonly by planting nets before their berries, wherein they soon entangle themselves. These four sorts cannot raise themselves upon the wing, from the land; but, if at any distance from the cliffs, waddle (for they cannot be well said to go, their legs being too infirm for that use, and placed much more backward than a Duck's, so that they seem to stand upright) to some precipice, and thence cast themselves off, and take wing: but from the water they will raise to any height.

William Camden, *Britannia*, 1586.

---

* Manx Shearwater

7.   *Ramsey Falcons*

I ought not to omit mentioning the falcons of these parts, which are large, and of a generous kind, and exercise a most severe tyranny over the river and land birds. King Henry II remained here some time, making preparations for his voyage to Ireland; and being desirous of taking the diversion of hawking, he accidentally saw a noble falcon perched upon a rock. Going sideways round him, he let loose a fine Norway hawk, which he carried on his left hand. The falcon, though at first slower in its flight, soaring up to a great height, burning with resentment, and in his turn becoming the aggressor, rushed down upon his adversary with the greatest impetuosity, and by a violent blow struck the hawk dead at the feet of the king. From that time the king sent every year, about the breeding season, for the falcons of this country, which are produced on the sea cliffe; nor can better be found in any part of his dominions.

Giraldus Cambrensis, *The Itinerary through Wales,* 1188.

8.   *Puffins Galore*

We had frequently been informed by friends of the vast numbers of Puffins that inhabited Skomer, but from their descriptions we were but little prepared for what we actually saw. As our boat approached the island we first came upon an immense mass of birds upon the water, that proved to be acre upon acre of Puffins; flocks were continually arriving, and others leaving the main body, and all over the surface of the sea there were smaller flocks. As we drew near to the shore we found the cliffs in front of us so thickly covered by Puffins as to look as if they were sprinkled with snow, and the air was thick with single Puffins flying off the water with ribbands of fish hanging from their mandibles, on their way to feed the young in their burrows. The birds were ridiculously tame, and when we landed, and were close to them, took but slight heed of us, only fixing their little round eyes upon us, and seeming to sit a little more upright upon the rocks. But there was a continual movement amongst them of those arriving and departing, and sitting down among the fern. We for some time watched the wonderful scene, and as we remained quiet, some of the birds were emboldened to alight almost within arm's reach, and presently we saw a pure white Puffin, white all over, save for the wings that were black, fly within a few feet of us. In Mr Vaughan Davies' house there is preserved a beautiful specimen of a perfect albino Puffin that had been obtained on the island, and we were informed that varieties are rare, and that this was the only albino that had ever occurred. Mr Dix related that on Caldy Island, where Puffins are also numerous, there was in his time a very cruel custom that we heartily trust has been put a stop to by the Sea Birds' Preservation Act, viz., the men and boys of Tenby used to slaughter the Puffins wholesale on Whit Monday, and adds: 'It is as much an institution with them as May Day with the sweeps.'

The Rev. Murray A. Mathew, *The Birds of Pembrokeshire,* 1894.

9. *An Invasion of Crossbills*

This time two years, there came a flock of birds (about a hundred) to a hemp-yard, at a place called Lhan Dewi Velfrey in Pembrokeshire; and in one afternoon destroyed all the hemp seed. They described the Cocks as to be all over red as scarlet; the hens greenish above, and red underneath about as big, or little less than Blackbirds; with bills more stubbed and bigger than a Bullfinch. I suspect these to have been Virgin Nightingales, otherwise I know not what to make of them.

— Edward Lhuyd, Letter from Swansey, Sept. 14 1696,
from *Early Science in Oxford*, Vol. XIV.

10. *The Birds of St Margaret's*

As we came out, we saw on the outside of (St Margaret's) island — that is to say, the seaward side — numbers of the Guillemots and Auks, young birds of the season, swimming on the smooth sea. These birds certainly do look, when swimming, exceedingly like ducks, and justify the mistake of the poor Welsh woman the boatmen were quizzing about. She had lived all her life without ever seeing the sea; but, coming to Llanelly in her old age, saw the young *Mers* swimming in the Bay. 'Oh, what a pity!' says the benevolent old woman; 'some poor body has lost their ducks, and here they are swimming in this great pond!'

Our old Palinurus was garrulous on the habits of birds. One or two things which he told me seemed worth recording, as I knew him to be a man of veracity. The Guillemot, or Mer, as he calls it, will never forsake her young while the latter are helpless; and if they be pursued and taken into a boat, the mother bird will follow, and shouts and even stones will not avail to drive her away. If true, this is a pretty trait of maternal affection.

A Cormorant was watching from the topmost edge of one of the slender columnar peaks. Suddenly he swooped down upon the sea, and disappeared beneath the surface, but presently emerged, bearing in his beak a silvery fish, which he carried back to his watch-tower. Then he gave a toss of his head upward, and without seeming to lose his grasp of the prey, so turned it, that it was swallowed head foremost. This is the universal custom with piscivorous birds, to swallow their finny victim head foremost; and the necessity of it will appear, when we consider the mode in which the fins and spines frequently project. But even instinct is sometimes at fault; and the incident we had just seen gave occasion to old Tommy to draw again on his stores of zoological memory.

'Once upon a time I was in Milford Haven: I see a Comoral (Cormorant) catch a gurnard. He had got 'un hold by the tail; and whether he forgot to throw 'un up, I don' know, but he tried to swallow 'un so. The prickles took him in the throat, and bless ye, Sir! he turned over in a minute!'

Philip Henry Gosse, *Tenby: A Seaside Holiday,* 1856.

11. *The Bishops and Clerks*

A seaboard this Island Ramsey rangeth in order the Bushop and his Clearkes being vii in nomber, all wayes seene at lowe water who are not without some small Quiristers, who shewe not themselves, but at spring tydes, and calm seas . . .

The Bushop and those his Clerkes preach deadly doctrine to their winter audience . . .

George Owen, *The Description of Penbrokshire,* 1603.

XII

Ships and the Sea

1. The Little Ships

The commodities carried in these little ships (which might range from 100 to 350 tons burthen) can be classified simply into exports and imports. The export included coal (or more often culm), salted herrings, cheese and woollens. The chief imports were Gascony wine, salt, sugar, some wheat, and general merchandise. These commodities call for little comment. The coal and culm were an obvious export from the South Pembrokeshire coalfield, where the Haven and its many branches cut right across the western end of the coalfield. Some of this coal and culm went to Spain and the continent generally, but most of it was destined for Ireland. The herrings, cheese and woollens are likewise the natural products of the environment. On the import side, salt was an obvious necessity as a preservative in the absence of refrigeration. The salting of meat and bacon was a well-known feature of the countryside. It must be remembered that the Pembrokeshire climate did not always allow grain crops (especially wheat) to mature fully. Bad harvests were common, and wheat and even barley had to be imported on occasions. Sugar was a tropical crop, and greatly prized by those wealthy enough to buy it. It usually reached the Pembrokeshire ports as a re-shipment from Bristol. Sometimes other tropical luxuries were involved in the incoming trade. In 1566 we hear of 'certain oranges with the mariners' at Milford. This is the first reference ever to the orange in Wales. Twenty years later, however, we hear of the same port handling '30,000 orendges and lemons' from France.

A brief comment is necessary on the importation of such large quantities of Gascony wine — one of the most common commodities handled in Pembrokeshire at this time — as well as on the general merchandise arriving regularly from Bristol into almost all these little ports.

It is well-known that in spite of some attempts to cultivate the vine in northern lands (South Pembrokeshire is no exception as we hear of attempts to grow the vine at Manorbier in the Middle Ages), wine and oil (particularly olive oil) were generally lacking, and had to be imported. The wine trade was particularly flourishing during the Middle Ages and, as time progressed, the commercial production of wines became concentrated in regions of specialised viticulture. In the late thirteenth century the wines of La Rochelle were pre-eminent, while in the fourteenth, they probably took second place after those of Gascony. By 1480 English merchants appear in force in the wine markets of Bordeaux, which was the chief port for exporting these wines to northern Europe. The large quantities of Gascony wine imported into Pembrokeshire in Tudor times are a good indication of the prosperity of the Tudor gentry in West Wales at this period, reflecting, as they do, English tastes in food and drink, as well as the atmosphere of the Royal Court with their own kinsfolk on the Throne. Furthermore, it must be remembered that especially before the Reformation, the wine ships did not return empty to the French ports; on the contrary, they offered ideal facilities for pilgrims and others desirous of travelling to France. Wherever pilgrims from Pembrokeshire, or elsewhere, were landed on French soil, they made for Bordeaux (if their ship did not go there directly). Bordeaux was the gathering place for the many thousands of pilgrims who journeyed annually to the famous shrine of St James at Compostella in north-west Spain. It is worth re-calling in this context that in St Mary's Church in Haverfordwest there is an interesting tomb of one of these pilgrims who had visited Santiago de Compostella. The stone carved figure of the pilgrim shows him dressed in pilgrim garments and wearing a satchel over the right shoulder with the three scallop sheels — the badge worn by all pilgrims who had visited Santiago — clearly shown.

E. G. Bowen, 'Seafaring along the Pembrokeshire Coast in the days of the Sailing Ships' in *The Pembrokeshire Historian*, No. 4, 1972.

2. *A Terrible Shipwreck*

A terrible shipwreck took place near Solva in 1773, when a large vessel, the *Phoebe and Peggy*, bound from Philadelphia to Liverpool, was dashed to pieces somewhere between Porth y Bwch and the entrance to Solva Harbour. Sixty souls and a valuable cargo were lost, although the vessel's own lifeboat came in safely.

Six or seven captains of vessels belonging to Solva went out to render assistance, but on the return journey their boats were swamped or struck the Black Rock and all were lost. The bodies of Henry John, William Woolcock and Peter Richard were afterwards washed ashore.

An old story says that the bodies of a woman and her baby were also washed in. A woman who lived in a cottage in the Gwadn Valley, and who was pregnant at the time, broke the lady's fingers in order to get off her gold rings and stripped the baby of its clothing for the use of her own child — but that was not to be — at the confinement both she and the baby died.

F. W. Warburton, *The History of Solva,* 1944.

3. *Shipments*

Herrings do not assume marked prominence in the earlier coasting books of Milford — though there is one out-shipment from Tenby in 1566, and one in-shipment of 'empty casks' from Bristol to St David's in the same year. The absence of herring shipments from the in-coasting traffic to the Pembrokeshire ports seems to indicate that Pembrokeshire fishermen supplied all the herrings necessary to meet the local sustenance demand. During the closing years of the century, however, there are clear indications of a fairly thriving herring industry, with exports of herrings — on the foreign side to France and Ireland — and on the coasting side to Bristol, Carmarthen, Chester, and Liverpool. The activities of the Pembrokeshire seamen in the Newfoundland fisheries were somewhat occasional. Newland fish, along with dry and wet fish, were sometimes imported from the Somerset and Devon coast. The oyster industry was not much developed — but there is reference to one out-shipment of 20,000 oysters from Tenby in 1582.

The out-traffic in minerals was not considerable. There are instances of minor shipments of lead, and a little surprising, only one shipment of slate-stones from Newport in Kemes. Pembrokeshire coal, mostly monopolised by the Irish market, entered the out-coasting trade in only very modest proportions. Examples, however, occur of the transport of local coal to Plymouth (1585), Dartmouth (1586), London (1586) and to Pwllheli and Aberystwyth (1587). Among other commodities (apart from the products of the local minor metal and leather industries), which entered the out-going trade from time to time, mention may be made of two other specialities of the premier county, namely — oreashes or kelps (apparently burnt sea-weed for use as manure) and Pembrokeshire mats.

E. A. Lewis, *The Welsh Port Books (1550-1603),* 1927.

4. *Trade*

In return, the Pembrokeshire ports received salt from France and Portugal, haberdashery from Bristol, cloth from Brittany and live-stock from Ireland, more especially horses. This trade grew appreciably from year to year, supplemented with consignments of horseshoes and spurs, and was valued more than any other. Wales was not a country that bred horses of quality, although some shires like Montgomeryshire had formerly been famed for their horses. By the end of the century, so many Pembrokeshire people were engaged in trade that it was accounted one of the principal means of livelihood. George Owen, the squire of Henllys, wrote of his own shire,

'The Countrey, especiallye of late years, is fallen much to trade to sea, and a great parte of the Countrye people are seamen and maryners . . . many of them contynuallye abroade at sea'.

It is a profession that has ever since engaged the affection of the inhabitants of Pembrokeshire.

G. Dyfnallt Owen, *Elizabethan Wales,* 1964.

5. *Coal of Rare Quality*

Most of the gentlemen of the shire are well served with wood for their fuel, but for the most part those that dwell near the coal or that may have it carried by water with ease, use most coal fires in their kitchens and some in their halls, because it is a ready fire and very good and sweet to roast and boil meat; and void of smoke where ill chimneys are, and doth not require a man's labour to cleave wood and feed the fire continually. Next unto the wood or rather to be preferred before it for smell is the coal fire for the generality of it, as that which serveth most people and especially the chief towns. This coal may be numbered as one of the chief commodities of this countrey and is so necessary as without it the countrey would be in great distress. It is called stone coal for the hardness thereof, and is burned in chimneys and grates or iron, and being once kindled giveth a greater heate than light, and delighteth to burn in dark places. It serveth also for smiths to work, though not so well as the other kind of coal called the running coal; for that when it first kindleth it melteth and runneth as wax, and groweth into one clod, whereas this stone coal burneth apart and never clingeth together.

This kind of coal is not noisome for the smoke, nor nothing so loathsome for the smell as the running coal is, whose smoke annoyeth all things near it, as fine linen and men's hands that warme themselves by it, but this stone coal yieldeth in a manner no smoke after it is kindled, and is so pure that fine cambric or lawn is usually dried by it without any strain or blemish, and is a most proved good drier of mault therein passing wood, fern, or straw. This coal for the rare quality thereof was carried out of this country to the city of London to the late Lord Treasurer Burleigh by a gentleman of experience to shew how far the same excelled that of Newcastle, wherewith the city of London is served, and I think, if the passing were not so tedious, there would be great use made of it. . .

The digging of this coal is of ancient time used in Pembrokeshire but not in such exact and skilful sort as now it is, for in former time they used no engines for lifting up of the coals out of the pit, but made their entrance slope, so as the people carried the coals upon their backs along stairs which they called landways, whereas now they sink their pits down right four square about six or seven foot square, and with a windlass turned by four men they draw up the coals a barrell full at once by a rope; this they call a downright door. The lord of the land hath either rent, or the third barrell after all charges of the work deducted . . .

They now most commonly sink down right twelve, fourteen or twenty fathom before they come to the coal whereas in old time four fathom was counted a great labour. When they find it, they work sundry holes, one for every digger, some two, some three or four, as the number of diggers are: each man working by candle light and sitting while he worketh. Then they have bearers, which are boys that bear the coals in fit baskets on their backs, going always stooping by reason of the lowness of the pit, each bearer carrieth this basket six fathom where, upon a bench of stone he layeth it, where meeteth him another boy with an empty basket, which he giveth him and taketh that which is full of coals, and carrieth it as far, where another meeteth him, and so till they come under the door where it is lifted up. In one pit there will be sixteen persons, whereof there will be three pickaxes digging, seven bearers, one filler, four winders, two riddlers, who riddle the coals when it is aland — first to draw the small coal from the big by one kind of riddle, then the second riddling with a smaller riddle with which they draw small coals for the smiths from the culm, which is indeed but very dust, which serveth for lime burning. These people will land about eighty or hundred barrels of coal in a day. Their tools about this work is pickaxes with a round poll, wedges and sledges to batter the rocks that cross their work.

All times of the year is indifferent for working, but the hot weather is worst by reason of sudden damps that happen, which often times causeth the workmen to swound, and will not suffer the candles to burn, but the flame waxing blue of colour will of themselves out. They work from six o'clock to six o'clock, and rest an hour at noon, and eat their allowance, as they term it, which is ob. (halfpenny) in bread to every man, and iiijd. in drink among a dozen: this is of custom on the charge of the pit, although they worke on their own charge. All their worke is by candle light throughout the year.

The dangers in digging these coals is the falling of the earth and killing of the poor people, or stopping of the way forth, and so die by famine, or else the sudden irruption of standing waters in old works. The workmen of this black labour observe all abolished holy days and cannot be weaned from that folly.

George Owen, *The Description of Penbrokshire,* 1603.

6. *Unlicensed Cargoes*

Wheat, barley and malt were shipped to Spain, the uncompromising enemy of Protestant England, from the havens of Pembrokeshire, and the merchants of Tenby and Milford made it no secret that they would counter any interference by Crown officials with force of arms if necessary. The Government had good reason to be perturbed, for, apart from the incorrigibility of the merchants, this clandestine traffic to Spain depleted the wheat resources of the shire causing the price of corn to rise — to the distress of the poorer classes, always a sore point with the Elizabethan authorities.

But Pembrokeshire must have been a constant source of irritation to the Government, and one reason was not far to seek. The searcher at Pembrokeshire in 1572, George Clerk, was a rogue of the deepest hue, if all the accusations levelled against him were true. He had accepted bribes right and left, from the mayor of Tenby, who, with others, had sent a shipload of leather to Spain, from George Devereux, gentleman, who had despatched a cargo of wheat to the same hostile country, and from other interested quarters which had not forgotten to add the gallant gesture of presenting his wife with a valuable mantle. Any attempt to put an end to his pernicious practices had been decisively crushed. His under-searcher had presumed to interfere and had been assaulted and wounded, once at the hands of the mayor of Tenby himself. His superior, the Customs Officer at Carmarthen, had undergone a series of tribulations when he had tried to interfere. They began with a spate of 'evil words' showered upon him by the inhabitants of Tenby, the words soon being replaced by blows, and ended with his being marooned on the island of Caldey by the crew of a French ship, whose unlicensed cargo of leather, wax and beans he had rather hastily tried to confiscate single-handed. Clerk's conduct, brutality and machinations were not surprising, for everyone in Pembrokeshire knew — although London could not be expected to share the knowledge — that he owned a tavern in Angle openly patronised by Callice and other notorious pirates.

G. Dyfnallt Owen, *Elizabethan Wales*, 1964.

7. THE FISHING LASS OF HAKIN

*A new sea song in the sea style set to a new sea tune sung at sea by a
seafaring man over a can of sea liquor called Phlip.*

Ye sailors bold both great and small
That navigate the ocean,
Who love a lass that's fair and tall,
Come, hearken to my motion;
You must have heard of Milford Haven
All harbours it surpasses,
I know no port this side of Heaven
So famed for handsome lasses.

In Milford on your larboard hand
We found a town called Hakin,
The snuggest place in all the land
For lads inclined to raking;
There all the girls were cleanly drest
As witty as they are pretty,
But one exceeded all the rest,
And this was charming Betty.

A fisherman her father was,
Her mother a fisherwoman,
And she herself a fishing lass
Perhaps possessed by no-man;
She'd bait her hook with lug or crab,
No fisherman so nimble,
And at her oar she was a dab,
But never at her thimble.

Assist me, all the wat'ry tribe,
I find my wit a-flagging
As I endeavour to describe
This precious pearl of Hakin;
Ye mermaids tune my merry song,
And Neptune bless my darling,
Your smoking altars shall ere long
Be spread with sole and sparling.

Her fishing dress was clean and neat,
It set me all a-quaking,
I loved her, and could almost eat
This maiden ray of Hakin;
If ere you saw a cuttle fish,
Her breasts are more inviting,
Like shaking blubbers in a dish,
And tender as a whiting.

Her cheeks are as a mackrel plump,
No mouth of mullet moister,
Her lips of tench would make you jump,
They open like an oyster,
Her chin as smooth as river trout,
Her hair as rockfish yellow,
God's Sounds! I view her round about
But never saw her fellow.

When hungry people write for bread,
Whom they call poetasters,
They talk of fires in topmast head,
Of Pollax and of Castor's;
Her eyes afford a brighter mark
Than all those flashy meteors,
Like Milford Lights even in the dark
Revealing all her features.

Whene'er a smile sits on her lip
I'm brisk as bottled cider,
I quite renounce and leave my ship
And never can abide her;
Whene'er she speaks, so sweet her tone
I leap like spawning salmon,
And when she sings I'm all her own,
I serve no Jove nor Mammon.

But if she frowns I'm gone to pot,
As dead as pickled herring,
The muscles of my heart must rot
And split from clew to earring;
Then in my hammock sink me deep
Within the sight of Hakin,
Then sure she'll melancholy weep
As turtles at their taking.

Let doctors kill, let merchants cheat,
Let courtiers cogg and flatter,
Let gluttons feed on costly meat,
Let me have Betty's platter;
To mess with her I'd spend my days
On pilchard and on poor-John,
Let richer folks have if they please
Their turbot and their sturgeon.

Lewis Morris (1700-65).

XIII

Food

1. Rural Delicacies

As the main component of a pie, a rabbit was superb. Mixed with pieces of old streaky belly bacon, well cured, and onions, with home-made crust enveloping all, it was a most delectable dish. Boiled with a lump of bacon it made a delicious *cawl*. Cold, the pieces of rabbit were a convenient meal with pieces of bread and butter. My sister often fried a disjointed rabbit using butter, bacon fat, or dripping. The work of the night being over, I'd fall into bed already occupied by a younger brother, callously placing my cold back against his warm one, to cull some instant warmth. The morning would come all too soon, with its cowshed chores, and then away to school half-doped by lack of sleep and fatigue. In my boyhood I suffered from the lack of two things, — sleep, and Bird's custard, which I thought was tastier than nectar. I suppose I never asked mother to make gallons of it, or she would have done so — but it was something for which I then had a craving. Now I can afford unlimited custard, I don't eat it at all. Other foods which I considered delicacies were Palethorpe's sausages, which like every other sausage, has never regained its pristine perfection; Hume's tinned salmon — and Skipper's Norwegian brisling in oil or tomato.

James Williams, *Give Me Yesterday*, 1971.

2. Salmon

I will speak of the river fish, whereof the salmon shall have the first place, partly for the plenty and store thereof taken in many parts and places of the country, but chiefly for the excellence and daintiness thereof . . . This fish is best in season, at his first coming from the sea, where he goeth to wash himself, and returneth into the fresh river, most bright, and shining, fat and delicate, and the longer he traveleth up the river, beating himself against the banks, rocks and shelves, the leaner he goeth; they are chiefly in season in the spring, and all the summer. This fish the sooner he be boiled after his taking, the more sweet, and delicate he proveth in eating.. . . . A merry writer, likening the parts of this fish to a fair woman, sayeth, that about the jaws, the eyes and the belly are the sweetest parts of the salmon.

George Owen, *The Description of Penbrokshire,* 1603.

3. *Sgadan Abergwaun*

Fishguard (Abergwaun being the Welsh for Fishguard, i.e. **Aber,** *river mouth,* **Gwaun,** *the name of the local river) Herrings are of exceptional quality and used in many unusual ways.*

8 medium-size filleted herrings
1 large peeled, cored and sliced apple
2lb. peeled and sliced potatoes
1 large peeled and sliced onion
1 heaped teaspoon made mustard
1 teaspoon chopped sage
1 level tablespoon butter or margarine
salt and pepper to taste
boiling water

Lay the fillets of fish flat, sprinkle with salt and pepper, and paint over a little of the mustard on each, then roll up the fillets. Lightly grease an ovenproof dish and line it with half the sliced potatoes, then layer it with the sliced apple, then onion and finally the herring rolls. Sprinkle with chopped sage and season again. Cover with the remaining potatoes, and half fill the dish with boiling water. Put the rest of the butter on top in small pieces, cover and bake in a moderate oven (350°F) for 45 minutes. Remove the lid, and allow the top to brown for a further ½ hour.

This recipe can also be used with mackerel fillets, anchovies, pilchards, John Dory, or tuna fish, and half cider and half water can be used if like.
Serves 4-6.

Theodora FitzGibbon, *A Taste of Wales,* 1971.

4. *Katt Pie*

Templeton Fair, Pembrokeshire (November 12th), specialised in Katt Pie for over two hundred years.

To make the pastry
Boil the suet in the water for 5 minutes, then stir in the flour mixed with the salt and mix very thoroughly until the mixture leaves the sides. Turn out quickly onto a thickly floured board and roll out to a thickness of just under ½ in. This should be done quickly before the suet hardens. When cool, cut into circles, or more easily into two large circles, and place on a greased tin the correct size. Arrange the filling in layers: currants, sugar and mutton, seasoned to taste. Moisten with water around the edges and put on the lid, pressing down tightly to keep the filling in. Make a small incision on top to let the air escape, brush over with milk or egg and bake in a moderate oven for about 30-40 minutes. Eat warm.

Nowadays when suet pastry is not often used, this pie can be made either with short-crust pastry, or butter or margarine can be substituted for the suet in the above recipe. Personally I prefer this pie made in a deep pie dish rather than in individual small ones, for the fruit, sugar and meat amalgamate in a delicious manner.

For the crust
1lb flour
8oz grated suet
½ teaspoon salt
1½ gills (¾ cup) boiling water

For the filling
1lb lean minced mutton or lamb
8oz (1 cup) currants
6oz (½ cup) brown sugar
salt and pepper
a little milk or beaten egg

Theodora FitzGibbon, *A Taste of Wales,* 1971.

5. *Oysters Galore*

Now for shell fish, this sea is also no niggard both for plenty and several kinds, among whom before all I will give place to the oyster which Milford Haven yieldeth, most delicate and of several sorts and in great abundance, and is a commodity much uttered in many shires, for by water they are transported to Bristol and to the Forest of Dean, from whence by land they are sent to Somerset, Gloucestershire and some parts of Wiltshire, and often-times up the river [Severn] as far as Worcester and Salop: they are also carried by land to the shires of Carmarthen, Cardigan, Brecknock, Radnor, Monmouth, Hereford, Montgomery, and (al)so to Ludlow and other parts of Shropshire. The chiefest places of taking these oysters is Lawrenny, Llangwm, the Pill and the Crow. The first is accounted the fattest, whitest and sweetest; the Pill oyster for that it is less washed with fresh water tasteth more salt, and therefore more pleasing to some, and is larger grown; and the Crow oyster striveth with them both for delicacy.

These oysters are taken by dredge (within Milford Haven), which is done with a kind of iron made with bars, having a piece of horse or bullock skin sewn to it like a bag in such sort as that it, being fastened to a rope's end, is cast into the bottom of Milford at eight or ten fathom deep, and is dragged at a boat's end by two rowers which row up and down the channel. And so the bag of leather, being made apt to scrape up all manner of things lying in the bottom, gathereth up the oysters that bred there over certain known beds, which bag being filled, they draw up and empty their oysters into their boat, applying their labour so all day. And when they have done they row to some appointed place near the shore at full sea, and there cast out oysters in a great heap which they call beds, where every tide overfloweth them, and so are kept for loading of boats to Bristol and other places.

Besides this Milford oyster there is a great kind of oyster, gathered at Caldy and Stackpool, which eaten raw seems too strong a meat for weak stomachs and must be parted in two, three or four before he may be eaten by reason of his exceeding bigness, and are not counted so pleasing as the former, and therefore is used in pies, stewings, broths, fried and boiled, wherein he is found most delicate. The oyster in ancient time were accounted seasonable in those months only that had 'R', but experience now teacheth that in May, June, July and August there are some found to be very sweet and wholesome.

George Owen, *The Description of Penbrokshire,* 1603.

6. *Black Butter*

Near St David's . . . especially at Eglwys Abernon, and in other places, they gather, in the spring-time, a kind of Alga or sea-weed, with which they make a sort of food call'd Lhavan or Lhawvan, in English Black butter. Having gather'd the weed, they wash it clean from sand and slime, and sweat it between two tile-stones; then they shred it small, and knead it well, as they do dough for bread, and make it up into great balls or rolls, which some eat raw, and others, fry'd with oatmeal and butter. It is accounted sovereign against all distempers of the liver and spleen.

William Camden, *Britannia.* 1586.

7. *Gathering Laver*

The carrying of burdens on the head, a survival of very old times, is less universal than it was ten years ago, but still is fairly common; only women carry in this manner, and it is wonderful what a weight even slight young girls can bear with ease, once it is placed on the head by a comrade: brimming pails of water or milk, or huge, ungainly bundles of drift wood. The custom gives a splendid, upright carriage and even, swinging walk, and it is a thousand pities that it should ever decline. The gathering of laver from the rocks is one of the chief industries of the Angle villagers, and one meets very picturesque groups returning from the shore, in patched and tattered garments (sea water being ruinous), with great bundles of drift wood poised on their heads. They collect the laver from the rocks beyond Freshwater Bay, about three miles from Angle, and have there built a number of little huts of wreck-wood, thatched with sedge, in which to store it (which go by the name of Little Angle); it is collected weekly and sent off by train to Swansea, where the Rhondda Valley miners consider it a great delicacy, eaten as a vegetable. In appearance it is something like what is known as Gold Beaters' Skin, sticking flat and close to the rocks; the picking of it, all wet with salt water, makes the fingers very sore at first.

Mary Beatrice Mirehouse, *South Pembrokeshire,* 1910.

8. *Killing the Pig*

With noisy fluency, the butcher honed a new knife, bigger and wider than the dagger-pointed killing blade, revolved the carcase on its creaking gambrel to catch the northern light, and drew the shining blade with careful precision between the two-seven-a-side lines of small virgin teats, until the pink guideline joined the gash in the throat. Then he cut in deeply, the walls of fat parted and opened, the voluptous reek of hot insides and vital fluids flooded the kitchen. He cut away the moorings and with effort lifted the squelching mass of streaming blue-grey gut into the galvanised bath.

Goodies were salvaged and segregated — brown kidneys, dark blood-frothed liver were placed in Nana's enamel dish, the big pluck of lights put by to boil for the Indian Game cockerels, the bladder, expertly excised, squeezed and emptied — a process which always produced a grin from the butcher — and passed to Llewelyn. Later, Schoolin would fill the touch bag with straining breath, tie it with a leather lace and hang it in the beams to dry, until it cured into a virtually punctureless winter football. Finally, the carcase was sluiced down with cold well water, a potato inserted to keep the mouth open and the door carefully secured against Boof and Butterpaws.

Schoolin and family went to bed agog with harvest excitement, nourished by back-kitchen visits, to bathe the carcase in the gold light of high-held candles, regaling themselves with the glory of the fulfilled and forgotten Blodwen. Ten o'clock the following day the butcher arrived, with his frail of cutting-up instruments. Pig was held motionless by Schoolin and Dafydd Moon as he cut off the head, carved through the tendons to remove the front feet, halved the carcase with short, sharp, cunningly-timed blows with his black-bladed butcher chopper and laid the two halves of the pig on the cold blue stone slab which ran the length of one wall. He measured, cut off, shaped, trimmed and tidied the hams, sides and shoulders. A piece from the backbone fillet was cut out for his own lunch which, when his task was finished, filled the kitchen with the nasal manna of fried fresh-killed pork.

The butcher mounted his bike, pedalled away with five shillings and a joint, and the family moved into the back kitchen to allocate pieces to those on the take-and-give list, especially on this occasion to Mrs Moon.

Using salt from the two 7-lb salt loaves, crunchingly flattened with the rolling pin, and heaped high in readiness from the previous night,

Nana began to rub pink flesh and snow-white fat with seven of salt to one of saltpetre mixture. The hams were later treated with brown sugar, and remained a week longer than the flitches and shoulders which were lifted, washed, drained, dried, and hung from the black-smith's rafter hooks after three weeks. (Curing was always a success except for one shameful year when a ham cut after four months in the rafters was found to be maggoty and, taken out after dark, given a felon's burial in the midden.) The head was boiled to make jellied brawn.

In the evening, chopped liver, pork scraps, heart, onions, leaves of dried sage and fresh parsley, were mixed with stale breadcrumbs in a deep-dish by Llewelyn's grandmother, who signified her completion, as she had for twenty years (as though accepting a *novitiate*), with the words 'bring on the veil', and the lacy membrance of lard which had enclosed Blodwen's stomach was cut into little squares. The old lady laboriously rolled helpings of the mixture into small balls in the hollow of her palm, encasing the savoury bombs with cut-up sections of the veil. Finally she cleaned the mix off her fingers, laid the faggots side by side in the baking dishes, sucked her wedding ring, and for the next fireside hour regaled her ancient nose with the rich fumes of her faggots which filled the kitchen with cargoes of fragrance, the memory of which gives Llewelyn jaw-ache after fifty years.

Llewelyn Jones, *Schoolin's Log,* 1980.

XIV

Sport and Leisure

1. The Squirearchy at Play

Race meetings were a popular sport in the social lives of the Pembrokeshire squires, the recognised meeting points being at Haverfordwest, Newgale Sands and Stackpole Court. The Haverfordwest races commenced as a yearly event in 1726 when the county gentry formed a society and arranged to contribute a purse of thirty-six guineas, to be run for on Portfield Common. After the races at Newgale the gentry were entertained with such rural amusements as men jumping in sacks for a new shovel and grinning for tobacco. On part of the Stackpole Court demesne there was a race course one mile flat, and, once every year, Lady Cawdor presented a silver cup to the fastest horse bred within the hundred of Castlemartin.

A frequent accompaniment to horse-racing was cock-fighting. This sport had been suppressed during the Interregnum but after the Restoration it was revived. That this sport was popular among the Pembrokeshire squires is apparent from the custom duties of many property leases which often enjoined the tenants to keep a cock and, more frequently, one or a number of dogs.

The latter were maintained by the tenantry in good condition for fox-hunting. In 1777 Lord Milford of Picton Castle owned a pack of twenty-eight hounds which were kept in this way. Fox-hunting was the sporting passion of the eighteenth century gentry and other squires, besides Lord Milford, had their own pack of hounds and a huntsman. In addition to these private packs there was the Pembrokeshire Hunt, a county pack cared for by a paid huntsman and maintained by subscriptions of the squires. The second week of November of each year was dedicated to the subscribers of the Hunt when three meetings of the hounds and three balls were held at Haverfordwest.

Shooting was another favourite activity of the squires, the game including rabbits, hares, pigeons, pheasants, partridges, woodcock and snipe. Great pains were taken in feeding certain of the game, and the game-laws preserved them for the exclusive sporting pleasure of the squire and his friends. Lord Cawdor's diaries between 1815 and 1819 reveal his great love of shooting. It has been estimated that the number of gun days on his estate at Stackpole usually ranged from a hundred to a hundred and fifty a year.

The summer sports of the Pembrokeshire squires were cricket and sailing. In 1832 Mrs M. D. Phillips of Clynfiew, North Pembrokeshire, wrote to her daughter, the Baroness de Rutzen of Slebech, informing her that 'we drove to the cricket match on Monday'. Much more popular, however, was sailing, and certain squires owned family yachts. Sir John Philipps of Picton noted in his diary for 10 August, 1759 — 'Went on yacht on ye River below Hubberston with my wife and daughters'. On 22 June 1798, Lord Cawdor and his family boarded their yacht, the *Speedwich,* at Stackpole Quay, and sailed round Caldy Island, dining on board. On certain occasions the gentry competed in sailing matches on Milford Haven, the prize being a silver cup presented by one of their number.

While Tenby was the local social centre for the Pembrokeshire squires in the summer months, Haverfordwest was the main attraction during the winter. The discomforts involved in travelling during this period led many families to maintain winter houses there. Balls, dinners, card-parties, and plays were organised for their amusement. During Assize Week balls were given by the sheriff, the county representative and the foreman of the jury. The ladies arrived at these balls in sedan chairs, and the dancing continued into the early hours of the morning. Haverfordwest was, too, one of the main meeting centres of the Society of Sea Sergeants, having Jacobite sympathies, a society to which many of the Pembrokeshire squires belonged. The round of balls, dinner parties and yachting trips during their festive week did much to add to the social gaiety of the town.

David Howell, 'Landed Society in Pembrokeshire, c. 1680-1830' in
The Pembrokeshire Historian, No. 3, 1971.

2. *Tenby Exalted*

The circumstances that conspired in the outset to exalt Tenby to consideration as a bathing place, are rather extraordinary, and may be best explained by the recital of a local anecdote that came to our knowledge while we remained for a few days in the town. It appears from this relation that the ancient Welsh custom of reading prayers for the success of the fishery before the men ventured to cast their nets into the sea was observed at this port with much religious scruple, till about five and twenty, or at most thirty years ago. There was a small chapel stationed on a rocky projection of the shore, that was appropriated solely to the performance of this singular service. Thither the parish priest repaired before the fishery began, to invoke a benediction on the draught, and there his deputy remained to receive the tythe of the capture when the fishery was over. This custom, which had prevailed in monastic times throughout the Principality, had been sensibly on the decline for the last sixty years. In most of the fishing towns it became extinct by degrees, till at length about the time before-mentioned it only remained in force at Tenby. The worthy incumbent, aware of this, conceived it might as well be laid aside in his district. To this the fishermen had no objection, provided he should wave his tythe with the ceremony. But, if the tongue of rumour reports true, he tenaciously insisted this could not be right. Although the prayers were deemed superfluous, he seems to have considered it as a matter both of conscience and of duty to demand his share of the capture as before. At last the altercation was happily terminated by mutual compromise, the clergyman consented to receive a moderate compensation in lieu of his tythe of fish, and the custom being abolished, the chapel was no longer useful to either party.

Thus the building remained deserted for some years, till an intelligent apothecary of Haverfordwest, Mr Esau Jones, struck with its admirable situation, for a bathing house, applied for leave to fit it up to his mind, for the accommodation of a few patients, to whom he had prescribed the use of the sea waters. This permission was no sooner obtained than put in execution, and thus the *ci-devant* chapel was transformed into a bathing-house; the first regular establishment of that kind ever projected at this fashionable watering place.

This event took place rather better than twenty years ago. In the first season the adventurer so far succeeded to his wishes, that on the summer following he enlarged his scheme, and was able to accommodate a greater number of patients than in the year preceding. Other speculative strangers, encouraged by his example, erected two or three houses on the cliffs for the use of the summer visitors; then the hotel arose, and speedily after the new range of lodging houses began to assume a more important figure. The inference is natural: some of the adventurers have already retired in easy circumstances, acquired by their judicious and well-timed speculations, the place has increased in respectability, and rising every year into higher consideration, promises, at no very distant period, to become a spot of greater resort in the summer season, than perhaps any other bathing place on the coast of Wales. — The civic honours of this ancient town ought not to be forgotten: Tenby is a corporate town, governed by a mayor and other proper officers. The parliamentary interest prevails in favour of Lord Cawdor, who has a splendid seat at Stackpole, fourteen computed miles to the westward. Tenby, from time immemorial, is celebrated for the amazing abundance and variety of the fish tribe that haunt its shores, and the sea immediately adjacent, in allusion to which the Welsh call it Dynbegh-y-Piscoid.

E. Donovan, *Descriptive Excursions through South Wales and Monmouthshire in the year 1804.*

3.   Bosherston: The Summer Fishing

If to me the chief glory of our Bosherston water is the pike fishing, there are others, of differing temperament perhaps, who would put the sport provided by its fine tench above it; and even though I myself give pike first place, I will not deny that the tench is a most exciting fish, a fine fish to catch and with its own beauty and set of associations. I have described how they can be seen from the big bluff cruising around the margins of the weedbeds (swimming, incidentally, rather faster than carp do when they can be seen on the surface) or drifting, as it seems, aimlessly, across the wide reaches of the lake, for from this height, and in this clear water, they can be seen a hundred yards and more out from the bank. They seem to be concentrated in their greatest numbers, here at the bottom of the bluff, but I have seen odd ones up as far as the Bosherston dyke, and observed the clouds of tiny bubbles that the fish send up as they feed. They have been taken nowhere else in the lake except in a small area near the Eightarch Bridge, and I have never heard of any being caught in the middle arm. But these observations are by no means conclusive. Who can guess what a clearing of the weed in certain parts of the lake will produce? The lake is full of surprises. Last week, tench fishing in the early hours, my companion's float shot away very much more quickly and suddenly than in usual with tench bites. He thought he had a roach at first, a nice one of nearly a pound, but when it was in the land-net we could see that it was unmistakably a rudd, the first that I had ever seen or even heard of from the lake.

There is a legend of carp also, but I am sure that if they were present they would have been seen, since they are much more inclined than tench to show themselves in sunny weather and the tench are plain enough to be seen. There are certainly great eels in the water, though the species is not there in great numbers, but these are fish I am not inclined to try for specially. A fellow club member does fish for them though, legering with a small dead roach: the best so far was just over five pounds, a specimen eel, I believe, and he has tales of being broken by much larger ones.

Clive Gammon, Hook, Line and Spinner, 1959.

4. *Deer-parks*

One indispensable adjunct to their estates, or so many gentlemen thought, was a deer park. It was a fashion much practised in England, where every manor house with any pretensions had a special enclosure for deer. Even the parsimonious Lord Burleigh had been known to spend a great deal of money on them. It meant a heavy outlay, since the parks had to be surrounded with walls or hedges to restrain the deer from wandering, but this consideration did not unduly worry the Welsh squires. The gentry of South Wales certainly spared no expense. Sir John Perrot erected a wall around his park at Carew in which he kept a good stock of fallow deer.

G. Dyfnallt Owen, Elizabethan Wales, 1964.

5. *Early Theatre*

The first play known to have been performed in Tenby was in 1790 — probably at the Blue-Ball tavern in Upper Frog Street. It was here that Nelson with Sir William and Lady Hamilton saw the 'Mock Doctor' performed in 1802. So great was the enthusiasm for such plays among the polite society of Tenby that, in the summer of 1810, a new theatre was erected in Frog Street from the generous sub-scriptions of such people as Lord Milford of Picton Castle, Sir William Paxton, Sir Henry Mannix and John Owen of Orielton. In August 1817 the 'gentlemen visitors' were induced to play all the parts in a performance of 'John Bull' and 'Miss in her Teens'. We are told the 'heroines' were greeted with much applause. This theatre was rebuilt in 1818 and became notable as the scene of a visit by Edmund Kean, one of the greatest actors of the London stage, in August 1828.

David Howell, 'Landed Society in Pembrokeshire, c.1680-1830' in
The Pembrokeshire Historian, No. 3, 1971.

6. *Chess*

But the thing most worthy of note is, that from time immemorial the inhabitants . . . were expert at the scientific game of chess; for George Owen says, 'In ancient times in this parish [Whitechurch in Cemais], the meanest and simplest sort of people, yea, the plain ploughmen were skilful at chess play, and being altogether Welshmen of language, had proper names for the chess board and the several sorts of men. The play they called Fristiol Tawlbwrdd; the kings and queen by their usual names; the bishop they termed Elphin; the rooks, Brain Owen ap Urien; the pawns, merely a corruption of the French Paons, they properly called Y Paenod bach, the little peacocks; they also knew the motions of every sort of men, and would artfully manage the game, they never being dwelling out of their parish, but unliterate and brought up at the plough and harrow altogether. There are living at this day a few old men that are most skilful therein, and I have seen in my time very many. This I laid down as worthy note, that such simple people should be skilled in this so rare a play, that in most countreys not but of the best sort and the quickest wits are found to be expert therein.'

Richard Fenton, *A Historical Tour through Pembrokeshire,* 1811.

7. *The Game of Cnapan*

Of these *cnapan* days in Pembrokeshire there were wont to be five in number, the first at the Bury Sands, between the parishes of Nevern and Newport upon Shrove Tuesday yearly. The second at Pont

Gynon, on Easter Monday, between the parishes of Meline and Eglwyswrw, the third on Low Easter Day at Pwll Du in Penbedw between the parishes of Penrhydd and Penbedw, the fourth and fifth was wont to be at St Meugans in Cemais between Cemais men of the one party, and Emlyn men, and the men of Cardiganshire with them of the other party, the first upon Ascension Day, the other upon Corpus Christi Day, and these two last were the great and main places, far exceeding any of the former in multitude of people, for at these places there hath oftentimes been esteemed two thousand foot besides horsemen.

The companies being come together, about one or two of the clock after noon, beginneth the play in this sort. After a cry made, both parties draw together into some plain, all stripped bare saving a light pair of breeches, bare headed, bare bodied, bare legs and feet, their clothing being laid together in great heaps under the charge of certain keepers appointed for the purpose, for if he leave but his shirt on his back in the fury of the game, it is most commonly torn to pieces.

The foot company thus meeting, there is a round ball prepared of a reasonable quantity, so as a man may hold it in his hand and no more. This ball is of some massy wood as box, yew, crab or holly tree, and should be boiled in tallow for to make it slippery and hard to be held. This ball is called *cnapan* and is by one of the company hurled bolt upright into the air, and at the fall he that catcheth it hurleth it towards the country he playeth for. For goal or appointed place there is none, neither needeth any, for the play is not given over until the *cnapan* be so far carried that there is no hope to return it back that night.

The *cnapan* being once cast forth you shall see the same tossed backward and forward by hurling throws in strange sort, for in three or four throws you shall see the whole body of the game removed half a mile and more, and in this sort it is a strange sight to see a thousand or fifteen hundred naked men to concur together in a cluster in following the *cnapan* as the same is hurled backwards and forwards. There is besides the corps or main body of the play certain scouts of fore-runners whose charge is always to keep before the *cnapan* which way soever it pass. These always be of the adverse part, between the other party and home, lest by surreption the *cnapan* should be snatched by a borderer of the game and so carried away by foot or horse to those scouts. You shall all day hear the body of the main play cry with loud voices continually 'cadw ol', that is, 'Look well to their backs'.

And in this sort you shall in an open field see two thousand naked people follow this ball backwards and forwards, east, west, north and south, so that a stranger that casually should see such a multitude so ranging naked would think them distracted. It is strange to behold with what eagerness this play is followed, for in the fury of the chase they respect neither hedge, ditch, pale or wall, hill, dale, bushes, river or rock or any other passable impediment, but all seemeth plain unto them wherein also they show such agility in running, such activity in leaping, such strength and skilful deliverance in hurling, such boldness in assaulting, such stoutness in resisting, such policy in inventing, such skill in preventing, as taking them out of their game they are not able to perform or invent half the prowess or devices shown in the same, a thing much noted of men of judgement.

The horsemen have monstrous cudgels of three foot and a half long, as big as the party is well able to wield, and he that thinketh himself well horsed maketh means to his friends of the footmen to have the *cnapan* delivered him, which being gotten he putteth spurs and away as fast as the legs will carry. After him runneth the rest of the horsemen, and if they can overtake him he summoneth a delivery of the *cnapan,* which should be thrice by law of the game, but now they scarce give it once till he be strike, and if he hold the *cnapan* it is lawful for the assailant to beat him with his cudgel till he deliver it . . .

But now at this play private grudges are revenged, so that for every small occasion they fall by the ears, which being but once kindled between two, all persons on both sides become parties, so that sometimes you shall see five or six hundred naked men beating in a cluster together as fast as the fist can go, and there part must be taken, every man with his company, so that you shall see two brothers, the one beating the other, the man the master, and friend against friend.

You shall see gamesters return home from this play with broken heads, black faces, bruised bodies and lame legs, yet laughing and merrily jesting at their harms, telling their adversaries how he broke his head, to another that he struck him on the face and how he repaid the same to him again, and all this in good mirth, without grudge or hatred.

George Owen, The Description of Penbrokshire, 1603.

8. Entertainment Lacking

George Owen described some Welsh towns as being 'indifferent for intertaignements'. The studious squire of Henllys, in Pembrokeshire, was probably lamenting the inadequacy of comfortable lodgings, and the difficulty sometimes of finding any accommodation at all. In such an emergency, it was customary for travellers to request a night's lodging in private houses, and the traditional hospitality of the Welsh generally overcame the lurking suspicions that the innocent-looking stranger might turn out to be a thief, which was only too often the case.

But other forms of entertainment were conspicuously lacking. Unlike English towns, for instance, there was a singular absence of organised pageantry and presentation of mystery plays and interludes based on scenes from the Holy Scriptures. . . Haverfordwest Corporation also was activated by a sentiment of sympathy for its citizens who were at a loss of distractions. It maintained a company of waits to entertain them with music and song, and clothed them at the public's expense in liveries of grey frieze faced with green taffeta and ornamented with green moccado and green buttons.

G. Dyfnallt Owen, *Elizabethan Wales,* 1964.

XV

War and Strife

1.   The Subduing of Ireland

The subduing of Ireland being a whole realm by Strongbow, Earl of
this county, and his people, and bringing it in obedience and subjec-
tion to the kings of this land, while out of this country is descended
some of the chief and principal men in Ireland, as the Geraldines of
whom the Earls of Desmond and Kildare draw their paternal descent,
the Viscount Baltinglass, the Lord Roche, the Lord Barry, the
Flemings, barons of Slane, Fitzmorris baron of Kerry, MacJordan
baron of Dysart, the Wogans of Green Castle, a great and mighty
people there in times past. If Pembrokeshire people then were the
means of subduing Ireland to the kings of England, the one being a
kingdom and the other a principality, what glory can be greater and
what praise more worthy, and what other counties in this land may
vaunt themselves of such valiant attempts and happy success, and
therefore no marvel that this county was magnified above all the rest
of Wales to be a County Palatine and well might the king of England
call this his *Little England beyond Wales.*

George Owen, *The Description of Penbrokshire, 1603.*

2.   The Landing of Henry Tudor

. . . it is from Polydore Vergil's Chronicle that we are given the
clearest indications of the exact location of the landing. Vergil, of
course, wrote long after the event, but was in a good position to have
reliable information on the point. He has frequently been cited by
modern historians as the authority for their statements on the matter,
but never hitherto with sufficient attention to the significant details
which Vergil provided. He does not say Henry landed *at* Dale. On the

contrary, he very precisely says that a little before sunset, entering Milford Haven, he forthwith landed, and took first a place called Dale, which he had heard had been garrisoned against his landing the previous winter. The next day at dawn he set out for Haverfordwest, 10 miles from Dale.

If this account is to be relied upon (as most probably it is), then Henry did *not* land at Dale, but at the first feasible landing place inside the Haven, which is in fact Mill Bay, immediately on the Dale side of St Ann's Head. Mill Bay is a small beach and cove, sheltered on the one side by St Ann's Head, entirely invisible from Dale Point, Roads, Beach, and Castle. It is, indeed, separated from Dale Point by two substantial promontories (the modern West Blockhouse Point and Watwick Point), and two beaches (the modern Watwick Bay and Castlebeach Bay) the ascent from both of which is much steeper than it is from Mill Bay. Into the latter falls what is now only a very slight stream, fed by two small watercourses, the left-hand one of which leads up from the beach to Snailston Farm, and the right one to Brunt Farm, situated 200 feet above sea-level, and less than a third of a mile distant. The spot on the beach nearest as the crow flies to Brunt Farm is known to this day as Harry's Carthouse, and this, according to local tradition, is the precise spot where Henry himself landed. This spot is now a small cove largely buried by rock-fall, and no satisfactory explanation of the meaning of the name can be offered. On the other side of the beach, into which the stream runs, are still the remains of an old mill, the date of which cannot be ascertained, and which may or may not have given the bay its name, but the bay was called Mill Bay at least as early as 1595. Exactly opposite to Mill Bay, about a mile and a half eastwards, is West Angle Bay, the first practicable landing place within the Haven on the southern shore (also invisible from Dale Castle and Beach, but not from the tip of Dale Point). The state of the tide at sunset on Sunday, 7 August 1485, appears to have been entirely favourable for a landing at either point.

S. B. Chrimes in *The Welsh History Review,* II, 2, 1964.

3.   *The Pembroke Yeomanry*

On March 5th, 1794, Mr Pitt outlined to the House of Commons various measures for strengthening the internal defences. Foot soldiers must either march, or else be moved by sea. There was a need for greater mobility, and he employed the expression 'Yeomen Cavalry' for the first time.

That month a plan was sent to the Lord Lieutenant of each County which contained provision for the raising of 'Bodies of Cavalry' to consist of 'gentlemen and yeomanry' who would be exempt from the Militia Ballot and Horse Duty. They were to provide their own horses, the Government their arms and accoutrements. Training was to be authorised by the Lord Lieutenant and he, or the High Sheriff of the County, could call upon them for 'the suppression of riots or tumults within their own or adjacent Counties' as well as in the event of invasion. In such circumstances they were to receive pay as cavalry and be subject to Military Law. The plan was accepted with enthusiasm all over the United Kingdom. Lord Milford presided over a meeting of Pembrokeshire gentlemen in London on April 19th, 1794, at which it was decided to raise the 'Pembrokeshire Company of Gentlemen and Yeomanry Cavalry'.

In 1795 the Army List showed the following officers, together with the dates of their commissions, under the heading of 'Gentlemen and Yeomanry, Pembroke':

> Captain Richard Lord Milford, 17th July, 1794.
> Captain John Campbell, 31st August, 1794.
> Lieutenant Dudley Ackland, 31st August, 1794.
> Cornet John Lloyd, 31st August, 1794.

Each Captain was to raise a Troop of 50 men, Lord Milford's to be known as the Dungleddy Troop and recruited from the neighbourhood of Picton and Haverfordwest. John Campbell, to be raised to the Peerage as Lord Cawdor in 1796, was to form the Castlemartin Troop from the district around Stackpole. The uniform was to consist of boots and white breeches; a blue coatee with buff collar, cuffs and lapels, and a leather helmet with a bearskin crest and a turban of moleskin. This helmet was to be edged with white metal, bearing the words 'Pembroke Yeomanry'. They were to be armed with swords and pistols, with an additional twelve carbines a Troop. From the condition that they must provide their own riding horses, it would appear that the recruits were to be persons of some substance and responsibility.

It was in the winter of 1796 that the Castlemartin Troop was first called upon for service, parading on market days in the Pembroke district after disturbances caused by the shortage of bread. Early in the morning of February 23rd, 1797, they rode to Haverfordwest, crossing the Haven by ferry, and that evening were at Fishguard with the 750 men commanded by Lord Cawdor who had been mustered to oppose the 1,400 Frenchmen under William Tate, safely landed at Carreg Wastad Point the night before.

R. L. Howell, 'The Pembroke Yeomanry' in *The Pembrokeshire Historian,* No. 2, 1966.

4.   *The French Invasion*

Numerous instances occurred of French soldiers, singly or in pairs, being captured by the country people whilst they were in the act of plundering, or were overcome by the effects of their excesses, and not a few of the French soldiers were saved from the fury of the peasantry by the intervention of British officers. But the hero, or heroine, of these exploits was one Jemima Nicholas, a tall and masculine woman who followed the trade of a cobbler in Fishguard. This Amazon is reported to have marched out to Llanwnda armed with a pitchfork. Finding a party of twelve French soldiers in a field, she brought them back to the town as her prisoners, and went out again to look for more. Whether she accomplished this feat by force of arms, or the persuasion of her tongue, is not recorded, but the incident gained sufficient credence for a tombstone to be erected to her memory in Fishguard churchyard some years ago.

At Brestgarn, residence of the Rev David Bowen, a ludicrous incident occurred. A French soldier entered the house, and the ticking of the clock conveyed to his fuddled senses the idea that a man must be concealed inside. Levelling his musket at the clock face, he fired and the bullet hole may be seen in it to this day as one of the very few exhibits which have survived the intervening hundred and fifty years.

Most of the women folk had got away on the previous evening, but at Cotts there was a poor woman who was lying in bed with a newborn infant, unable to move. One unkind historian has said that her husband had left her to get on as best she could. However, when the French soldiers entered the house she pleaded her condition and was spared. Mary Williams of Caerlem was not so fortunate, although financially she did very well out of the invasion. On seeing a party of French soldiers approaching the house, she attempted to escape, but was brought to the ground my a musket ball in the leg, and was otherwise ill-treated. For this she received a Government pension of £40 per annum, and survived the event to enjoy it for fifty-six years.

There was not a house nor a cottage in the whole district of Pencaer which escaped the attentions of these *banditti,* and nearly a thousand pounds was paid out in compensation afterwards. The church of Llanwnda was entered and spoliated. The church records and registers were destroyed and the Communion plate stolen. Some days later a French officer on parole in Carmarthen had the temerity to offer it for sale, explaining that the inscription on the chalice **POCULUM ECCLESIAE DE LLANUNDA** showed that it had come from La Vendée. Perhaps it is needless to add that this subterfuge did not deceive Commissary Propert to whom it was offered, and the plate was returned to the churchwardens of Llanwnda . . .

If the part played by the red-cloaked women in compelling the French troops to lay down their arms is difficult to determine at this distance of time, it is but natural that so picturesque an incident should have captivated popular fancy sufficiently to lend itself to some degree of embellishment in the course of a century and a half, and the story varies considerably with the strength of the narrator's imagination. In its most ingenious version the Welsh women are arranged in some kind of military order, and made to march from the top of the Bigney Hill to the bottom, when, out of sight of the French, they are supposed to have wheeled left along a lane and back to the top of the Bigney to repeat the process all over again. In another form Lord Cawdor is said to have armed these women with firearms, roasting spits, pokers, and other implements, and lined the stone walls with them so that they could take part in the defence of the locality . . .

One imagines that if Cawdor had any muskets to spare he would have needed them for the gentlemen and volunteers who had joined up with him on his march, and that he was too much occupied with other matters to spend his time falling-in an assemblance of garrulous country-women, with the enemy undefeated and in full view. For the sake of historical accuracy it must be stated that to have had any effect on determining Tate to make his offer of surrender, this incident would have had to have taken place on the Thursday afternoon, but the exact time, or day, on which this martial array of women took place is not specified . . . That this tradition, for such it has become in the passage of time, is founded on fact, is proved by two original letters written at the time, showing that the women were there beyond a shadow of doubt, and ready to join in the fray if necessary.

No one will have the last word on this engaging episode, but from the foregoing it should be evident that the women must at least share the credit with the armed forces, and men of the countryside, in bringing the enemy to so speedy a surrender. Certain it is that this tradition will be perpetuated until the end of time.

E. H. Stuart Jones, *The Last Invasion of Britain,* 1950.

5.   *Surrender*

After receiving the message of acceptance of his terms on Friday morning, Lord Cawdor rode over to Trehowel to receive the surrender of Tate and his companions in arms.There, in the parlour of the old Pembrokeshire farmhouse the articles of capitulation must have been signed, if they were ever signed at all, and *The Times* of 6 March 1797 informs us that the articles were signed by Tate and Lord Cawdor. Yet, curiously, no trace of this important military document, no yellowing parchment with the signature, 'Wm Tate' and 'Cawdor', in fading ink at the bottom, has ever been found in the archives on either side of the Channel. The popular opinion is that a treaty was signed at the Royal Oak, but as Tate never got to Fishguard this can hardly be in accordance with fact.

Tate, and those officers for whom horses could be provided, were escorted by Major Ackland and a guard direct from Trehowel to Haverfordwest by way of Llangloffan, Plumstone Mountain, and Camrose. At Haverfordwest they were confined in a room at the Castle Inn for the night. The next day most of them were sent on under an escort of the Yeomanry Cavalry to Carmarthen. They spent a night at the Ivy Bush Inn, the principal hostelry in the town, where Tate had perforce to wash his hands at the inn pump, and was not even allowed a rough towel to dry them. After a brief sojourn at the Ivy Bush they were lodged in the county gaol.

E. H. Stuart Jones, *The Last Invasion of Britain,* 1950.

6.   *War Scare, 1803*

At an adjournment of a general meeting of the Lieutenancy of the said County held at Haverfordwest, this 15th day of August, 1803. It is ordered, that horses, cattle and sheep be sent off in the following manner, on a signal given of the appearance of an enemy on their landing on the coast, viz.

Hundred of Narberth
Horses, cattle and sheep to be driven over Llanvalteg and Llanglwydwen Bridges, and to meet at Maengwynhir mountain, and proceed from thence through Hanwidde to Penboyr Rhos.

Hundred of Castle Martin
Horses, cattle and sheep to be driven through Tavernspite, Whitland to Llanwinie over Treleach mountain and Penboyr Rhos.

Hundred of Dungleddy
Horses, cattle and sheep to be driven to Llandisilio Rhos, Llanglwydwen Bridge, Maengwynhir, and Penboyr Rhos.

Hundred of Roose
Horses cattle and sheep from the lower part of Roose, to be driven over Portfield, the remainder over Treffgarne Mountain to Spittal, Poletax Inn, Maenclochog, Manachlogddu, Llanvirnach, and Penboyr Rhos.

Hundred of Kilgerran
Horses, cattle and sheep to assemble on Penboyr Rhos over Pontressely, Bwlchydwmen and Penboyr Rhos.

Hundred of Kemes
Horses, cattle and sheep to follow in the same tract.

Hundred of Dewsland
Horses, cattle and sheep to Kilkeffeth mountain, New Inn Maenclochog, Manachlogddu Llanvirnach and Penboyr Rhos.

If circumstances require they are to proceed from Pemboir Rhos to Kevencoch, near Abergwissin, on the borders of Radnorshire, with as little delay as possible. The Act directs that horses with carriages shall move off immediately their oxen after that the other horned cattle, lastly the sheep and pigs.

It is recommended that the different proprietors do immediately mark their cattle with a brand.

It is the opinion of the Lieutenants that the Lord Lieutenant should be applied to, to appoint proper persons to alarm the country by lighting a fire whenever orders are received from him, on the following conveniences, viz., Prescelly, Frenin Fawr, Carew Beacon, and Roch Castle.

Pembrokeshire Antiquities, 1897.

7. *The Rebecca Riots*

The [*Report on a Constabulary Force,* 1839] draws attention to the increasing frequency of the outbreak of disorders associated with the practice of employing the *ceffyl pren* (the wooden horse), and it is particularly important to notice that these disorders occurred in precisely the area which saw the beginning of the Rebecca Riots a few years later. The practice of holding someone up to derision by carrying him, in person or in effigy, on a wooden pole or ladder is common to the folk-custom of many lands. It may have been derived from the riding of the hobby horse in ancient revelry and in Christmas games, and the phallic significance of this posture may have retained for it a suggestion of obscenity which made it particularly appropriate, to rural minds, as a punishment for marital infidelity. Edward Crompton Lloyd Hall professed to believe that it was sanctioned as a punishment for this by the laws of Hywel Dda. But its application was far wider than that. The practice varied from land to land, and even from place to place, yet the incidents almost invariably bore certain characteristics. They always happened at night; the mob nearly always blackened their faces, and frequently the men dressed themselves in women's clothes; they generally acted a sort of pantomime or mock trial of the person concerned, and the whole proceedings were accompanied by a great deal of noise, such as the beating of drums or the firing of guns. These, as we shall see, were also the characteristics of the Rebecca Riots . . .

The winter of 1838-9 was one of fitful disturbance and uneasiness in the countryside. Successive bad harvests had produced a state of semi-starvation and of spiritual malaise. The *ceffyl pren* stalked the Pembrokeshire hills . . . The first Rebecca Riot broke out on 13 May

1839, just as the lime-burning season was beginning, with the destruction of a gate at Efailwen which had been erected to catch lime-carters who were evading the tolls . . . The trust re-erected the gate, whereupon notices were posted on public doors facetiously summoning a meeting on 6 June 'for the purpose of considering the necessity of a toll gate at Efailwen'. The magistrates hastily swore in seven special constables and sent them to protect the gate. The mob, three to four hundred strong, arrived at 10.30 p.m. on the appointed night. They made much noise, clamouring that they would have 'free laws'. They were all disguised, some having their faces blackened and some being dressed in women's clothes. They drove away the special constables and chased them into the neighbouring fields. Then they set to work, smashing the gate with large sledge hammers and dismantling the house to within a yard of the ground (at Efail-wen). On Wednesday afternoon, 17 July, a large crowd assembled, again with blackened faces and in women's clothes, but this time in broad daylight. The constables who were guarding the chain took to their heels, except a lame man who failed to get away and was severely manhandled. On this occasion the leader was addressed as Becca, and the name 'the Rebecca Riots' thereby came into use. Local tradition has always identified him with Thomas Rees, a pugilist who farmed the little homestead of Carnabwth nearby, in the parish of Mynachlog-ddu. It is said that there had been difficulty in finding women's clothes large enough to fit him until he succeeded in borrowing those of Big Rebecca, who lived in the neighbouring parish of Llangolman. From that day to this the name of Twm Carnabwth has been inseparably associated with the Rebecca Riots in popular tradition, but the truth is that he played no further part whatsoever in them, nor did any subsequent riot take place within eight miles of Efail-wen.

David Williams, *The Rebecca Riots,* 1955.

8. *H.M.S. Warrior*

Of no other warship in the history of the world could it be claimed, as it was of *Warrior,* that she was a military match for all warships afloat put together.

She was built of iron, which permitted an extraordinary length of 380 feet. Over half her long, low length was sheathed in armour plating $4\frac{1}{2}$ inches thick, backed by 2 foot thick teak timbers, impenetrable by any gun then in service. As well as being the world's biggest warship, she was also the fastest. The engines, made by Penn of Greenwich, were by far the most powerful ever made for any navy and her two-bladed propeller, over 23 foot diameter, drove the leviathan through the seas at over 14 knots. With an armament of mixed seven-inch and eight-inch muzzle loading rifled guns, the *Warrior* was virtually invincible . . .

She never fired her guns in anger and, unlike the *Victory,* had no association with great admirals or brilliant victories. The *Warrior* was paid-off as a seagoing ship in 1884 and was laid-up for 16 years. In 1900 she was converted into a hulk to support the torpedo school at Portsmouth. When the school moved to shore accommodation in 1928, the old ship was transferred to Pembroke Dock — the forerunner of the mighty *Dreadnought* fleets of the past 100 years; Jellicoe's *Iron Duke* was a descendant, as was Beatty's *Lion* and Cunningham's *Warspite.* The *Tirpitz* and *Bizmarck* were mere grandchildren and have since faded from the waters.

Lawrence Phillips in the *Western Mail,* 27 March 1976.

9. *D-Day Rehearsal*

The Wiseman's Bridge Inn claims the distinction of having entertained Sir Winston Churchill who had come to see the rehearsal here in 1943 of the invasion of Normandy, when this vast beach from Pendine to Saundersfoot swarmed with soldiers, landing-craft, guns and all the paraphernalia of seaborne attack. As it happened the weather was rough for the rehearsal on Pembrokeshire's coast (as it was for the real thing in France) with the same piling up and stranding of barges and equipment.

R. M. Lockley, *Pembrokeshire,* 1969.

10. *U-Boat Menace*

In January, 1915, a German submarine — Otto Hersing's *U-21* — made a pilot raid into the Irish Sea, after slipping through the English Channel defences. It marked the beginning of a terror campaign against merchant shipping unprecedented in the history of warfare. Pembrokeshire, so strategically placed to command the main shipping routes, played a major part in the fight against the U-boats. The county also became a refuge for the hundreds of survivors from ships which fell victim to the German submarines.

By the end of March, 1915, the 16 U-boats then on operational patrol in British waters had sunk 28,000 tons of shipping. And the shocks of the war at sea hit home for the people of Pembrokeshire on successive days — March 27th and 28th — when the liners *Aguila* and *Falaba* were torpedoed by Baron von Forstner's *U-28*.

The ships were sunk well off the Pembrokeshire coast — the *Aguila* going down 47 miles south-west of the Smalls, and the *Falaba* 38 miles west of that position — but Milford Haven and Fishguard became reception centres for the crews and passengers. The Yeoward Bros. steamship *Aguila* was on a voyage to Lisbon and the Canary Islands when she was sighted and chased by *U-28*. The liner increased speed to 14 knots but was soon overhauled by the submarine and compelled to stop after a shot had been fired across her bows.

While boats were being lowered, the U-boat began shelling the vessel. The chief engineer and two men were killed and 20 shells struck the ship before a torpedo split her in half. Eight lives were lost in the attack, including a woman passenger and a stewardess who drowned when one of the liner's boats capsized. The thirty-eight survivors, who included the captain, were picked up by the steamer *St Stephen*, and the trawler *Ottilie* which put into Fishguard.

Von Forstner struck again the following day. The Elder Dempster liner *Falaba* was on passage from Liverpool to Sierra Leone when the U-boat ordered her to stop. She responded by increasing speed, but when a second signal was received ordering — 'Stop or I will fire into you' — the *Falaba* hove to, knowing the submarine could outpace the ship. The passengers and crew began abandoning ship, but only five boats had been swung out when *U-28* fired a torpedo into the liner without warning. Of the one hundred and fifty-one passengers and ninety-six crew, one hundred and four died — either by drowning or in the explosion when the torpedo struck. Survivors arriving at Milford Haven spoke of the German submariners laughing and jeering as their victims struggled in the water. Those who had been sucked under when the liner sank, bobbed to the surface desperately attempting to grab at wreckage to stay afloat.

The drifter *Eileen Emma* played a leading part in the rescue operations and her skipper, George Wright, was awarded a piece of plate by the Board of Trade in recognition of his services.

At John Cory's 'Sailors Rest and Bethel' at Milford Haven, a tablet was later erected to commemorate the crews of the torpedoed ships, and particular reference was made to the men, women and children saved from the *Falaba*. Among those lost in the disaster was an American citizen, Leon Thresher. His death caused a storm of protest in the United States and further losses of American lives, including those who went down with the liner *Lusitania*, finally resulted in the U.S.A. entering the war against Germany in 1917.

Ted Goddard, *Pembrokeshire Shipwrecks*, 1982

XVI

Divers Wonders

1. Beyond the Veil

That isolated cape which forms the county of Pembroke was looked upon as a land of mystery by the rest of Wales long after it had been settled by the Flemings in 1113. A secret veil was supposed to cover this sea-girt promontory; the inhabitants talked in an unintelligible jargon that was neither English, nor French, nor Welsh; and out of its misty darkness came fables of wondrous sort, and accounts of miracles marvellous beyond belief. Mythology and Christianity spoke together from this strange country, and one could not tell at which to be most amazed, the pagan or the priest.

Wirt Sikes, *British Goblins*, 1879.

2. Of Divers Wonders of Pembrokeshire

1. The shaking stone near within half a mile of St David's, towards the sea cliff, . . . is mounted upon diverse other stones about a yard high from the ground, and so equally poised as that with one finger a man may so shake it, as that you may sensibly see it move.

2. A well spring on the top of a high rock near St David's aforesaid, half a mile and more from the sea, the water being fresh and sweet, and keepeth course with the sea, in ebbing and flowing twice every xxiiij hours.

3.   There is not far from the shaking stone at a place called Porthmawr out of a chamber a passage under ground a quarter of a mile leading to the sea.

4.   Another matter I will note here is a strange and rare thing that is shells of fishes, as oyster shells, mussel shells, cockles, limpets and other shells of sea fish found in digging of marl, and this upon high hills where the marl is found, iij or iiij miles from the sea; and this xx foot deep under the earth, so that of necessity these shells must have remained there since the flood of Noah, being now 3909 years since.

5.   Another rare and strange thing is to be remembered of certain roots of timber which about xij or xiij years past were seen on the sands at Newgale.

6.   There is also a pit in the earth in Bosherston parish which is called Boshersmere . . . and when the sea is tempestuous the surges enter the concavity with great fury and the place being hollow, yieldeth strange and loathsome noises.

7.   In the parish of Whitchurch in Kemes . . . there was never seen any adder alive, although in the parishes round about they are found continually as in other places of the country: this being true, as I am persuaded it is, is a thing to be wondered at in deed, what affinity this parish only and none other should have with the land of Ireland.

8.   Another thing worth the noting is the stone called Maen-y-gromlech upon Pentre Ifan land; . . . the stones whereon this is laid are so high that a man on horseback may well ride under it, without stooping.

9.   And because I have read of wonders of diverse countries which most commonly I have found to be ix in number let me make up the like number with a strange event, that happened in this country in the beginning of June in the year of our Lord God 1601 which was this.
    There happened that suddenly as if the same had fallen by a shower out of the air, a great piece of ground to the quantity of cc English acres, was covered in a manner with a kind of caterpillars or green worms, having many legs and bare without hair, they were found in such abyndance that a man treading on the ground should tread upon xx or xxx of them, and in this sort they continued for the space of three weeks or more, . . . and after they had continued there iij weeks there resorted thither an infinite number of seamews and crows . . . This for the rare event thereof I thought good to note among the

wonders, although it be not permanent, yet more strange than any of the other.

George Owen, *The Description of Penbrokshire,* 1603.

3.   *Unclean Spirits*

In this part of Penbroch, unclean spirits have conversed, not visibly, but sensibly, with mankind, first in the house of Stephen Wiriet [Orielton] and afterwards in the house of William Not; manifesting their presence by throwing dirt at them, and more with a view of mockery than of injury. In the house of William, they cut holes in the linen and woollen garments, much to the loss of the owner of the house and his guests; nor could any precaution, or even bolts, secure them from these inconveniences. In the house of Stephen, the spirit in a more extraordinary manner conversed with men, and, in reply to their taunts, upbraided them openly with everything they had done from their birth, and which they were not willing should be known or heard by others. . .

Another instance occurred, about the same time, of a spirit's appearing in the house of Elidore de Stakepole, not only sensibly, but visibly, under the form of a red-haired young man, who called himself Simon. First seizing the keys from the person to whom they were entrusted, he impudently assumed the steward's office, which he managed so prudently and providently, that all things seemed to abound under his care, and there was no deficiency in the house. Whatever the master or mistress secretly thought of having for their daily use or provision, he procured with wonderful agility, and without any previous directions, saying, 'You wished that to be done, and it shall be done for you'. He was also well acquainted with their treasures and secret hoards, and sometimes upbraided them on that account; for as often as they seemed to act sparingly and avariciously, he used to say, 'Why are you afraid to spend that heap of gold or silver, since your lives are of so short duration, and the money you so cautiously hoard up will never do you any service?' He gave the choicest meat and drink to the rustics and hired servants, saying that

'Those persons should be abundantly supplied, by whose labours they were acquired!' Whatever he determined should be done, whether pleasing or displeasing to his master or mistress (for, as we have said before, he knew all their secrets), he completed in his usual expeditious manner, without their consent. He never went to church, or uttered one Catholic word. He did not sleep in the house, but was ready at his office in the morning.

He was at length observed by some of the family to hold his nightly converse near a mill and a pool of water; upon which discovery he was summoned the next morning before the master of the house and his lady, and, receiving his discharge, delivered up the keys, which he had held for upwards of forty days. Being earnestly interrogated, at his departure, who he was? he answered, 'That he was begotten upon the wife of a rustic in that parish, by a demon, in the shape of her husband'.

Giraldus Cambrensis, *The Itinerary through Wales*, 1188.

4.   *Baal's Bogey*

When I was a child and insisted upon crying instead of going quietly to bed, my father and nurse always used to call 'Bw'ci Bâl' to come and eat me as a bad little boy. Upon that kind of provision I was assured the 'Old Dog of Baal' regularly made his supper!

But when I came to years of reason I learnt that Baal's Old Black Dog had far more important work to do in the world than making his supper off chubby babies who would not go to sleep. I also discovered that he is sooty black, of huge size, and has a rattling chain round his neck, which crashes and rings as he trots along, and his flaming eyes, as big as oysters, paralyse the beholder with horror. Have I seen him, then? No! but several of my acquaintance assured me they had, and from the mental photographs of one of them the above description is taken.

My informant was a sea-faring man of pronounced rollicking habits, and one night, as he was returning from the Cefn-y-dre, Fishguard, to the Cwm, on reaching the bridge over the Gwaen, he saw the great black Dog of Baal rushing open-mouthed, to seize and carry him off for his sins to the very hot regions where Baal dwells, both body and soul together. As the dog came for him with a muffled roar like the sound of distant breakers in a hurricane, my friend had just enough presence of mind left to cry to God for mercy and pardon, and to seek salvation, he said, through the Sacred Name, before Hen Gi Bâl had closed his teeth in his leg — and as soon as the Name was uttered, the brute, with a yell of rage that rang to the top of Pen Tŵr on one side and Carn Mawr on the other side of the valley, started back, glared for a moment with fiendish fury, and, as my friend continued to pray for salvation, then leaped into the river and disappeared!

His intended victim, when he saw the Cwm end of the bridge clear of the enemy, rushed to the door of his brother, with whom he lodged when on land, and as soon as it was opened to his furious kicks fell like a corpse on the threshold! This latter portion of his experiences I verified from his brother and sister, so we must take the earlier part of his relation as equally accurate.

Ferrar Fenton in *Pembrokeshire Antiquities*, 1897.

5.   *The Bitch of Aber Deu Gleddyf*

Arthur said, 'Which of the marvels is it now best to seek first?' 'It is best to seek for the two whelps of the bitch Rhymhi.' 'Is it known where she is?' asked Arthur. 'She is,' said one, 'at Aber Deu Gleddyf.' Arthur came to the house of Tringad in Aber Cleddyf and asked him, 'Hast thou heard of her in these parts? In what shape is she?' 'In the shape of a she-wolf,' answered he, 'and she goes about with her two whelps. Often has she slain my stock, and she is down in Aber Cleddyf in a cave.'

Arthur went to sea in his ship Prydwen, and others by land to hunt the bitch, and in this wise they surrounded her and her two whelps, and God changed them back into their own semblance for Arthur. Arthur's host dispersed, one by one, two by two.

The Mabinogion: trans. Gwyn Jones and Thomas Jones, 1949.

6.   *Ghosts*

I fancy South Pembrokeshire folks enjoy a somewhat livelier faith in ghosts generally than do the inhabitants of other counties. Athoe, the wicked Mayor of Tenby, used to haunt the bridge by Holloway water. A deceased Stepney walked in Prendergast, near Haverfordwest; and a white lady, presumably a Devereux, haunts the ruins of Lamphey Court. Perhaps the most interesting spectre is that nameless pre-historic hopgoblin who has compelled the wayfarers to make a path for night use round the Parc-y-Marw. Headless apparitions, both human and bestial, are a strangely inexplicable relic of some forgotten faith. These occur in one or two localities. A headless horse haunts the entrance gate to Llangwarren, near Fishguard, and a ghostly party, consisting of two horses, a coachman and a lady (all headless), are supposed to travel with a coach from Tenby to Sampson Cross Roads, near Stackpole. Our forefathers had no troublesome doubts as to the personality of the Devil, for many of them had seen him; but his business was generally rather with the dead than the living. No one doubted that he carried off the corpse of John Meyrick, Chief Justice of South Wales, from Bush House. So thoroughly was this tale believed that an old gentleman who resided at Carew, considering that his life had been such as to give the devil a lien on his carcase, inserted a clause in his will to the effect that immediately after decease his body should be burned, and afterwards his ashes carried up to the top of Carew Church Tower and there riddled rhough a sieve to the four winds of heaven.

Edward Laws, *The History of Little England Beyond Wales*, 1888

7. *Corpse Candle*

Morris Griffith was once schoolmaster in the parish of Pontfaen, in Pembrokeshire, but subsequently became a Baptist preacher of the Gospel. He tells this story: 'As I was coming from a place called Tre-Davydd, and was come to the top of the hill, I saw a great light down in the valley, which I wondered at; for I could not imagine what it meant. But it came to my mind that it was a light before a burying, though I never could believe before that there was such a thing. The light which I saw then was a very red light, and it stood still for about a quarter of an hour in the way which went towards Llannerch-Llawddog church. I remained waiting to see it come out, and it was not long before it came out, and went to a certain part of the churchyard, where it stood a little time, and then vanished out of my sight. A few days afterwards, being in school with the children about noon, I heard a great noise overhead, as if the top of the house was coming down. I ran out to see the garret, and there was nothing amiss. A few days afterwards, Mr Higgon of Pontfaen's son died. When the carpenter came to fetch the boards to make the coffin, (which were in the garret), he made exactly such a stir, in handling the boards in the garret, as was made before by some spirit, who foreknew the death that was soon to come to pass. In carrying the body to the grave, the burying stood where the light had stood for about a quarter of an hour, because there was some water crossing the way, and the people could not go over it without wetting their feet, therefore they were obliged to wait till those that had boots helped them over. The child was buried in that very spot of ground in the churchyard, where I saw the light stop after it came out of the church. This is what I can boldly testify, having seen and heard what I relate — a thing which before I could not believe.'

Wirt Sikes, *British Goblins*, 1879.

8.   *The Green Meadows of Enchantment*

There are sailors on that romantic coast who still talk of the green meadows of enchantment lying in the Irish channel to the west of Pembrokeshire. Sometimes they are visible to the eyes of mortals for a brief space, when suddenly they vanish. There are traditions of sailors who, in the early part of the present century, actually went ashore on the fairy islands — not knowing that they were such, until they returned to their boats, when they were filled with awe at seeing the islands disappear from their sight, neither sinking in the sea, nor floating away upon the waters, but simply vanishing suddenly. The fairies inhabiting these islands are said to have regularly attended the markets at Milford Haven and Laugharne. They made their purchases without speaking, laid down their money and departed, always leaving the exact sum required, which they seemed to know, without asking the price of anything. Sometimes they were invisible, but they were often seen, by sharp-eyed persons. There was always one special butcher at Milford Haven upon whom the fairies bestowed their patronage, instead of distributing their favours indiscriminately. The Milford Haven folk could see the green fairy islands distinctly, lying out a short distance from land; and the general belief was that they were densely peopled with fairies. It was also said that the latter went to and fro between the islands and the shore through a subterranean gallery under the bottom of the sea.

Wirt Sikes, *British Goblins*, 1879.

9.   *Dog of Hell*

As Mr David Walter, of Pembrokeshire, 'a religious man, and far from fear and superstition', was travelling by himself through a field called the Cot Moor, where there are two stones set up called the Devil's Nags, which are said to be haunted, he was suddenly seized and thrown over a hedge. He went there another day, taking with him for protection a strong fighting mastiff dog. When he had come near the Devil's Nags there appeared in his path the apparition of a dog more terrible than any he had ever seen. In vain he tried to set his mastiff on; the huge beast crouched frightened by his master's feet and refused to attack the spectre. Whereupon his master boldly stooped to pick up a stone, thinking that would frighten the evil dog; but suddenly a circle of fire surrounded it, which lighting up the gloom, showed the white snip down the dog's nose, and his grinning teeth, and white tail. 'He then knew it was one of the infernal dogs of hell.'

Wirt Sikes, *British Goblins*, 1879.

10.   *Wicked Tanglost*

There is a story that Bishop John Morgan (about 1503) seized a certain lady, Tanglost, and imprisoned her at Llawhaden, because of her ill fame. Thomas Wyriott of Orielton came to her rescue with mounted troops and successfully stormed the castle. But the woman, persisting in her wicked ways, was once again imprisoned and Wyriott now asked the bishop to pardon them both. On her release Tanglost went to Bristol and engaged a witch to put a spell on the bishop. Waxen effigies of the prelate were made and stuck full of pins. Hearing of this, the bishop was frightened and appealed to the

"Mayor and Corporation" of Bristol to convict Tanglost. All ended well: Tanglost repented and reformed forthwith.

R. M. Lockley, *Pembrokeshire*, 1957.

11.   *Toad of Toad's Town*

In an out-of-the-way locality about two miles north of Nevern stands a farmhouse called Trellyfan, *anglice* Toadstown. The origin of this singular name is explained by the following story, narrated by no less an authority than the famous Giraldus Cambrensis.

One day in the course of his travels Giraldus fell in with an exceedingly tall young man, who, owing to the length of his limbs, was known as Sitsyllt of the Long Legs. The career of this ill-starred individual was cut short in a strange and tragic manner, the unhappy Sitsyllt being worried to death by *toads*, in spite of the fact that his friends had very considerably hung him up in a sack, to save him from the molestations of these malignant reptiles!

As a memento of this incident, the marble effigy of a toad was built into a chimney-piece at Trellyfan, where it was treasured for many generations. The toad was afterwards cut away and removed from its place in the farmhouse, but eventually came into the possession of its present owner, a resident at Haverfordwest, by whose courtesy we are enabled to give a sketch of this venerable relic. The toad in question is carved in a dark-green veined marble, about as large as the palm of a woman's hand, and is reputed to be the work of an Italian artist.

H. Thornhill Timmins, *Nooks and Corners of Pembrokeshire*, 1895.

12.   *Led Astray by Fairies*

An old man who died in St Dogmell's parish, Pembrokeshire, a short time since (viz., in 1860), nearly a hundred years old, used to say that that whole neighbourhood was considered 'fou'. It was a common experience for men to be led astray there all night, and after marvellous adventures and untellable trampings, which seemed as if they would be endless, to find when day broke that they were close to their own homes. In one case, a man who was led astray chanced to have with him a number of hoop-rods, and as he wandered about under the influence of the deluding phantom, he was clever enough to drop the rods one by one, so that next day he might trace his journeyings. When daylight came, and the search for the hoop-rods was entered on, it was found they were scattered over miles upon miles of country. Another time, a St Dogmell's fisherman was returning home from a wedding at Moelgrove, and it being very dark, the fairies led him astray, but after a few hours he had the good luck (which Sir John Franklin might have envied him) to 'discover the North Pole', and by this beacon he was able to steer his staggering barque to the safe port of his own threshold. It is even gravely stated that a severe and dignified clerical person, no longer in the frisky time of life, but advanced in years, was one night forced to join in the magic dance of St Dogmell's and keep it up till nearly daybreak. Specific details in this instance are wanting; but it was no doubt the Ellyllon who led all these folk astray, and put a cap of oblivion on their heads, which prevented them from ever telling their adventures clearly.

Wirt Sikes, *British Goblins*, 1879.

13. *Cocking and Other Customs*

Easter Monday was the great cocking festival; mains were fought at Gumfreston and Begelly. This was a very favourite sport in Pembrokeshire. The remains of cock-pits are to be seen at Haroldston, the old home of the Perrots, near Haverford, and at Rhosmarket. Oddly enough they are not pits, but raised tables of earth. Even now it is not very safe for a diffident youth to enter a hayfield, for it is quite possible that the women and girls employed therein will bind him hand and foot with hay-bands and leave him to consider the question of ransom; this is termed 'stretching his back'. Formerly the men treated female trespassers after the same fashion, and called it 'giving them a green gown'.

At St Florence (and most likely elsewhere) a curious custom was practised during Lammas-tide. The farm servants (boys and girls) constructed for themselves huts of green branches, lit them up with candles, and spent the night therein. Naturally this proceeding proved objectionable, so it was suppressed in the interests of morality about forty years ago. Not improbably the Lammas houses were originally raised to shelter harvesters in outlying districts, or herds tending cattle, whom as we have seen George Owen deemed a cruelly mistreated class.

On St Crispin's-eve, October 24th, this saint's effigy was hung on the church steeple, cut down on the holiday and carried round the town in derision of the shoemakers, who avenged themselves on the carpenters by treating their patron, St Clement, in like fashion on November 23rd.

Love-lorn maidens availed themselves of Hallow E'en (universally considered an eerie time) to discover their future husbands. The blade-bone of a shoulder of mutton having been procured, the girl put it under her pillow; at the dread hour of midnight she stabbed her bone with a steel fork, repeating the while:

> 'Tis not this bone I mean to prick,
> But my love's heart I wish to prick;
> If he comes not and speaks to-night,
> I'll prick and prick till it be light.

Edward Laws, *The History of Little England Beyond Wales*, 1888.

14. *Country Courting*

There were some who believed that no maid was more easily seduced than she who had been to an emotional prayer meeting, or a sermon with a *hwyl*, or above all a singing festival. A good intake of Handel or Bach would apparently lower the lady's defences sufficiently for her to stoop to folly. Tutors at theological colleges would advise their students not to go a-courting on Sunday, an emotional day, when *les girls* were most inclined to be permissive. During the winter months a singing rehearsal was held after the evening service, to get ready for the singing festival the following June. The likely lads would escort the chosen and willing back home to the farms often 2 or 4 miles away with the last part of the journey nearly always down an unmetalled rutted farm lane. There would be connivance by the employer at the late arrival home of his maid servant. Then there was the old established *caru trwy'r nos* or 'Courting all night'. The girl would leave a ladder conveniently placed near or beneath her bedroom window and usually on a Saturday night the man of her choice would arrive, clean-shaven and smelling of scented soap, his Amlwch shag-tobacco-laden breath disguised by the heavy exotic perfume of 'Sen-Sen' cachous. He would strip to his vest and long drawers both of heavy Welsh wool with a black vertical stripe in the drawers, and then with the nice protection of a blanket between them they'd commence to giggle and cuddle, protest and counterprotest, all very pleasureable no doubt. Occasionally the blanket proved insufficient insulation, and some months later a hurried marriage would be arranged — with the whole community rejoicing and congratulating the happy virile couple. Some of the happiest and most successful marriages in Wales have started on this basis.

James Williams, *Give Me Yesterday*, 1971.

15. *Bidding Notice*

October 15th, 1849

As we intend to enter the Matrimonial State, on Thursday, the 25th Day of October, inst., we purpose to make a BIDDING on the occasion, the same day at our Dwelling-House, called Porth, Abercych, when and where the favor of your good company is most humbly solicited, and whatever donation you will be pleased to confer on us that day, will be thankfully received, and cheerfully repaid whenever called for on a similar occasion,

By your obedient humble Servants,

THOMAS JONES,
ELIZABETH EVANS.

The Young Man's Father and Mother, desire that all Gifts of the above nature due to them, be returned to the Young Man, on the above day, and will be thankful for all favors granted. — Also, the Young Woman's Father and Mother, her Grand-father (John Davies, Shambles), desire that all Gifts of the above nature due to them, be returned to the Young Woman, on the said day, and will be thankful for all favors granted.

The Young Man's Company will meet that Morning at his Father's House, called Penrhiwoleu, Kenarth; and the Young Woman's Company at Porth aforesaid.

John Ballinger, 'Further Gleanings from a Printer's File' in *West Wales Historical Records*, Vol X, 1924.

16.   *Floral Wedding*

At Tenby, when the High Sheriff's son was married to the Rector of Tenby's daughter, in 1877, garlands of flowers were hung across the High Street, bearing pleasant mottoes, while flags and banners fluttered from house-tops in all directions. Children strewed flowers in the bride's path as she came out of church, while the bells in the steeple chimed a merry peal, and a park of miniature artillery boomed from the pier-head. This custom of children strewing flowers in the path of the new-made bride is common; so also is that of throwing showers of rice after the wedded pair, by way of expressing good wishes — a pleasanter thing to be thrown under these circumstances than the old shoes of tradition. However, since fashion has taken up the custom of rice-throwing and shoe-throwing, the shoes have become satin slippers.

Wirt Sikes, *British Goblins*, 1879.

17.   *Romantic Divination*

The customs of Rhamanta, or romantic divination, by which lovers and sweethearts seek to pierce the future, are many and curious, in all parts of Wales . . .

In Pembrokeshire a shoulder of mutton, with nine holes bored in the blade bone, is put under the pillow to dream on. At the same time the shoes of the experimenting damsel are placed at the foot of the bed in the shape of a letter T, and an incantation is said over them, in which it is trusted by the damsel that she may see her lover in his every-day clothes.

Wirt Sikes, *British Goblins*, 1879.

18. *The Wooden Horse*

Divorce did not have a place in the countryman's code, but there were several corrective devices which had become folk customs and through which any obvious breach of the ideal of married life could be rectified. These customs constituted an unofficial legal system (which often came into conflict with the law of the land) deriving its efficacy from the power of popular feeling in communities in which each man knew the business (and secrets) of his neighbour.

In south-west Wales the name given to a local form of penal custom was *y ceffyl pren* (the wooden horse). The practice consisted of carrying a person, or his effigy, on a wooden pole in order to make him the laughing stock of the community. In Tenby, Pembrokeshire, when domestic strife became too great — usually because the wife wanted to assume mastery of the home — 'the neighbours step in with the *ceffyl pren* or wooden horse. An effigy of the offender is dressed up, seated on a chair, placed on a ladder, and carried on men's shoulders, a crowd in procession preceding and following the *ceffyl pren*, shouting, screaming, and beating tin saucepans' etc. Halting at intervals, the nature of the offence is thus described by the spokesman:

> Ran-dan-dan!
> Betty Morris has beat her man.
> What was it with?
> 'Twas not with a rake, nor yet with a reel,
> But 'twas with a poker, that made him feel.

At other times the neighbours are not contented with a mere effigy. When a man or woman are faithless to their marriage vows, the mob seize the offending parties, fasten them back to back, mount them on the wooden horse, parade them about, proclaiming their shame, and pelting them with rotten eggs and other offensive missiles. After continuing the exposure for some time the culprits are taken down, and followed with hooting and execrations to their respective dwellings where they are left to digest the bitter reproaches of their injured partners.'

Trefor M. Owen, *Welsh Folk Customs*, 1974

19.   *A Welsh Wake*

The 'Wylnos' (wake night), or, as it is better known in North Pembrokeshire, 'Y Wynglos', is a very ancient custom, and still known to some extent in some parts of North Pembrokeshire. The 'Wylnos' is a ceremony held at the house of the dead, where candles are kept burning all night, and two or more persons are kept 'watching' till the day of burial. But, although this old custom of watching and illuminating the chamber of the dead is still practised, it has lost its most peculiar features, namely, the drawing up of the corpse through the chimney of the house where death had occurred, before it was conveyed to its last resting-place. The process of this extraordinary and mysterious custom was as follows: A certain number of persons would be engaged to remove the corpse from its coffin to a convenient place near the fire, where the pinioning of the dead would be performed. This was done by tying a rope to the upper part of the body, the other end was afterwards passed up the chimney by means of a long stick or pitchfork. Then a sufficient number of men (possibly according to the weight of the corpse), would be told off to go up to the top of the chimney from the outside of the house, which they did by means of a ladder, and having got there, and fixed themselves as securely as such a perilous situation would allow them, they took hold of the rope which had been sent up inside the chimney, and when they were ready for their work, they gave a sign to those inside by crying 'Hir wen gŵd' (words probably referring to the long white shroud with which the dead was clad), and those who were inside the house would answer by saying, 'Chware'n barod' words equivalent to 'We are ready', and slowly up the chimney went the corpse; when it had been brought to the top, it was carefully lowered, and eventually re-placed in its coffin. I am told that the last of such ceremonies in North Pembrokeshire took place at a cottage on the glebeland known as 'Old Mill', in the parish of Pontfaen, some hundred and fifty years ago.

Many curious tales are told as to the mysterious events which occasionally took place at these 'Wylnosau', and I may be permitted to relate one, and incredible as it seems, the person who told it me vouches for the truth of it. Here it is:

A notoriously ungodly man died in North Pembrokeshire; he was placed in his coffin, the 'Wylnos' went on, the candles were burning, and the watchers were wide awake.

Suddenly they heard the sound of feet as of a large concourse of people approaching the house; they came in, put out all the candles, and at last the house was filled with them; those who were of the household heard the bustle, and actually felt the crush. After a while, the intruders left the house, but had the courtesy to re-light the candles before taking their leave. When everything was over, and the house cleared of these audacious visitors, the relatives and those with them in the 'wake' were anxious to ascertain what it all meant and what had happened. After looking round the kitchen where they had sat in awe and silence during all this ado, they mustered enough courage to enter the room where the dead man lay, but to their horror nothing remained but the coffin — the corpse was gone — and gone for ever! The coffin was afterwards filled with stones and buried. It was believed by the people in that house and by those in the neighbourhood, that the intruders were 'evil spirits', and that they had come to carry away the body of a man who had spent such an evil life.

Whatever may have been the cause, the removal of the corpse appears to be well authenticated.

D. Jenkyn Evans, *Pembrokeshire Antiquities*, 1897.

20. *Mutinous Women*

1644, *circa* September 8. Haverfordwest.

ROGER BEAVANS, MAYOR, WILLIAM MEYLER, ETHELRED WOGAN, JOHN DAVIDS AND JOHN SYNETT TO THE HONOURABLE MAJOR GENERAL [ROWLAND] LAUGHARNE.

On Monday last the commissioners for the excise came to this town and having shown us their commission we yielded obedience unto it and thereupon they sent out their warrants for the summoning of the inhabitants before them. And having sat yesterday in the afternoon on it there came to the town hall a company of the poorest sort of women of this town and there made a mutiny and forced the commissioners thence to their lodgings. And they having complained unto us, we thought by the authority of the civil power to supress them and for that purpose entreated the commissioners to sit again this day and that we would assist them therein. And we and the said commissioners being in the town hall thinking to proceed on the service, the said women came again and would have forced into the hall, whereupon we committed some of them to the sheriff thinking they would have yielded obedience thereunto, but they fell again into such mutiny that for safeguard of the commissioners' lives we were forced to leave the hall, and having repaired with them to their lodging with an intent to see them safe out of town the said women followed us thither and would have forced on them in their chamber in such manner as for the space of six hours we could not pacify them. This being the truth of the proceedings we thought good to certify your honour whereby some course may be thought fit by your honour for the punishing of these idle women, which leaving to your honour's consideration we subscribe ourselves to be your humble servants to serve you.

Pembrokeshire Life 1572-1843, ed. B.E. & K. A. Howells, 1972.

21. *Wetting the Plough*

In the middle of the nineteenth century, according to a north Pembrokeshire account, Christmas Day marked the beginning of a three-weeks period of holidays (*Y Gwyliau*) during which farm work was suspended. As a symbol of this the plough was carried into the home and placed under the table in the room where the meals were eaten (*rŵm ford*). Christmas Day itself was marked only by a sumptuous dinner of goose, beef and pudding, etc., at the large farms in each neighbourhood to which all the other farmers and cottagers were invited. As for the rest of the holiday period till Epiphany, 'parties of men went about from house to house and were invited into the *rŵm ford*, where they sat around the table, regaling themselves with beer, which was always kept warm in small neat brass pans in every farm house ready for callers. But the peculiar custom which existed amongst these holiday-makers was that they always wetted the plough which lay dormant under the table with their beer before partaking of it themselves, thus indicating that though they had dispensed with its service for the time, they had not forgotten it, and that it would again, in due course be brought out on the green sward and turn it.'

Trefor M. Owen, *Welsh Folk Customs*, 1959.

22.   *Local Boy . . .*

I can tell you now one thing you will hardly believe, but which is as true as the gospel.

That a man who became our principal tenant, paying £400 a year for his farm at Orielton out there [in Tasmania], was transported for life for stealing one sheep. He had lived at Temperness on the hillside, near Rosebush in Pembrokeshire, where I see the Laburnums and the Sycamores that he planted still growing.

Fancy my taking the governor, Colonel Gore Brown and Sir Valentine Fleming, the Lord Chief Justice of the Colony (lately dead), Quail shooting to his farm, and our having one of the grandest dinners in all my colonial experience at his house. Now and again I could see the tear trickling, but I changed the subject.

John Owen, *Memories of Half-a-Century*, 1888.

23.   *Recantation*

Whereas, I David Evans, of the Village and Parish of St Dogmells, in the Country of Pembroke, Mariner, Master of the Sloop Leech of Cardigan, lately made use of most improper and indecent language affecting the character & credit of Margaret Edwards, wife of John Edwards of the Cwmgloyn Arms, in the same Village & Parish, Mariner; for which proceedings in the Ecclesiastical Court have been most justly threatened against me: but they in consideration of my acknowledging my error, and paying the expences already incurred, and also the expence of Printing this my Recantation, kindly consented and agreed to forego such proceedings. Now, I the said David Evans, do hereby acknowledge that the imputations which the Language made use of by me as aforesaid, were capable of conveying and which tended most materially to injure the character and credit of the said Margaret Edwards, were totally false and unfounded; and I do hereby very sincerely express my sorrow and contrition for having uttered the same. As Witness my hand, the 21st Day of January, 1832.

DAVID EVANS

Witness,

DAVID JENKINS.

John Ballinger, 'Further Gleanings from a Printer's File' in *West Wales Historical Records*, Vol XI, 1926.

24.   *A Crock of Gold*

1572, September 10. Wiston.

JOHN WOGAN, SHERIFF OF PEMBROKESHIRE, TO LORD BURGHLEY.

Whereas it is my duty, be[ing] sheriff of the shire, to advertise Her Majesty or some of Her Highness's most honourable council of every thing or causes which does concern Her Majesty's commodity by any manner [of] means, therefore these are to advertise your honour that I [am] credibly informed and the report is . . . that about Easter last Jeuan Canton, [illegible] Hurte and Thomas Probert of this county of Pembroke have found at an old pair of [walls] at Spittell in the said county a great quantity of treasure, gold and silver, contained in a certain crock of brass as is supposed, and that they had knowledge thereof by the advertisement of one Sir Lewis, a priest dwelling in Carmarthenshire not far from Kayo.

For further consideration whereof I have sent unto your honour the depositions of such as were examined before me, and am ready for my part to execute your lordship's further commandment in this matter or any other cause wherein I may do your lordship any service. But I gather that the truth of this mater will never be bolted out without that the priest be examined and the parties also menaced with some torture or extremity. All which I remit to your lordship's further discretion, and for this time do most humbly take my leave of your good lordship. Your lordship's most assured and poor kinsman at commandment.

Pembrokeshire Life 1572-1843, ed. B. E. & K. A. Howells, 1972.

25.   *Beating the Bounds*

What makes the Lordship of Kemes so interesting is that it is the only one of all the Lordships Marchers about which there is any authentic history. Kemes was a very important and enormously rich lordship: it was divided into 25 knights' fees, 34 plough lands, and 4 boroughs. This old feudal Barony is about 60 miles in circumference, and up to a very few years ago the marching of the boundaries was a picturesque survival of old times. The last ceremonial perambulation took place in 1888, and official ones have been made periodically since. It occupied 5 days, and about 300 people followed the procession on foot. The following gives an idea of the order:

THE PROCESSION

The Flag of the Barony of blue and silver.
The Pioneers in scarlet tunics with silver buttons and red caps carrying mattocks ornamented with ram's horns and rosettes.
The Band on horseback.
The Steward of the Barony.
The Homagers of the Barony of Kemes.
The Tenants and Homagers on horseback.
Handsome blue and red Flag surmounted with a golden eagle carried by a Pioneer being the special
Boundary Flag.
The Lord Marcher and Lady.
Tenants and Homagers on foot all carrying banners.
The general crowd.

The procession was about a mile long, and those attending were regaled with bread and cheese and beer each day. The most impressive scene of all was when the Lord Marcher and his Lady stood in the centre of the Court Baron surrounded by the officials and jury; outside again being a dense ring of homagers and tenants, interspersed with flags of almost every colour and device, to receive the homage of the oath to keep inviolable the bounds of the Barony. In olden days a boy was kicked over the boundary to make him remember it!

Katharine H. Lloyd, *Lords of Kemes*, 1930.

26. *Mari Lwyd*

The decoration of the *Mari Lwyd* or *Cynfas-Farch* as practised in the St David's district of Pembrokeshire was somewhat different. A canvas sheet a couple of yards square such as was 'used for carrying odds and ends of corn chaff etc. or the *brethyn rhawn* (horse-hair sheet) used over the kiln for drying corn . . . was sewn at one of the corners for about a yard to form a snout and head of an

Ichthyosaurus or any other animal of such beauty! The eyes were represented by large buttons and two brown harvest gloves tacked on for ears, the head tightly stuffed with straw. The man stood underneath the canvas and a long pitchfork stuck into the straw enabled him to turn the head about in every direction. It was then carried about and the first intimation often received was the sight of this prowling monster peeping around into the room, or sometimes shewing his head by pushing it through an upstairs window. One case was recorded, by my mother, of a sudden death through fright of this. It almost always created a collapse of some and the scamper of others.'

Trefor M. Owen, *Welsh Folk Customs*, 1959.

27.   *Hunting the Wren*

An early description of the custom in Pembrokeshire is that given by Edward Lhuyd (1660-1709) in his *Parochialia*. He writes 'Arverant yn swydh Benfro &c dhwyn driw mewn elor nos ystwylh; odhiwrth gwr Ivank at i Gariad, sef day nae dri ai dygant mewn elor a ribane; ag a ganant gorolion. Ant hevyd i day ereilh lhe no bo kariadon a bydh kwrw v. &c. A elor o'r wlad ai galwant Kwlli (*sic* Kwtti) wran.' [They are accustomed in Pembrokeshire etc. to carry a wren in a bier on Twelfth Night; from a young man to his sweetheart, that is two or three bear it in a bier (covered) with ribbons, and sing carols. They also go to other houses where there are no sweethearts and there will be beer etc. And a bier from the country they call Cutty Wran.] Some of the main features of the custom are referred to in this description: the link with Twelfth Night, the decorated bier carried by two or three bearers, carol-singing and the name 'Cutty Wren'. These elements were still to be found in the Pembrokeshire countryside in the nineteenth century, and the Welsh Folk Museum's collection includes a wren-house from Marloes in that county which was made in 1869. Like the elor or 'bier' described by Lhuyd it is decorated with ribbons and was carried in procession on Twelfth Night, the wren having been caught and imprisoned beforehand. The song sung was as follows:—

Joy, health, love and peace; we're here in this place;
By your leave here we sing concerning our King.

Our King is well drest in silks of the best
And the ribbons so rare, no King can compare.
Over hedges and stiles we have travelled many miles.
We were four foot-men in taking this wren.
We were four at watch and were nigh of a match
Now Christmas is past, Twelfth Day is the last.
To the old year adieu, great joy to the new.
Please turn the King in.

In the same county the custom is also recorded in Tenby where the details were as follows: 'Having procured a wren, and placed it in a small ornamented box, or paper house, with a square of glass at either end, two or four men would carry it about, elevated on four poles fixed to the corners, singing the while a long ditty . . . The four men would then enter the doorway, groaning under the weight of their burden, and looking as if they had just relieved Atlas of his shoulder-piece.' The song sung in Tenby included the following verses:

1.   O! where are you going? says Milder to Melder,
     O! where are you going? says the younger to the elder,
     O! I cannot tell you, says Festel to Fose,
     We're going to the woods, says John the Red Nose.
2.   O! what will you do there? . . . Shoot the Cutty Wren.
3.   O! what will you shoot her with? . . . With bows and with arrows.
4.   O! that will not do . . . With great guns and cannons.
5.   O! what will you bring her home in? . . . On four strong men's shoulders.
6.   O! that will not do . . . On big carts and waggons.
7.   What will you cut her up with? . . . With knives and with forks.
8.   O! that will not do . . . With hatchets and cleavers.
9.   What will you boil her in? In pots and in kettles.
10. O! that will not do . . . In brass pans and cauldrons.

Trefor M. Owen, *Welsh Folk Customs*, 1959.

28. *The Guisers*

Christmas-tide brought the Guisers with their dramatic entertainment. Apparently this was a degenerate relic of the

Mysteries or Miracle plays of an earlier time. Usually there were but three actors in a Guiser company, and as six characters were introduced into their play, some of them had to double their parts. The *dramatis personae* were: Father Christmas, St George, a Turkish knight, a doctor, Oliver Cromwell, and Beelzebub. Perhaps this rather inconsequential drama which some of us have laughed at, was based on that played during the Carew Tournament, held in honour of St George at the beginning of the 16th century. It is observable that although St George is the hero, Oliver Cromwell (his copper nose notwithstanding) is represented as a patriot. Beelzebub plays pantaloon; there is no villain, but the Turkish knight could not have expected much sympathy from his audience, seeing that Algerine corsairs had cruised in Tenby bay . . .

The fishermen had a masquerade of their own. One member disguised in mask and bedecked with evergreens, representing the 'Lord Mayor of Pennyless Cove', was borne on the shoulders of four comrades through the town, the rest gathered in what coppers they could from the spectators.

Edward Laws, *The History of Little England Beyond Wales*, 1888.

29. *New Year's Water*

The custom of New Year's water has been recorded principally in south Wales, especially Pembrokeshire. Early on New Year's morning, about three of four o'clock, crowds of boys visited the houses of the neighbourhood carrying with them a vessel of cold spring water, freshly drawn that morning, and a twig of box, holly, myrtle or other evergreen (sometimes a branch of rosemary also). According to one account the vessel was kept out of sight. The hands and faces of every person whom they met on their rounds were sprinkled with water in return for a copper or two. In every house which they entered each room would be sprinkled with New Year's water and the inmates — who would often still be in bed — wished a Happy New Year. The doors of those houses which they were not allowed to enter were sprinkled. In Pendine, Carmarthenshire, where the custom was practised on Old New Year's Day, 'the best families would say to those they liked and respected "Bring us New Year's Water". They always gave to the bringer five shillings or half a crown.' While sprinkling the visitors sang (or recited) the following verse:

> Here we bring new water from the well so clear,
> For to worship God with, this Happy New year;
> Sing levy dew, sing levy dew, the water and the wine,
> With seven bright gold wires, the bugles that do shine;
> Sing reign of fair maid, with gold upon her toe,
> Open you the west door, and turn the old year go;
> Sing reign of fair maid, with gold upon her chin,
> Open you the east door, and let the new year in.

Trefor M. Owen, *Welsh Folk Customs*, 1959.

30. REMEMBERANCE

One blissful moment as the sun is setting,
A mellow moment ere the night comes on,
To bring to mind things which are long forgotten,
Now lost in dust of eras that are gone.

Now like the foam breaking on lonely beaches,
Or the wind's song and no one there to hear,
I know they call on us in vain to listen, —
The old forgotten things men loved so dear.

Things wrought through cunning skill in early ages,
Neat little dwellings and resplendent halls,
And well-told stories that are lost for ever,
And olden gods on whom no suppliant calls.

The little words of languages once living,
Lively was then their sound on lips of men,
And pleasing to the ear in children's prattle,
But now, no tongue will fashion them again.

O countless generations of earth's children,
Of dreams divine, and fragile godlikeness,
Is there but stillness for the hearts that quickened,
That knew delight and knew grief's bitterness?

Often when evening falls and I am lonely
I long once more to bring you all to mind,
Pray, is there no-one treasures and holds dear
The old forgotten things of humankind?

Waldo Williams, translated from the Welsh by D. M. Lloyd.

Bibliography

ATKINSON, R.J.C.
  Stonehenge. Hamish Hamilton, London. 1956.
BALLINGER, JOHN.
  Further Gleanings from a Printer's File. *West Wales Historical Records*, XI. Carmarthen. 1926.
BARRETT, J.H.
  Life on the Seashore. *Pembrokeshire Coast National Park Guide*. London. 1973.
BOWEN, E.G.
  Seafaring along the Pembrokeshire coast in the days of the sailing ships. *The Pembrokeshire Historian*, No. 4. 1972.
BEYNON, T. (trans.)
  Howell Harris's Visits to Pembrokeshire. Aberystwyth. 1966.
CAMDEN, WILLIAM
  Britannia. 1610.
CHARLES, B.G.
  The English Element in Pembrokeshire Welsh. *Studia Celtica*, VI. 1971.
  The Second Book of George Owen's *Description of Penbrokeshire*. *The National Library of Wales Journal*, V 4. 1948.
  The Records of the Borough of Newport in Pembrokeshire. *ibid.* VII 1. 1951.
CHRIMES, S.B.
  The Landing Place of Henry of Richmond, 1485. *The Welsh History Review*, II 2. 1964.
CONDRY, WILLIAM
  Exploring Wales. Faber & Faber, London. 1970.
DAVIS, T. A. WARREN
  Flora and Vegetaion. *Pembrokeshire Coast National Park Guide*. London. 1973.
DONOVAN, E.
  Descriptive Excursions through South Wales and Monmouthshire in the year 1804. London. 1805.

EVANS, D. JENKYN
Welsh Wake. *Pembrokeshire Antiquities*. 1897.
EVANS, J.J.
Sir Watkin Lewes. *Dictionary of Welsh Biography*. London. 1959.
EVANS, OLWEN CARADOC
Marine Plans and Charts of Wales. The Map Collectors' Circle, London. 1969.
EVANS, P.C.C.
Sir John Perrot. *Dictionary of Welsh Biography*. London. 1959.
FAIRBURN, ELEANOR
The Golden Hive. Heinemann, London. 1966.
FENTON, FERRAR
Baal's Bogey. *Pembrokeshire Antiquities*. 1897.
FENTON, RICHARD
A Historical Tour through Pembrokeshire. London. 1811.
FITZGIBBON, CONSTANTINE
The Life of Dylan Thomas. Dent, London. 1965.
FITZGIBBON, THEODORA
A Taste of Wales. Dent, London. 1971.
FRASER, MAXWELL
Introducing West Wales. Methuen, London. 1956.
FREEMAN, E.C. & GILL E.
The Story of Lord Nelson and Sir William & Lady Hamilton's Tour in Wales & Monmouthshire. 1962.
GAMMON, CLIVE
Hook, Line and Spinner. Heinemann, London. 1966.
GEORGE, T. NEVILLE
Geology and Scenery. *Pembrokeshire Coast National Park Guide*. London. 1973.
GIRALDUS CAMBRENSIS
The Itinerary through Wales. Dent, London. 1908.
GOSSE, PHILIP H.
Tenby: A Seaside Holiday. London. 1856.
GRIMES, W.F.
Archaeology. *Pembrokeshire Coast National Park Guide*. London. 1973.
GUEST, LADY CHARLOTTE
The Mabinogion. Dent, London. 1906.
HAWKES, JACQUETTA
A Guide to the Prehistoric and Roman Monuments in England and Wales. Chatto & Windus, London. 1976.

HAWKINS, GERALD S.
Stonehenge Decoded. Fontana/Collins. 1970.

HOWELL, DAVID
Landed Gentry in Pembrokeshire c. 1608-1830. *The Pembrokeshire Historian.* 1971.
Pembrokeshire Gentry in the Eighteenth Century. *Carmarthen Studies.* Carmarthen. 1974.

HOWELL P. & BEAZLEY, E.
The Companion Guide to South Wales. Collins, London. 1977.

HOWELL, R.L.
The Pembroke Yeomanry. *The Pembrokeshire Historian.* 1966.

HOWELLS, B.E. & K.A.
Pembrokeshire Life 1572-1843. Pembrokeshire Record Society. 1972.

HOWELLS, E.J.
The Centenary of Milford Haven Parish Church. Church Army Press, Oxford. 1908.

HUBBARD, C.L.
The Pembrokeshire Corgi Handbook. London. 1952.

JAMES, J.W. (trs.).
Rhigyfarch's Life of St David, University of Wales Press, Cardiff. 1967.

JENKINS, J. GERAINT
Pembrokeshire and the Woollen Industry. *The Pembrokeshire Historian.* 1966.
Nets and Coracles. David & Charles, Newton Abbot. 1974.

JENKINS, R.T.
Thomas Rees. *Dictionary of Welsh Biography.* London. 1959.

JENNET, SEAN
South-west Wales. Darton, Longman & Todd. London. 1967.

JOHN, AUGUSTUS
Chiaroscuro. Jonathan Cape, London. 1952.

JONES, E.H. STUART
The Last Invasion of Britain. University of Wales Press, Cardiff. 1950.

JONES, FRANCIS
From Norman Times Onward. *Pembrokeshire Coast National Park Guide.* London. 1973.
Foreword. *Sheriffs of the County of Pembroke.* Haverfordwest. 1976.
Llanrheithan. *The Pembrokeshire Historian.* 1971.

The Pageantry of Picton. *The Slebech Story*. 1948.

Some Further Slebech Notes. *National Library of Wales Journal* XIV 3. 1966.

Some Farmers of Bygone Pembrokeshire. *The Transactions of the Honourable Society of Cymmrodorion*. London. 1946.

Town and County of Haverfordwest. 1479-1974.

JONES, GARETH

The Gentry and the Elizabethan State. Christopher Davies, Swansea. 1977.

JONES, GWYN & JONES THOS.

The Mabinogion. Dent, London. 1949.

JONES, LLEWELYN

Schoolin's Log. Michael Joseph, London. 1980.

LAWS, EDWARD

A History of Little England beyond Wales. London. 1888.

LEACH, ARTHUR L.

The History of the Civil Wars (1642-49) in Pembrokeshire. Witherby, London. 1937.

Charles Norris 1799-1858. Tenby. 1949.

LELAND, JOHN

The Itinerary in Wales. Bell, London. 1906.

LEWIS, E.A.

The Welsh Port Books (1550-1603). London. 1927.

LLOYD, SIR J.E.

Asser. *Dictionary of Welsh Biography*. London. 1959.

LLOYD, KATHARINE A.

The Lords Marcher of Kemes. Carmarthen. 1930.

LHUYD, EDWARD

Parochialia in *Early Science* in Oxford, W. Gunter: Clarendon Press, and *Archaeologia Cambrensis*, 1911.

LOCKLEY, R.M.

The Island. Andre Deutsch, London. 1969.

In Praise of Islands. Frederick Muller, London. 1957.

Grey Seal, Common Seal. Andre Deutsch, London. 1966.

Pembrokeshire. Robert Hale, London. 1957.

MALKIN, BENJ. H.

The Scenery, Antiquities and Biography of South Wales. London. 1804.

MARPLES, THEO.

The Sealyham Terrier. Manchester, 1921.

MATHEW, MURRAY A
  The Birds of Pembrokeshire. London. 1894.
MILES, DILLWYN
  The Royal National Eisteddfod of Wales. Christopher Davies,
  Swansea. 1978.
  John Owen. *Dictionary of Welsh Biography.* London. 1959.
MIREHOUSE, MARY B.
  South Pembrokeshire. London. 1910.
MORTON, H.V.
  In Search of Wales. Methuen, London. 1932.
OWEN, G. DYFNALLT
  Elizabethan Wales. University of Wales Press, Cardiff. 1964.
OWEN, GEORGE
  The Description of Penbrokshire (1603), ed. Henry Owen.
  London. 1906.
OWEN, TREFOR M.
  Welsh Folk Customs. National Museum of Wales, Cardiff. 1959.
PHILLIPS, W.D.
  Old Haverfordwest. Haverfordwest. 1925.
REES, SIR J.F.
  Lucy Walter. *Dictionary of Welsh Biography.* 1959.
REES, VYVYAN
  South-West Wales. Faber & Faber, London. 1963.
ROSCOE, THOMAS
  Wanderings and Excursions in South Wales. London. 1844.
SENIOR, MICHAEL
  Portrait of South Wales. Robert Hale, London. 1974.
SIKES, WIRT
  British Goblins. London. 1880.
SMITH, PETER
  Houses of the Welsh Countryside. HMSO, London. 1975.
SQUARE, OWEN
  (John Owen)
  Memories of Half-a-Century. London. 1889.
SUTHERLAND, GRAHAM
  Welsh Sketch Book. *Horizon*, V 28. 1942.
THOMAS, W.J.
  Bartholomew Roberts. *Dictionary of Welsh Biography*. London.
  1959.
TIMMINS, H. THORNHILL
  Nooks and Corners of Pembrokeshire. London, 1895.

TRIPP, JOHN
Apricot Sponge with a Sage. *The Old Man of the Mist and Other Stories*, ed. Lynn Hughes. Martin, Brian & O'Keeffe. 1974.

WARBURTON, F.W.
The History of Solva. London. 1944.

WILLIAMS, A.H.
John Wesley in Wales. University of Wales Press, Cardiff. 1971.

WILLIAMS, DAVID
The Rebecca Riots. University of Wales Press, Cardiff. 1955.
The Pembrokeshire Elections of 1831. *The Pembrokeshire Historian*. 1960.

WILLIAMS, GLANMOR
Thomas Young. *Dictionary of Welsh Biography*. London. 1959.

WILLIAMS, JAMES
Give Me Yesterday. Gwasg Gomer, Llandysul. 1971.

Acknowledgements

The publishers and the editor gratefully acknowledge copyright and permissions kindly granted by the following:

Professor R. J. C. Atkinson and Hamish Hamilton, Ltd, for the extract from *Stonehenge*. J. H. Barrett, the late T. A. Warren Davis, the late Professor T. Neville George, Professor W. F. Grimes, Major Francis Jones, Wales Herald of Arms Extraordinary, and the Controller of Her Majesty's Stationery Office for passages from *Pembrokeshire Coast: National Park Guide No. 10.* Professor Emeritus E. G. Bowen, David Howell, Lieut.-Col. R. L. Howell, J. Geraint Jenkins, Major Francis Jones, the Executors of the Estate of the late Professor David Williams, and the Pembrokeshire Local History Society for excerpts from *The Pembrokeshire Historian.* Dr B. G. Charles, Major Francis Jones and the National Library of Wales for the extracts from *The National Library of Wales Journal.* S. B. Chrimes and the University of Wales Press for the extract from *Welsh History Review*. William Condry and Messrs Faber & Faber, Ltd, for the excerpts from *Exploring Wales*. Olwen Caradoc Evans and the Map Collectors' Circle for the extract from *Marine Plans and Charts of Wales*. Eleanor Fairburn and Wm. Heinemann, Ltd, for the passage from *The Golden Hind*. Constantine FitzGibbon and J. M. Dent & Sons, Ltd, for the extract from *The Life of Dylan Thomas*. Theodora FitzGibbon and J. M. Dent & Sons, Ltd, for the recipes from *A Taste of Wales*. The Executors of the Estate of the late Maxwell Fraser and Methuen London, Ltd, for the extracts from *Introducing West Wales*. E. C. Freeman and Edward Gill for the excerpt from *The Story of Lord Nelson and Sir William and Lady Hamilton's Tour in Wales and Monmouthshire*. Clive Gammon and Wm. Heinemann, Ltd, for the extract from *Hook, Line and Spinner*, Jacquetta Hawkes and Chatto & Windus, Ltd, for the extracts from *A Guide to the Prehistoric and Roman Monuments in England and Wales*. Gerald S. Hawkins and Fontana/Collins for the extract from *Stonehenge Decoded*. David Howell and Dyfed County Council for the excerpts from *Carmarthenshire Studies* edited by T. Barnes and N. Yates. Peter Howell and Elisabeth Beazley and Wm. Collins, Sons & Co, Ltd, for the passage from *The Companion Guide to South Wales*. B. E. & K. A. Howells and the Pembrokeshire Record Society for the letter from *Pembrokeshire Life 1572-1845*. J. W. James and the University of Wales Press for the extract from *Rhigyfarch's Life of St David*. J. Geraint Jenkins and David & Charles, Ltd, for the excerpt from *Nets and Coracles*. The Executors of the Estate of the late Sean Jennett, Laurence Pollinger, Ltd, and Darton, Longman & Todd, Ltd, for the extracts from *South-west Wales*. The Executors of the Estate of the late Augustus John and Jonathan Cape, Ltd, for the extracts from *Chiaroscuro*. The Executors of the Estate of the late Cmdr. E. H. Stuart Jones for excerpts from *The Last Invasion of Britain*. Major Francis Jones and The Honourable Society of Cymmrodorion for the extract from *The Transactions of The Honourable Society of Cymmrodorion, 1943-44*; and the Haverfordwest Town Council for the passage from *Town and County of Haverfordwest 1479-1974*. Gareth Jones and Christopher Davies, Ltd, for the extract from *The Gentry and the Elizabethan State*. Professor Gwyn Jones and Mrs Mair Jones and J. M. Dent & Sons, Ltd, for the extracts from *The Mabinogion*. Llewelyn Jones and Michael Joseph, Ltd, for the passage from *Schoolin's Log*. R. M. Lockley and his publishers for extracts from *The Island* and *Grey Seal, Common Seal* (Andre Deutsch), *In Praise of Islands* (Frederick Muller, Ltd), and *Pembrokeshire* (Robert Hale, Ltd). Geraint Dyfnallt Owen and the University of Wales Press for extracts from *Elizabethan Wales*. Trefor Owen and the National Museum of Wales for the excerpts from *Welsh Folk Customs*. Lawrence Phillips and the *Western Mail* for the article *H.M.S. Warrior*. J. W. Hammond & Son for the extract from *Old Haverfordwest*. Vyvyan Rees and Messrs Faber & Faber, Ltd, for the extracts from *South-West Wales*. Michael Senior, David Higham Associates, Ltd, and Robert Hale, Ltd, for the extracts from *Portrait of South Wales*. Peter Smith and the Controller of Her Majesty's Stationery Office for the excerpt from *Houses of the Welsh Countryside*. John Tripp and Martin, Brian & O'Keefe, Ltd, for the extract from the story *Apricot Sponge with a Sage* from *The Old Man of the Mist and Other Stories* edited by Lynn Hughes. Wynford Vaughan Thomas and Webb & Bower, Ltd, for the passage from *The Countryside Companion*. A. H. Williams and the University of Wales Press for the excerpt from *John Wesley in Wales*. The Executors of the Estate of the late Professor David Williams and the University of Wales Press for the extracts from *The Rebecca Riots*. The Executors of the Estate of the late James Williams and J. D. Lewis & Sons, Ltd, Gwasg Gomer, Llandysul, for the passages from *Give Me Yesterday*. The Executors of the Estate of the late Dylan Thomas and David Higham Associates, Ltd, for the poem *In Pembroke City* from *Under Milk Wood*. Tony Curtis and Pembrokeshire Handbooks, Ltd, for the poems *Peninsula Run* (John Tripp), *Poem from Manorbier* (Raymond Garlick), *Encounter at Pentre Ifan* (Jeremy Hooker), *Skokholm* (John Stuart Williams) and *Seal Island* (Alison Bielski) from *Pembrokeshire Poems*. Meic Stephens and Gwilym Rees Hughes and Christopher Davies, Ltd, for the poem *Cwm yr Eglwys* by Gwyn Williams from *Poetry Wales*. D. M. Lloyd for *Remembrance*, his translation of Waldo Williams's poem *Cofio*, in *A Book of Wales* edited by D. M. & E. M. Lloyd and published by Wm Collins, Ltd. Anthony Conran and Penguin Books, Ltd, for *Praise of Tenby* and *Elegy for Rhys Gryg* from *The Penguin Book of Welsh Verse*. Professor Gwyn Jones and the Oxford University Press for *In Two Fields*, from *The Oxford Book of Welsh Verse in English*, by permission of J. D. Lewis & Sons, Ltd, Gwasg Gomer. The British Library for permission to reproduce a page from the 'Haroldston Calendar'. The National Trust for the cover illustration. Hilary Davies for help with typing.

While every effort has been made to trace copyright holders, in some cases this has proved fruitless. Anyone laying claim to a copyright not acknowledged should contact the publishers so that a proper arrangement for any future editions can be made.

The editor's and publisher's special thanks are also due to Ieuan Jones, late of *Cambria Depicta*, Llandovery, for his help with the illustrations, the prints and engravings, maps and charts from his private collection which embellish the text of this book.

I must thank Wynford Vaughan Thomas for his spontaneous and elegant Foreword.

Finally, I wish to express my warm and sincere gratitude to Lynn Hughes for his editorial guidance and help with every stage of the preparation of this publication for the press.

DILLWYN MILES

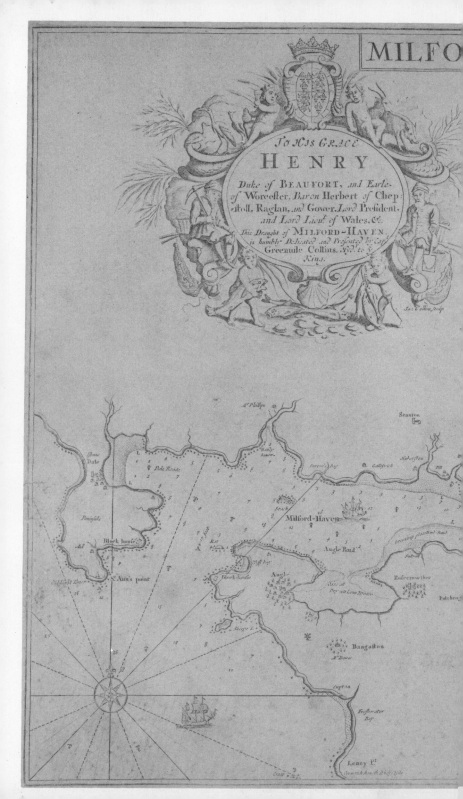

MILFO

To HIS GRACE
HENRY
Duke of BEAUFORT, and Earle
of Worcester, Baron Herbert of Chep-
stoll, Raglan, and Gower, Lord Prefident,
and Lord Lieut of Wales, &c.
This Draught of MILFORD-HAVEN
is humbly Dedicated and Prefented by Capt.
Greenvile Collins, Hydr. to ye
King.

Jas. Collins Sculp.

Stanton

Mr. Phillips

Stone
Dale

Dale Roads

Sahceston

Pennells

Block houfe

Butcers Bay   Gallifwick

Stack

Milford-Haven

Angle Road

Drawing place Red-Road

Patch

St. Ann's point

Old Light houfe

Block houfe

Angl

Site of
Pryetts Iron Braver

Roferowther

Patchro

Sheep I.

Bangafton

Mr. Davis

Gupton

Frofhwater
Bay

Lenny Pt.